Country Music Legends

Country Music Legends

in the Hall of Fame

CHET HAGAN

Thomas Nelson Publishers
/ Country Music Foundation Press
NASHVILLE

Published in Nashville, Tennessee, by Thomas Nelson, Inc., and distributed in Canada by Lawson Falle, Ltd., Cambridge, Ontario.

Printed in the United States of America.

Design by *Design for Publishing, Bob Nance*

Production supervised by *Harold Leach*

Photographs from the collection of *Les Leverett*

Library of Congress Cataloging in Publication Data

Hagan, Chet.
    Country music legends in the Hall of Fame.

    1. Country musicians—United States—Biography.
I. Title.
ML394.H34   784.5'2'00922 [B]   82-6457
ISBN 0-8407-4104-9   AACR2

Contents

Foreword

In October of 1979, President Jimmy Carter stood on the stage of historic Ford's Theatre in Washington, D.C., to introduce a special country music television show. In his remarks he said: *"The country in country music is America."*

The phrase had originated with Joseph Cates, the veteran TV producer-director who was the executive producer of that program. But it was significant that it had been included in the text of a President of the United States, especially one who had come out of the rural South in which country music was spawned. Mr. Carter knew better than most that country music had burst out of its southern bonds and had, indeed, become the music of *all* America.

There have been numerous scholarly treatises on the origins of country music, technical papers on the musical patterns inherent in "country," and psychological studies of the motivations of the songwriters. In the broadest sense, however, country music has been simply a documentation of the American experience. It has dealt with the realities of human happiness and tragedy, of true love and infidelity, of strength in the face of adversity and frailty in contending with the stresses of living, of working and loafing, of sobriety and drunkenness, of heroics and cowardice, of faith and doubt, of life and of death.

Nowhere is that better illustrated than in the Country Music Hall of Fame and Museum in Nashville, where singers and musicians and songwriters and "movers" responsible for the popularization—and preservation—of country music are honored. A widely-based special electors committee, made up of veterans of the country music industry (each has *at least* twenty years experience), votes by secret ballot for new members of the Hall of Fame. The vote comes after a smaller nominating committee, following careful study, presents the electors with a group of nominees each year. The announcement of the new Hall of Fame member(s) is made during "Country Music Month" in October.

And the backgrounds of those already elected are as varied as their songs: A mule wagon driver, a railroad brakeman, a governor, a telegrapher, a Broadway actor, a cotton picker, a radio announcer, a garment factory worker, a finishing-school product, a minor league baseball player, an operatic tenor, a pallbearer, a Tin Pan Alley songwriter, a Nova Scotia seaman, even an immigrant Englishman.

Their cumulative music holds up a mirror to all of us—whether we work on a production line in Michigan or a cattle ranch in Texas, in a corn field in Iowa or a "glass box" high-rise office in New York—and reflects back to us what we really are.

Their personal stories deserve retelling, because, like their music, their lives are the warp and woof of the American fabric. In total, the members of the Country Music Hall of Fame *are* America.

That is reason enough for this book.

CHET HAGAN
February, 1982

*I'm trying to pick up a couple of musicians to work with me
. . . Boys who'll be willing to work whatever date I can
get—schoolhouse, barn dance, roadhouse, beer joint—
anything . . . Folks everywhere are gettin' tired of all this
Black Bottom-Charleston-jazz music junk.*

1

Jimmie Rodgers

Elected to the Country Music Hall of Fame: 1961

His story is the stuff of fiction.

Poor, ill-educated, motherless at four, in bad health all of his life,
dead at the age of thirty-five in a strange hotel room far from home, and,
yet, an entertainment star of the first magnitude, an influence on an entire
generation of country music artists and beyond. That was Jimmie Rodgers,
called, by some, "The Father of Country Music." His plaque in the Country
Music Hall of Fame uses less pretentious words: ". . . the man who started it
all."

And what he started was the *commercial* era of country music. He
wasn't the first million-seller on records; that was Vernon Dalhart. He never
played the legendary *Grand Ole Opry* radio show. He never made a personal
appearance outside the southern states. He never imagined that his music
was significant. He never took on the lavish trappings of stardom; he always
remained himself. What he did was sing to *survive*, in a life where survival
seemed so tenuous.

Once given the opportunity to sell his clearly unique talents, to merchandise them, he did so with a vengeance. He used whatever he needed to use to make commercial records: musical saws, jug players, whistlers, ukelele pickers, and the talents of Hawaiian guitarist Lani McIntire, trumpeter Louis Armstrong, and jazz pianist L'il Armstrong. In all, he made 111 recordings (only 110 were released; one master was inadvertently destroyed) in the short span of six years. A phenomenal twenty million of them were sold!

Roy Horton, veteran music publishing executive with the Peer-Southern Organization, reported: "Legend has it that in his heyday, general store customers would approach the counter and say: 'Let me have a pound of butter, a dozen eggs, and the latest Jimmie Rodgers record.' "

The why of that is what makes the Jimmie Rodgers story so fascinating.

He was born in 1897 near Meridian, Mississippi, the son of a section gang foreman on the Mobile and Ohio Railroad. His mother died of tuberculosis when he was only four years old. There followed a growing up in cheap boarding houses, foster homes, being shunted from one relative to another in a succession of small towns in Mississippi and Alabama. He was always frail with TB, his poor health making his formal schooling a sometime thing. In 1911, when he was approaching his fourteenth birthday, his school days ended once and for all. It was then that he took a job as a water boy on the railroad, a task normally assigned to black youngsters. In retrospect, it might have been the first good thing that ever happened to him.

It was on the railroad that he was exposed to the songs of the black workers, and where he learned to play the guitar and banjo. Slowly, almost by cultural osmosis, he absorbed the blues idiom of the blacks, and his natural musical talent refined it into a style peculiar to himself. And he added something: a clear, mournful, wide-ranging yodel. He became a white blues singer. There was no specific moment when this all came together; it simply evolved.

But life, hard and uncompromising, went on. He continued to work on the railroad, but he had to contend constantly with his ill health, which sometimes made work impossible. Jimmie married Carrie Williamson in 1920; a daughter was born in 1921, and another in 1923. During that summer, desperately needing money to support his family, he went on the road with a medicine show that toured the tiny towns of Kentucky and Tennessee. He would black his face, play the banjo, and sing his special brand of the blues. For a time, things seemed to go reasonably well; well enough, in fact, for Jimmie to put the few dollars he had into a Hawaiian tent show of his own. A storm, with high winds, destroyed it all. The bottom came when he had to pawn his banjo to return home to Meridian for the funeral of his baby daughter, June Rebecca, who died at the age of six months.

Matters got worse. In 1925, after fourteen years of railroading, doctors told Rodgers he'd have to quit; the work was too strenuous for him. There seemed little left to him but his music. He formed a three-piece dance combo: himself on banjo and guitar, one Slim Rozell on violin, and his sister-in-law, Elsie McWilliams, on piano. Elsie was important to Jimmie. A talented composer, she wrote songs with him, and she introduced him to a large repertoire of popular songs.

Nevertheless, it was a "coffee and cakes" existence, and the Rodgers family life became a nomadic one. Seeking part-time work and a better climate, they went first to Florida (where Jimmie tried for a time to hold down a job as a brakeman on the Florida East Coast Railroad), then to Tucson, Arizona, and San Antonio, and Galveston. In January of 1927, Carrie Rodgers and their daughter, Anita, returned to Meridian, and Jimmie went on to Asheville, North Carolina, for a job on radio station WWNC. He formed what he characterized as a "hillbilly ork"—formally known as the Jimmie Rodgers Entertainers—and they had a regular program sponsored by the state's tourist department. It was a success; audience reaction to Rodgers and his distinctive yodeling style was enthusiastic. But after only six weeks, the sponsorship ran out. The Jimmie Rodgers Entertainers began barnstorming the southeastern states for small money.

Enter Ralph Peer. He was a Victor Records talent scout who was scouring the South for acts. It came to Jimmie's attention that Peer was going to set up his portable recording equipment in Bristol, a hill town straddling the border between Tennessee and Virginia. Rodgers' band headed for Bristol, but all was not well within the group. In an apparent dispute over billing, the other musicians abandoned Rodgers and recorded on their own as the Tenneva Ramblers.

Jimmie, with only his guitar for accompaniment, persuaded Peer to let him record as a solo artist. Strangely, the two songs he elected to record were slow ballads, offering little of his blue yodeling style. One was an old lullaby, Sleep, Baby, Sleep, and the other was a song he had written after a close friend had been killed in the service, The Soldier's Sweetheart. Peer must have liked what he heard, because he signed Rodgers to a Victor contract.

(In one of those oddities of coincidence, Peer also made a deal in that same first week of August, 1927, with a group that had come to Bristol from Maces Spring, Virginia—the Carter Family.)

So, Jimmie had become a recording artist. He was nearly thirty years old, his tubercular cough was beginning to wrack his body with greater frequency, and, when he received his first royalty check for twenty-seven dollars, it seemed to be just another disappointment in his dismal life. Before the end of 1927, however, it became clear that the public was discovering Jimmie Rodgers. His second royalty check was for four hundred dollars.

He was rushed back into the Victor recording studio in Camden, New Jersey, and, with his sister-in-law, Elsie, by his side (along with nine of her original songs), he began what has been considered to be one of the most important recording sessions in the history of country music. One of the songs he cut was his first blue yodel, *T for Texas*. It captured the imagination of the American public. There was a great clamor for his recordings. In almost no time at all, Rodgers had gone from being an impoverished nonentity to a major star earning two thousand dollars a week, and more.

Ralph Peer, well aware of what he had discovered, became the publisher of Rodgers' songs and booked him for a northern states tour on the famous RKO vaudeville circuit at a salary of one thousand dollars a week. It was a tour Jimmie was never to make because of his continuing poor health. He had to restrict himself to appearances in the South: on the Loew's vaudeville circuit, with the Paul English Players, and with other major tent show groups. Rodgers always appeared as a solo artist. He was never again—probably remembering what had happened with his musicians in Bristol—to put together his own band. The labels on the Victor records never mentioned anyone but Jimmie Rodgers.

Hit followed hit: *Dear Old Sunny South by the Sea, My Lovin' Lucille (Blue Yodel #2), Evening Sun Yodel (Blue Yodel #3), Waiting for a Train, California Blues (Blue Yodel #4), Any Old Time, Black-headed Mama (Blue Yodel #5), Everybody Does It in Hawaii, Blue Yodel #6, Hobo Bill's Last Ride, Jimmie's Texas Blues, In the Jailhouse Now, The One Rose, Anniversary Blue Yodel #7*, and on and on. In all, there were to be twelve blue yodels and dozens of other songs in the same vein. And the money poured in.

Rodgers, always a happy-go-lucky type in spite of his difficult life, was enjoying himself. In May of 1929, he built a fifty-thousand-dollar mansion in Kerrville, Texas, and called it Blue Yodeler's Paradise. And he bought big cars. There is one picture of Jimmie standing proudly by a new, long sedan; on the photo he wrote: "When better cars are built I will buy one."

With all of his good fortune, however, the tuberculosis got worse. Often it sent him to bed for days, with high, weakening fever. Always slim, he got thinner. Long coughing spells overtook him, and he was spitting up blood with more frequency. One of his close friends, fiddler Pappy McMichen, expressed his concern one day, suggesting that Rodgers ought to get additional treatment. The man who had written a song called *The TB Blues* had a ready answer.

"I'm not gonna lay in one of those hospital rooms," Jimmie said, "and count the fly specks on the wall. I want to die with my shoes on."

It was probably that spirit that took him to New York City on May 17, 1933, for yet another recording session at Victor's studio on Twenty-fourth Street. He was so frail that a cot was placed in the studio so that he could rest between songs. The plan was to record twenty-four sides, but by May 24, only half of his goal had been accomplished. Jimmie was returning from dinner on May 25 when he began to hemorrhage, and he was put to bed in his room in the Manger (later the Taft) Hotel. He lapsed into a coma. By the early morning hours of May 26, 1933, he was dead. One of the last songs he had recorded was titled *My Time Ain't Long*.

A great multitude met the train carrying Rodgers' body when it was returned to Meridian, Mississippi. One eye witness recalled that the train's whistle was "a low, mellow whistle, not the usual train whistle, but a long moaning that grew in volume as the train crept toward the terminal, never ceasing until the powerful engine breathed to a rest." Jimmie Rodgers, "The Singing Brakeman," had come home for the last time.

In a sense, that was only the beginning of the story. Rodgers' influence on commercial country music was so profound that it cannot be adequately measured. The record, however, is clear. A young Gene Autry, on his way to becoming a recording star himself as the thirties began, so closely followed the Rodgers style in his early releases that it was almost impossible to distinguish between his records and those of Rodgers. Others followed. Ernest Tubb came out of Benjamin, Texas, as an avowed devotee of Jimmie Rodgers; Hank Snow left Nova Scotia as "The Yodeling Ranger"; the imprint of Rodgers could be heard in the work of Hank Williams, Jimmie Davis, Slim Whitman, Elton Britt—even Eddy Arnold, Grandpa Jones, and Merle Haggard. It's probably significant that Autry, Tubb, Snow, Williams, Davis, Arnold, and Jones are all members of the Country Music Hall of Fame.

When the time came, in 1961, for the Country Music Association to establish a Hall of Fame, Jimmie Rodgers was the first performer selected.

Early in 1978, U.S. Postmaster General Benjamin F. Bailar came to Nashville to unveil the design for a commemorative stamp honoring Jimmie Rodgers. It went on sale in May during the Jimmie Rodgers Festival in Meridian. Fittingly, it was the first stamp in a new series on American Performing Arts and Artists.

Earlier (in June, 1953), a Jimmie Rodgers Memorial had been dedicated in Meridian. Ernest Tubb, who had never met his hero, was there to join Mrs. Carrie Rodgers and daughter Anita in unveiling the monument.

On it are inscribed these words:

The silver tones of his voice, the magic strumming of his guitar, the haunting melody and the heartthrobs of his American folk songs brought comfort, joy and inspiration to the millions who heard him on stage, in broadcasts and on recordings. Through long years of hardship to the triumphs of his fame, his simple philosophy of life and his devotion to family and friends remained unchanged because his religion was love.

James Charles Rodgers, born Meridian, Mississippi, September 8, 1897; died New York City, May 26, 1933.
Married, Carrie Williamson, 1920. (Two daughters: Carrie Anita, June Rebecca.)

We pride ourselves in being 'a very intelligent people' and good Americans, but are we? We put on our best 'bib and tucker' and make quite an affair of spending an enjoyable evening being entertained with Italian, Russian, French, etc., 'folklore' (we call it 'opera' and 'music appreciation') . . . but what do we say about our good ol' American 'folklore'? We call it 'hillbilly' music, and sometimes we're ashamed to call it music . . .

2

Fred Rose

Elected to the Country Music Hall of Fame: 1961

If Fred Rose had never been anything but a songwriter, he would have merited his fame.

If Fred Rose had never been anything more than a musician, or a record producer, or a song publisher, he would have deserved all of the accolades of the music industry.

If Fred Rose had never been anything more than the molder of the career of Hank Williams, he would have earned his place in the front ranks of country music.

But Fred Rose was all of those. And more! And it was eminently fitting that he was elected to the Country Music Hall of Fame in its first year.

Rose fit none of the stereotypes usually associated with country music. He was not a farm boy; he grew up in the urban environments of St. Louis and Chicago. He didn't pick out his first tunes on a guitar or a fiddle; his instrument was the piano, which he played with deceptive ease. He didn't write initially of walking behind a plow or of picking cotton; his early songs were for night clubs, and jazz halls, and Broadway.

Fred Rose was a Tin Pan Alley pop music songwriter who made his transition to country music because his prolific talent constantly forced him to do more. In making that transition, he became one of country music's leading defenders, as much responsible for its commercial development as any one individual, before or since.

He was born in Evansville, Indiana, in 1897, but his earliest days were spent in St. Louis, where he lived, apparently not in the happiest of circumstances, with his mother's relatives. Fred was a child prodigy on the piano; at a very early age (there are indications that it may have been when he was only ten years old) he was playing for tips in St. Louis saloons. He left grammar school in the third or fourth grade. When he reached his teens he went to Chicago, where he made a living of sorts as a musician, playing tough South Side clubs, cutting piano rolls for player pianos (Fats Waller was one of his contemporaries at the QRS piano roll company), and playing in theater pits for silent movies.

It was in Chicago, too, that he began to write songs. He was, quite literally, a song machine; songwriting seemed so simple for him. But a good many of those early songs were written just for eating money, or, in truth, for drinking money.

In 1916 he married a young lady named Della Braico, and shortly thereafter they had two sons: Wesley in 1918 and Lester in 1920. Fred's songwriting output increased, and he began to solidify his reputation as a writer. A lot of his early songs were published with shared credits, indicating a practice prevalent in those days of "cutting in" orchestra leaders for part of the royalties on the songs in order to get them performed. Fred had songs copyrighted with such collaborators as Paul Whiteman, Abe Lyman, Ted Fiorito, and Isham Jones.

The sheer versatility of Rose's songwriting is indicated in some of the titles of his songs from the early twenties: *Cease Bernice; Charlestonette; Down in Hindu Town; The Ghost of Mister Jazz; Here Comes the Hot Tamale Man; I'll Be Your Regular Sweetie, But I Won't Be Your Once in a While; Ireland Is Heaven to Me; Mississippi Choo-Choo; Sweet Mama, Pappa's Gettin' Mad; You Can Take Me Away From Dixie But You Can't Take Dixie From Me; Wish That I Could But I Can't Forgive You Blues; Don't Bring Me Posies, It's Shoesies That I Need*, to detail only a very few.

In November of 1923, with collaborators Gilbert Wells and Bud Cooper, Fred wrote *Red Hot Mama*, which was to become the theme song, and a major hit, for the flamboyant night club star, Sophie Tucker, who billed herself as "The Last of the Red Hot Mamas."

There was a kaleidoscopic quality to Rose's career in that period. He became a recording artist in his own right on the Brunswick label. He was a popular radio entertainer, teaming with Elmo Tanner (later to be a whistling star with the Ted Weems Orchestra) in an act called the Tune Peddlers. For a brief time, Rose and Tanner even played clowns on a children's show on a Chicago radio station. But Fred's marriage, under stress from the demands of his career and his drinking, ended; in 1929 he remarried, this time to Helen Holmes. He began to recognize the commercial value of minstrel show songs and wrote a large number of them in the late twenties and early thirties. He also wrote at least four different musical comedies in that period. It was clear, however, that his career was in a decline; his song production fell off as his drinking increased, and he lost his radio shows. There was need for a change.

Through the aegis of the Vagabonds, a vocal group he had known in Chicago and which was then featured on the *Grand Ole Opry*, Rose learned of a possible opening on WSM radio in Nashville. In May of 1933, he drove to Nashville and made a deal for a nightly fifteen-minute spot on WSM called *Freddie Rose's Song Shop*, a program on which he played the piano and chatted about songs, sometimes writing simple tunes on the spur of the moment on themes suggested by listeners who telephoned the studio. Unfortunately, his move to Nashville was accompanied by the break-up of his second marriage.

By the mid-thirties, he returned to New York to try to revive his flagging songwriting career. There he had a religious conversion, committing himself to Christian Science, apparently under the guidance of a songwriting colleague, Ed G. Nelson. It was a significant move in terms of his health.

In March 1935, he married again; his third wife was Lorene Harmon, a woman he had met in Nashville. And what was before him, as his life began to change, were associations with three men who were to be vastly important to him and to all of country music: Gene Autry, Roy Acuff, and Hank Williams.

The relationship with Gene Autry began in the spring of 1938, at a time when Autry was clearly the "cock of the walk" in Hollywood. Rose was introduced to Autry by Ray Whitley, a cowboy singer-composer who had earlier recorded Fred's matching event songs, *Will Rogers, Your Friend and My Friend* and *The Last Flight of Wiley Post*. Whitley had written some songs for Autry, and still had ahead of him the creation of the star's theme song, *Back in the Saddle Again*. A topflight country music promoter, J. L. (Joe) Frank, who had been instrumental in the development of Autry's career, also played a role in bringing Autry and Rose together. In any event, they became collaborators (at times joined by Johnny Marvin, Jimmy Wakely, and Whitley) on a total of forty-nine songs.

It was a landmark collaboration, highlighted by such major hits as *Be*

Honest With Me, nominated for an Academy Award in 1941, *Tears on My Pillow,* and *Tweedle-O-Twill,* all with words and music by Fred Rose and Gene Autry.

Rose didn't go to Hollywood without some experience in the cowboy-song genre. In 1936 he had written a song with Ed G. Nelson, a frequent co-writer, titled *Horse Op'ry, Yip Addy Yipi Addy Aye,* and two years later he had another song, *We'll Rest at the End of the Trail,* written with Curt Poulton, recorded by both Bing Crosby and Tex Ritter.

There have been some questions about the nature of the collaborative efforts of the Rose-Autry partnership—primarily, who did what? The answer is of little importance, perhaps, because it's always difficult to gauge individual contribution in a true collaboration. But it is known that Autry frequently supplied the basic idea, coming up with a commercial title to match, and Rose put the flesh on those bones.

A key example was the Autry hit, *At Mail Call Today*. It happened in 1945, while Autry was still in the service. He called Rose from Dallas with an idea that had been generated by his reading a poignant letter in a soldier's magazine. Responding to Gene's request, Rose flew from Nashville to meet him in Dallas, and the song that Autry envisioned was quickly completed. It was the number three country chart song of the year.

The Rose-Autry collaboration was a happy one, and it continued into the early fifties. By that time, Fred Rose was established as the industry's leading country music publisher, in partnership with yet another superstar: Roy Acuff.

Acuff provided the impetus for the association. "People out of New York and California and all," Roy recalled, "were comin' in here tryin' to buy my songs, and I refused to sell 'em. But I realized that what I should do is get with some company to place my songs where they would be protected. When I first recorded they stole every song from me, and I was a young man and didn't know anything about it. I was green. But when I recorded the songs the record company just copyrighted them. They stole them."

At the time—it was 1942—there was frequently no protection for the less sophisticated country songwriter, and Acuff wanted to correct that. He wanted Rose to start a music publishing company. Fred, uncertain about becoming a businessman, hesitated. Acuff pressed him and Rose, after seeking the advice of Chicago music publisher Fred Forster, finally agreed.

Acuff remembered: "I said: 'Fred, I got twenty-five thousand dollars I'll place in the bank in your name. You use any amount of it you want to. I will never bother your publishing company.' He took my word, we went into a fifty-fifty agreement on it—a gentlemen's agreement. This was our main point: That we were going to make sure that it be run as an honest company; that no man, or girl, that entered our door would be cheated out of a song, or one penny of anything that they've got coming. I said: 'Fred, if I ever find anything crooked about it, my name'll come off of it.'"

Roy's desires for integrity matched those of Rose and, on October 13, 1942, Acuff-Rose Publications was started. What most people didn't realize was that the formal partnership agreement was between Fred Rose and *Mildred Acuff*, Roy's wife. The "Acuff" in Acuff-Rose was, in the legal sense, not Roy himself. In spirit it was, of course.

Rose took two important steps to assure the future of the company. Almost immediately, he licensed the company's country music catalog with the comparatively new Broadcast Music, Inc. (BMI), receiving an advance of $2500. That money was used to meet the early expenses of the then-small company, and Rose never had to touch Acuff's initial investment of $25,000. Second, unwilling to tie himself down with business details that he feared would interfere with his songwriting, Rose persuaded his eldest son, Wesley, to join the company. Wesley wasn't sure he wanted to make the move from Chicago; he was a well-paid accountant with the Standard Oil Company, and he really didn't know his father too well. Their contacts had been limited over the years. But the elder Rose guaranteed his son that he would be in full charge of the business end, and Wesley, with the title of general manager, joined the fledgling company.

Acuff delighted in the songwriting ability of his new partner. "I remember one time Fred being backstage at the Opry," Roy said, "and he heard me sing *Unloved and Unclaimed*, the one about the girl laying on a cold marble slab at the morgue, with thousands viewing her but none knew her name. They don't get no sadder than that. Well, Fred said: 'Lord, ain't nobody gonna want to hear that morbid thing.' And I said: 'I don't know, people love to cry, Fred.' Well, he went home and right away wrote *The Day They Laid Mary Away*." Roy roared with laughter at the recollection.

Acuff-Rose Publications was a huge success. At the end of the first year, Fred Rose also put together a publishing company to license some songs with the American Society of Composers, Authors and Publishers (ASCAP). It was called Milene Music, a name devised by using syllables from the first names of Mildred Acuff and Rose's wife, Lorene.

All that had gone into Fred Rose's life up to that time was enough to make him a successful man; his accomplishments had brought him both respect and money. But in 1946, there was yet another development that is the meat of legend. He met Hank Williams.

It's an oft-told story, but one that becomes more fascinating with the retelling. The Roses, father and son, were engaged in a Ping-Pong match at the WSM radio studio (Ping-Pong is still a way of life at Acuff-Rose). The game was interrupted by a skinny young man and his pretty blonde wife: Hank and Audrey Williams. Hank wanted to audition for them, and he sang a half-dozen of his songs, among them *Six More Miles to the Graveyard* and *When God Comes and Gathers His Jewels*. The young man's raw talent was obvious, and he was immediately signed to a contract with Acuff-Rose; the first *exclusive* songwriter's contract issued by the company.

To say that Hank Williams would not have become a star without Fred Rose would not be defensible; but to say that Williams' stardom would not have reached the magnitude it did without Rose is simply stating fact. Hank was an unschooled musician; the songs he heard in his head came out on scraps of paper, on the backs of envelopes, on matchbook covers. The Williams-Rose association was a perfect blending of two geniuses—Hank's poignantly realistic songs, born of his real-life experiences, and Fred's considerable trained skills as a song editor. What made it work so well was Rose's ability to change a note here, and a lyric line there, and still retain the realism of Williams' original composition.

Fred's contribution to the Williams songs might have merited co-writing credit on all of them. That was not done. Only 6 of the 130 songs attributed to Hank Williams in his tragically short life carry Rose's name as a collaborator: *Kaw-Liga* (plus *Minni-Ha-Cha*, another version of the same song), *I'll Never Get Out of This World Alive*, *A Mansion on the Hill*, *If I Didn't Love You*, and *You're Barking Up the Wrong Tree Now*.

Rose was also Williams' record producer for MGM, with a constant eye (and ear) on keeping the recording quality high without stifling the natural style of Hank. But Williams wasn't Rose's only performing protege; he also guided the careers of Molly O'Day, Rosalie Allen, and the Bailes Brothers.

Fred's greatest joy, however, came when he was working with young songwriters, helping them to polish their skills and using his editing talent to improve their output. There were dozens of those associations.

And through it all, Fred had built up his own catalog of hits: *Blue Eyes Cryin' in the Rain*, *'Deed I Do* (with Walter Hirsch), *Honest and Truly*, *I Hope You're Satisfied*, *I'll Never See Sunshine Again*, *I'm Trusting in You*, *More Precious Than Silver and Gold* (with Cowboy Copas), *Roly Poly*, *Take These Chains From My Heart* (with Hy Heath), *Wait for the Light to Shine*, *We Live in Two Different Worlds*, plus the hits he wrote under the pseudonym of Floyd Jenkins. Included among those were *Fire Ball Mail*, *Home in San Antone*, *Low and Lonely*, and *Pins and Needles (In My Heart)*.

Fred Rose was a prodigious talent. In retrospect, the most interesting speculation about him is how many hit songs he *really* wrote that never carried his name.

Knols Fred Rose, born Evansville, Indiana, August 24, 1897; died Nashville, Tennessee, December 1, 1954.
Married, Della Braico, 1917. (Two sons: Wesley, Lester.) Divorced.
Married, Helen Holmes, 1929. (Two children: Gene, Patricia.) Divorced.
Married, Lorene Harmon, 1935.

When a hillbilly sings a crazy song, he feels crazy. When he sings 'I Laid My Mother Away' he sees her a-layin' right there in the coffin. He sings more sincere than most entertainers, because the hillbilly was raised tougher than most entertainers . . . You got to have smelt a lot of mule manure before you can sing like a hillbilly.

3

Hank Williams

Elected to the Country Music Hall of Fame: 1961

Hank Williams was a man of brilliant light and dark shadows. Fortunately, it's the light that prevails—light shining through the one hundred thirty songs that he wrote, light reflecting from his eleven gold records, light illuminating the impact of his personal appearances.

He lived only twenty-nine years; in only the last six of those years could he have been considered to be a nationally known figure. Yet, no performer in the history of country music has had more impact than Hank Williams.

And why? Perhaps it was his universal commonality.

Mitch Miller, one-time head of the popular music division of Columbia Records, said Williams was in a class with Stephen Foster as an American songwriter. "He had a way of reaching your guts and your head at the same time," said Miller.

Music commentator Allan Rankin wrote: "He had a voice that went through you like electricity, sent shivers up your spine, and made the hair rise on the back of your neck with the thrill. With a voice like that he could make you laugh or cry."

Minnie Pearl said: "He had real animal magnetism. He destroyed the women in the audience."

Little Jimmy Dickens, who watched Williams in front of the Grand Ole Opry audiences, commented: "You could hear a pin drop when Hank was working. He just seemed to hypnotize those people. It was simplicity, I guess. He brought his people with him. He put himself on their level."

And that's the key. Hank Williams wrote of life—the joys and the sadnesses of it—and he sang those songs in a manner that convinced everyone of the sincerity of what he had written. He *was* those people in the audience, those millions who bought his records. And when the stories surfaced about his considerable problems with alcohol and pills, and about his domestic battles with his wife, those millions nodded their heads collectively in understanding. Real understanding. They could believe that an ill-educated country boy from Alabama would have problems with sudden wealth and fame. They'd have difficulties with it, so why not Hank Williams? He was, after all, one of them.

Hank was born in 1923 (in a log cabin, actually) in the little community of Mt. Olive, Alabama, some sixty miles south of Montgomery. His father was a sometime lumber-train engineer, sometime store owner, sometime berry picker. When Hank was seven, his father entered a Veterans Administration hospital, effectively removing him from the young boy's life. It was his domineering mother, Lilly, a country version of the Hollywood stage mother, who raised him. She was the posthumous source of much of the myth associated with her son. Lilly was a church organist, and young Hank sat on the bench beside her during many evangelistic services. In later years, although never a churchgoer, that upbringing manifested itself in the numerous country gospel songs that are included in his small catalog, and in the moralistic recitations he recorded as "Luke the Drifter."

At about the age of five he was on the streets, selling peanuts and shining shoes. "The first day," his mother recalled, "he made thirty cents, and I remember how proud he was. He brought home stew meat, tomatoes, and rice. 'Mama, fix us some gumbo stew—tonight, we're gonna eat.' Hank always liked gumbo."

Lilly bought him his first guitar (others have claimed the same distinction), a secondhand $3.50 instrument. And he had one teacher on it—and only one. He was a black man named Rufe Payne, widely known as "Tee Tot." From him, Williams learned chord progressions, bass runs, and the basic style of accompaniment. The techniques were nothing complex, but they were sprinkled liberally with the blues idiom of the southern black; a musical background very similar to that of Jimmie Rodgers.

When Hank was twelve, the family moved to Montgomery. He sang his first original song, *The WPA Blues*, in an amateur night contest at Montgomery's Empire Theater, and he won the fifteen-dollar first prize. The die was cast. "He told me," his mother said, "he wanted to make a profession of singing and playing. He wanted to play the night clubs and honky-tonks. He was only twelve, but I let him do it. It was rough going."

Encouraged by Lilly (or pushed?), Williams started his own band at thirteen—the first version of the Drifting Cowboys—and performed for a time on WSFA radio in Montgomery. Lilly rationalized later: "He didn't learn much in school. It was too bad that Hank, worn out by playing and singing all night, often slept through his classes in school. But, in a way, it turned out to be lucky. Too much learning might have spoiled the natural flow of his songs."

By the time he was seventeen, Lilly claimed her son knew "what makes a song." It was "love that makes the best songs," Hank was supposed to have told her. "Never in the history of country music," the mother said expansively, "has so much come out of a love of one boy for a girl, as in the case of Hank and Audrey. They loved each other like lovers in the old ballads."

Williams met Audrey Shepherd (already married at a young age and the mother of a daughter, Lycretia) at a medicine show in Banks, Alabama, and the romance was stormy from the beginning. Audrey was ambitious and given to prolonged nagging. Hank, who had started drinking at the age of twelve, during those long nights in the tough honky-tonks, had frequent bouts with alcohol. Nevertheless, they were married in December of 1944 at a gas station near Andalusia, Alabama, during a brief respite from the rigors of a road tour.

Two years later, Williams, apparently prodded by Audrey to make the effort, went to see Fred and Wesley Rose in Nashville, was signed by Acuff-Rose Publications, and the national career of Hank Williams was launched. Fred put him on the MGM record label and arranged for him to be a regular on the *Louisiana Hayride* radio show in Shreveport. "My father," Wesley Rose explained, "knew he'd get a straight reaction to Hank in Shreveport. The people there were real country fans."

It was Wesley who made the deals that took Hank's songs out of the country genre and made them popular hits as well. The most notable of those crossover successes was Tony Bennett's recording of *Cold, Cold Heart*, a million seller and a number one hit on the pop charts.

Williams' recording career was vastly impressive on the country charts, of course. In a very short time he earned eleven gold records, symbolic of million-seller singles: *Lovesick Blues; Jambalaya; Cold, Cold Heart; Your*

Cheatin' Heart; My Bucket's Got a Hole in It; Long Gone Lonesome Blues; Moanin' the Blues; Hey, Good Lookin'; Ramblin' Man; Honky Tonk Blues; and *I'll Never Get Out of This World Alive.*

Those who followed the Hank Williams rocket to stardom could not help but be impressed by the reactions to his personal appearances. There was June 11, 1949, for example, when Hank made his debut on the Grand Ole Opry, singing *Lovesick Blues.* Ed Linn, writing in *Saga* magazine, said: ". . . he stopped the show colder than it has ever been stopped, before or since . . . After Hank had gone through six encores, Red Foley had to make a little speech to quiet the place down and get the show back on schedule."

Perhaps even more dramatic was Hank's contribution to the 1951 Hadacol Caravan tour, promoted by the flamboyant Dudley J. LeBlanc, inventor of the patent medicine, Hadacol. Hank Williams and the Drifting Cowboys was the only country act on the star-studded tour. And as the tour progressed, LeBlanc kept moving Hank on the program, getting him closer and closer to the top-billed closing spot. Finally, in Louisville Williams was next-to-closing in the order of performance, just before Bob Hope.

Jerry Rivers, the fiddler with the Drifting Cowboys, recalled that "the packed stadium seemed to explode, the ovation was so great." All efforts to quiet the crowd after Williams had finished were unsuccessful and, when Hope was introduced, the cheering for Hank still continued. "They just brought Hope on anyway," Rivers wrote, "and he stood there in front of the microphone for several minutes while the applauding gradually died down. When the roar was down to a point where his voice could be heard over the sound system, Bob pulled a big ragged cowboy hat down on his ears and said, 'Hello, folks, this is Hank Hope . . .' The roar went up again, and Bob Hope shared some of Hank Williams' glory."

The glory wasn't to last, however. Hank's drinking seemed out of control, and it was accompanied by pill-popping in an effort to kill some of the constant pain he had in his back from an earlier injury. Even that injury is part of the Hank Williams lore. There was one story that he was thrown from a bucking bronco; another said he fell on some rocks while fishing. Whatever the cause, he was in almost continual pain. So he was taking pills—a lot of them—and he was drinking a great deal.

The drunkenness got him fired from the Grand Ole Opry, and dozens of promoters around the country were burned by Williams showing up intoxicated, or not showing up at all. His tempestuous marriage to Audrey finally broke up (she got half of all his future song royalties in the divorce settlement), and Hank moved into a small apartment in Nashville with a young protege singer from Texas named Ray Price.

The brilliant career quickly turned seedy. Just a few weeks after his aberrant behavior got him canned from the Grand Ole Opry in August of 1952, Hank married nineteen-year-old Billie Jean Jones Eshlimar, a recent divorcee herself. It was a move apparently undertaken to spite Audrey. The singer, encouraged by the no-holds-barred promoter Oscar (The Baron) Davis, opted for a public ceremony during an engagement at the New Orleans Municipal Auditorium. Davis arranged to sell out the house for a matinee "rehearsal" of the wedding, and again in the evening for the "actual ceremony." Both were phony; the couple had been married by a justice of the peace the evening before.

No one seemed to care anymore; neither Hank nor those who attached themselves to his falling star. One of those was a paroled forger who had passed himself off as "Doctor" Toby Marshall and was supplying the singer with bogus prescriptions for the sedative chloral hydrate, a strong heart depressant that is sometimes used to treat alcoholics.

Hank's end came just about three months after the marriage to Billie Jean, in a manner that fleshed out the Hank Williams legend. He had booked himself for a major New Year's Night show in Canton, Ohio, and had sent out word to the Drifting Cowboys to meet him there. There was a widespread snowstorm, so he hired a young man named Charles Carr to drive him in his Cadillac from Montgomery to Canton. Hank sat in the back, apparently sleeping most of the time. At Oak Hill, West Virginia, a concerned Carr tried to rouse him and found him dead. The date was January 1, 1953; Hank Williams had not yet reached his thirtieth birthday. Official cause of death was "alcoholic cardiomyopathy"; simply put, heart disease brought on by excessive drinking.

In Canton that night a spotlight was played on an empty theater stage while a recording of Williams' best-known gospel song, *I Saw the Light*, blared over the speakers. The audience wept.

Several days later, Hank's funeral in Montgomery was a massive outpouring of grief. Twenty-five thousand people tried to crowd into a city auditorium that had seats for only twenty-seven hundred. Women fainted; men cried openly. One reporter wrote that the funeral was "the greatest emotional orgy in the city's history since the inauguration of Jefferson Davis." Ernest Tubb, standing beside the silver casket, sang *Beyond the Sunset;* Roy Acuff performed *I Saw the Light,* and Red Foley, choking back tears, sang *Peace in the Valley*.

There followed, of course, the inevitable "tribute" songs. Both of his wives went on tour, billing themselves as "Mrs. Hank Williams." His own records, especially *I'll Never Get Out of This World Alive*, dominated the country music charts in 1953. For a time the charts were so full of Hank Williams that several record companies complained to the music trade journals on behalf of their living artists, denied places on the charts by the posthumous appeal of Williams.

Later, there was a dreadful biographical movie, *Your Cheatin' Heart*, which conveniently managed to ignore the pills, his divorce and second marriage, and the fact that there was alcohol associated with his tragic death. The movie was profitable. (It is worth noting that Hank Williams, Jr., sang the songs on the movie sound track. Only four years old at the time of his father's death, "Bocephus" knew the elder Williams only as a legend, as the man in the countless stories, many of them cruel, that survived him. It is the mark of Hank, Jr., that he was able to overcome the pressures of the Hank Williams legend and carve out his own substantial career.)

What happened after Hank's death proved something: No matter how grossly the Williams story was handled, his music could not be subverted. All of the deep shadows of his life could not hide the light of his great talent.

In a commercial sense, the Williams song catalog (seemingly devoid of any really weak songs) is worth millions of dollars. In an aesthetic sense, the value of the songs is incalculable. His plaque in the Country Music Hall of Fame declares: "The simple beautiful melodies and straightforward, plaintive stories of his lyrics of life as he knew it will never die."

Capitol Records executive Ken Nelson said: "His songs were accepted in the pop field because they were realistic, and they were melodically and lyrically understandable to everyone."

Music historian Bill C. Malone has written: ". . . no one communicated as well as Hank Williams. . . . He sang with the quality that has characterized every great hillbilly singer: utter sincerity."

Minnie Pearl may have summed it up best: "Hank was just as authentic as rain."

King Hiram Williams, born Mt. Olive, Alabama, September 17, 1923; died Oak Hill, West Virginia, January 1, 1953.
Married, Audrey Shepherd, 1944. (One son: Randall Hank.) Divorced.
Married, Billie Jean Jones, 1952.

I'm one of the boys who's tried to work hard here at the Grand Ole Opry to make it in country music, and I don't deserve the title of being called the 'king.' I don't deserve the title of being called anything but 'Roy Acuff' . . .

4

Roy Acuff

Elected to the Country Music Hall of Fame: 1962

In the summer of 1932, Roy Acuff, already twenty-eight years old and not settled on a career, went on the road with Doctor Hauer's Medicine Show, working mountain hamlets in east Tennessee and Virginia. There was no lightning-strike decision involved in Acuff's show business debut; he joined Dr. Hauer's show because it seemed to be something he ought to try for a season.

Young Acuff had dreamed other dreams; dreams that had turned to nightmares.

He had been a superb high school athlete, nicknamed "Rabbit" because of his speed and quickness, and he had earned thirteen varsity letters at Central High School in Fountain City, Tennessee, the county area outside of Knoxville. He had four letters in football (he was a player in the first football game he ever saw), four in basketball, and five in baseball. He was only five feet seven and weighed a mere 130 pounds. But he was tough—very tough. And he never turned his back on a brawl, even when it might involve a police officer or two.

"There was nothing I loved as much as a physical fight," he has said, "an actual physical fight! It was a joy!"

Physical work, however, never had a high priority with him. As a teen-ager, he loathed farm work. Some of his time in the fields was spent learning to balance a small hand-plow on his chin. He once went to Detroit for a production line job at the Ford Motor Company and lasted two hours. His most permanent job, covering a period of nearly three years, was as a callboy on the Louisville and Nashville Railroad. But the tenure of that job might be attributed to the fact that he also played on the L&N semi-pro baseball team at the same time.

Baseball was his first love, and those young dreams were of major league stardom. In the spring of 1929, New York Yankee scouts came through the Knoxville area, and it seemed that "Rabbit" Acuff was going to be given an opportunity to go to the Yankee training camp in 1930. It was not to be. Early in the summer of '29, he went on a fishing trip to Florida and suffered a blistering sunburn. Later, while playing for the L&N baseball team in Knoxville, he collapsed in the dugout, violently ill. Doctors diagnosed it as a sunstroke. Three times more that year, as he tried to resume normal activities, he collapsed. The warning came: Another attack might be fatal.

The next two years he spent at home; a good part of 1930 was spent in bed, recuperating, and regaining his strength. During that time he picked up his father's fiddle and began to teach himself to play. Guidance came from his father, Neill Acuff, who was both a preacher and a lawyer, and from Victrola records of Fiddlin' John Carson and Gid Tanner and the Skillet Lickers.

He learned something, too, from his sister, Sue, who was a semi-professional light opera singer. Roy would mimic her and, as he did, he learned to sing from his diaphragm. Later he would say: "That's how I learned to rear back and sing, and come out with a lot of oomph. I used to knock some of the small stations off the air. They weren't used to my style. I was one of the first who ever put a real strong voice into country music."

By 1931, Acuff had recovered enough to make short trips to the corner drugstore, and there he discovered the yo-yo, a national fad at the time. His natural athletic ability made him expert with the yo-yo, and he was never to put it down again. More than forty years later he would demonstrate the use of the yo-yo to a President of the United States (Richard Nixon) on the stage of the new Grand Ole Opry House.

Yet, his fiddling and singing around the house and his mastery of the yo-yo did little to dispel the darkness of his life in those years. "When I found I was knocked out of a career of baseball," he recalled, "I just couldn't see any light at all—everything was dark." The fiddle, however, was to bring the light.

He sat one evening, early in 1932, on the porch of his home, idly playing a fiddle tune. It was heard by a neighbor, one Dr. Hauer, who ran a medicine show and who sold a homemade remedy called Mocoton Tonic, said to cure dyspepsia, sick headaches, constipation, indigestion, torpid liver, and countless other things. Dr. Hauer offered him a job. Roy accepted.

"I didn't make much money at it, but I got a pretty good background in show business," he explained. "And when I found that I could fiddle, and I found out that I could sing a song, or sell a song, and I found out that people appreciated me, I began to see a new light, and that light has been brighter for me than the world of sports."

When the medicine show season ended in the fall of 1932, Roy Acuff was in show business to stay. But it was difficult. Money was scarce in those Depression days. Musicians often played an engagement for fifty cents. Roy played first with a Knoxville group called the Three Rolling Stones. Then, in 1933 and 1934, they grew to the Tennessee Crackerjacks. In 1935, with some personnel changed, the band landed a regular daily show on radio station WROL, Knoxville, and became the Crazy Tennesseans. They began to tour in an old Reo sedan Acuff had purchased from Dr. Hauer, the medicine show man. "The height of my ambition," Roy said, "was to play a date where the box office receipts would total as much as a hundred dollars."

It was during that period that Roy heard a song titled *The Great Speckled Bird*, performed by a singer named Charlie Swain. The original six verses, based on the ninth verse, twelfth chapter of Jeremiah, had been written by a Reverend Guy Smith; the melody was a traditional English tune. (That melody also is heard in the Carter Family's *I'm Thinking Tonight of My Blue Eyes*, Hank Thompson's *Wild Side of Life*, and Kitty Wells' *It Wasn't God Who Made Honky Tonk Angels.)* Charlie Swain was paid fifty cents to copy down the words for Acuff. It became Roy's song.

By October of 1936, the Crazy Tennesseans had achieved enough of a reputation to be asked to record for the American Record Company. "They wanted *The Bird*," Roy said, "they didn't want me." But the band went off to Chicago for its first recording session. They did twenty songs, including, of course, *The Great Speckled Bird*. Also recorded on that first session was *Wabash Cannonball*, but Acuff didn't sing it at that time. The vocal fell to band member Red Jones. Acuff's own vocal of *Cannonball*—his theme song, really—wasn't recorded until 1947.

In the thirties, the goal of all country music performers was the WSM radio show in Nashville, the *Grand Ole Opry*. The 50,000 watts of the clear channel station carried the program to two thirds of the nation every Saturday night. In October of 1937, Acuff's band was finally invited to appear on the Opry for an audition. But he was hired only to play the fiddle. That had been made clear by the Opry brass. "I was scared to death," Acuff recalled, "and I did an awful job of fiddlin'." So, after two fiddle tunes, Acuff sang *The Great Speckled Bird*. He crooned it, however, and the whole audition was a failure.

In February of 1938, Acuff and the band got another chance on the Opry. This time Roy reared back and sang *The Great Speckled Bird* while imagining that he was performing it for the medicine show audience, without benefit of a public address system. By the next Monday afternoon mail had begun to pour into WSM "by the bushel baskets." Roy Acuff and the Crazy Tennesseans became regulars on the Grand Ole Opry. Opry officials wanted a name change and got it; the act was thereafter called Roy Acuff and the Smoky Mountain Boys.

In those days, a regular job on the Grand Ole Opry paid no money. Income had to be generated from personal appearances booked by the Opry Artists Service. For ten years, Acuff and his group worked every night on the road, except on Saturday nights when they had to be back in Nashville to play the *Opry* broadcast. ("Only bad sickness or death was accepted as an excuse for not bein' there.") It was hard work. Roy's wife, Mildred, would meet him at the Opry every Saturday with a suitcase filled with clean clothes, and would take from him a suitcase filled with dirty clothes. The band would be off on the road again right after the Opry broadcast.

Yet, in a surprisingly short time, Acuff was a front-rank star in country music. October of 1939 saw the R.J. Reynolds Tobacco Company sponsoring a portion of the *Grand Ole Opry* on the NBC Red Network, titling it the "Prince Albert Show." Acuff was the star and host. In May of 1940, Roy and the band went to Hollywood to appear in a Republic Pictures film, *Grand Ole Opry*. He was to make a total of eight feature films for Republic and Columbia Pictures in the next seven years; after the first one he always received star billing. There was an effort made to keep him in Hollywood, to develop him into yet another "singing cowboy," but he turned down the overtures.

In 1942, Roy took the most important step in his career, a step of incalculable value to the entire country music industry. With only a handshake to seal the deal, and with $25,000 of "seed money" from Acuff, a partnership was struck with a veteran songwriter and musician, Fred Rose. Acuff-Rose Publications was the first music publishing company established exclusively for country music writers. It was an immediate success; over the years it has brought to the public the songwriting talents of Hank Williams, Don Gibson, Dallas Frazier, Pee Wee King and Redd Stewart, the Everly Brothers, Roy Orbison, John D. Loudermilk, Boudleaux and Felice Bryant, Mickey Newbury, Eddy Raven, and dozens of others.

With the Grand Ole Opry as the foundation, and with Acuff-Rose as the building blocks, a new "city" was built in Nashville— *Music City, U.S.A*. It is not surprising that Roy Acuff was a key in both of them.

Roy himself became an international figure. During the battle of Okinawa in World War II, a Japanese banzai attack on U.S. Marine positions began with the cry: "To hell with Roosevelt! To hell with Babe Ruth! To hell with Roy Acuff!" Later, an Armed Forces Radio Network popularity poll was won by Acuff. He beat out another singer named Frank Sinatra.

In the 1950s, when war came to Korea, Acuff and the band began touring military installations under U.S.O. auspices, and continued the annual tours, most of them at Christmastime, for twenty-five years. He was headlining a U.S.O. show in Istanbul, Turkey, in November of 1962, when he was notified that he had been elected to the Country Music Hall of Fame—the first living performer so honored. That was certainly the key honor among the hundreds he has received over a half a century as a performer. His popularity even got him into the Tennessee gubernatorial campaign in 1948—reluctantly. He lost the race, but he ran up the largest Republican vote that had been recorded in Tennessee up to that time.

The enduring strength of Roy Acuff is found in the songs he has recorded over the years; songs of "real life" and simple faith— *The Precious Jewel, Pins and Needles (In My Heart), Wreck on the Highway, Unloved and Unclaimed, Don't Make Me Go to Bed and I'll Be Good, Blue Eyes Cryin' in the Rain, Lonely Mound of Clay*. And, of course, *Wabash Cannonball* and *The Great Speckled Bird*.

An old baseball friend, St. Louis Cardinals pitching star Dizzy Dean, gave Acuff perhaps his most lasting accolade. Appearing together with Roy on a show in Dallas, Dean dubbed him "the king of the hillbillies." The media soon edited that to "the King of Country Music." Roy has always modestly issued disclaimers.

But it doesn't work. Because Roy Acuff is, indeed, the King of Country Music. And he always will be.

When the new Grand Ole Opry House was opened in 1974, Acuff was assigned Dressing Room Number One—the only artist with a permanently assigned dressing room. On the door of that room is a small plaque that may well serve as a summary of his life: *Ain't nothin' gonna come up today that me and the Lord can't handle*.

Roy Claxton Acuff, born Maynardville, Tennessee, September 15, 1903. Married, Mildred Douglas, 1936. (One son: Roy Neill.)

They say that Virginia is the Mother of Texas. We never knew who the Father was, but we kinda suspected Tennessee.

5

Tex Ritter

Elected to the Country Music Hall of Fame: 1964

When Tex Ritter was inducted into the Country Music Hall of Fame, BMI executive Frances Preston, then chairman of the board of the Country Music Association, said of him: ". . . He is powerful, yet gentle. He is commanding, yet attentive. He is forceful, yet compassionate. When you talk he listens . . . when he talks everybody listens. If personal problems are being discussed, they are never his. If there is an inconvenience, it is never his. But when you need him, he is always there."

That was the measure of the man who became the first representative of "western" music named to the Hall of Fame. Big, gruff, quick to laugh, Tex was scholarly, but not pretentious. He was successful—a major star, certainly— and yet, there is a suspicion that Tex Ritter might have been more successful had he not thought so much of others, if he had not seen it as a duty to always be there.

He was born in 1905 at Murvaul, Panola County, Texas, in the piney woods section of east Texas, an area not known to be really close to any legitimate cowboys. (Indeed, he wasn't called "Tex" until he got into show business; his name was Woodward.) He was the youngest of six children, and perhaps a bit spoiled. A cousin, J. Rex Ritter, remembered that "he never showed any enthusiasm in becoming a farmer and got away being lazy since he was the baby."

As youngsters, the Ritters attended a two-teacher school very near their home; the principal boarded with them. And the cousin recalled: "On cold mornings one of the three boys had the job of starting a fire in the wood stove at the schoolhouse. One such morning, Woodward had the job. He must have loaded the stove pretty good, and the extra firewood must have been too close, because on our way to school we were astounded to see the schoolhouse going up in flames. . . . Several of the neighbors were unkind enough to suggest that the only way Woodward got out of school was to burn it down."

But young Woodward was a good student. By the time he was of high school age, the family moved to Beaumont where Tex graduated from South Park High School at the top of his class. He entered the University of Texas, taking pre-law courses. The twig was bent there, but not toward law. At the university he met Frank Dobie, the renowned authority on southwestern history; John A. Lomax, the well-known collector of American folk music; and Oscar J. Fox, a composer of cowboy songs and the director of the university Glee Club. Joining the Glee Club, Ritter threw himself into its activities with such enthusiasm that his studies were sometimes neglected.

In 1928, the Shubert Company's operetta, *Maryland, My Maryland*, played the Hancock Opera House in Austin, and Tex never missed a performance. When the show left town, Woodward Ritter was with it as a singer in the male chorus. The road led to New York City.

"The first two years were lean ones," Tex told an interviewer in later years. "I remember one Thanksgiving when I woke up with ten cents in my pocket. I took the dime to a restaurant and ordered French fries and poured ketchup all over them. This Greek that ran the joint gave me hell for using so much of his ketchup."

Ritter persisted. He landed a spot in the men's chorus of the Hammerstein-Romberg musical, *The New Moon* (the program listed his name as "W.M. Rytter"), playing on Broadway and on the road. There wasn't much money in it and when the show reached Chicago he decided to resume his law studies at Northwestern University. Once more, however, show business intruded. He wrote a letter to his professor from Milwaukee: "I regret to inform you that I find it necessary to leave the law school on the eve of examinations. You will remember my telling you that I was with *The New Moon* company, and that the Chicago run ended last Saturday. . . . From January 19 to the 26th my address will be Shubert Theater, Indianapolis, and from the 26th to Feb 9.

the Shubert Rialto Theater, St. Louis. . . . I hope to re-enter in the summer." Those hopes never became reality.

In December of 1930 he opened in a Theatre Guild Production on Broadway, *Green Grow the Lilacs*, playing a cowboy (Cord Elam) and understudying the star, Franchot Tone. During the course of the play he sang *Git Along Little Dogies*, *The Old Chisholm Trail*, *Good-bye, Old Paint*, and *Bury Me Not on the Lone Prairie*. The play was a hit, but not once did Tone miss a performance; Tex never got an opportunity to play the lead role of Curly McClain. (Years later, when Rodgers and Hammerstein were turning that play into the musical, *Oklahoma!*, Tex auditioned privately for Oscar Hammerstein II for the lead role—unsuccessfully.)

Ritter's role in *Green Grow the Lilacs* brought him wide acceptance in New York. He was to appear in two more Broadway shows: *The Roundup* and *Mother Lode*. But it was in radio that he was the busiest. He appeared on *The Lone Star Rangers* and *Maverick Jim*, both on WOR, and he had dramatic roles on such network shows as *Gang Busters*, the *ENO Crime Club*, and *Bobbie Benson*. And he starred locally on *Tex Ritter's Campfire*, the *WHN Barn Dance*, and the very popular *Cowboy Tom's Roundup*.

In New York Tex began his recording career with the veteran A&R (Artists and Repertoire) man, Uncle Art Satherley. His first release in 1933 was *Rye Whiskey*, backed by *Good-bye, Old Paint*. In 1935, when Satherly seemed to lose interest in Ritter, Tex signed with Decca Records and producer Dave Kapp.

With 1936 there came what seemed to be the inevitable summons to Hollywood. Two years earlier Gene Autry had burst onto the movie scene and had become a major box office draw for Republic Pictures as the first of the singing cowboys. Producer Edward F. Finney, associated with Grand National Pictures, wanted to duplicate that success. He selected Ritter after hearing him on *Cowboy Tom's Roundup* on WINS. A deal was quickly struck and by late November of 1936, Tex's first starring picture was released. Titled *Song of the Gringo*, the picture got excellent reviews ("Ritter . . . has an engaging personality . . . should be a drawing card") and was highlighted by Tex's big hit song, *Rye Whiskey*.

In less than two years, there followed eleven more Grand National "oaters," starring Tex Ritter and his horse, White Flash. In his fourth picture, *Trouble in Texas*, Ritter's love interest was a young actress named Rita Cansino, later to be known as Rita Hayworth. Although the Ritter "B" films made money consistently, Grand National's major pictures were big losers, and the company folded. Ritter and producer Finney moved to Monogram Pictures.

In his third picture at Monogram, *Song of the Buckaroo*, Jinx Falkenberg, a young model from New York, played the female lead. And in a big part was Dorothy Fay, an actress from Arizona, who was already starring opposite cowboy star Buck Jones at another studio. Within two months, she was signed to be the leading lady in Ritter's *Sundown on the Prairie*, and she was also to co-star in *Rollin' Westward* and *Rainbow Over the Range*.

In all, Ritter and Finney made twenty pictures for Monogram. They parted company, apparently amicably, and Tex signed with the bigger Columbia Pictures. With the benefit of hindsight, that was a mistake. At Columbia, he was co-starred with Bill Elliot, who played the popular role of Wild Bill Hickok. Tex did all of the singing in the pictures, but Elliot seemed to get the lion's share of the publicity.

The year of 1941 was more fortunate in another way. On June 14, Tex Ritter and Dorothy Fay Southworth were married in what could only be described as the social event of the season in Prescott, Arizona, Dorothy Fay's hometown.

Just a year later, Ritter made another important move, signing with the brand new Capitol Records label under the guidance of songwriter-producer Johnny Mercer. Tex's first single was the Frank Loesser pop western tune, *Jingle, Jangle, Jingle*. It was a solid hit, and was followed shortly by another, *There's a New Moon Over My Shoulder*.

Dissatisfied with the Columbia Pictures deal, Ritter left the company at the conclusion of his nine-film contract and moved to Universal Pictures. But there he ran into the same problem: Universal teamed him with star Johnny Mack Brown, and this time he had to share his songs as well. The comic character actor, Fuzzy Knight, was given a song in each picture, further diluting Tex's star image.

In 1944, he switched production companies again, joining PRC Pictures, where he was promptly teamed with Dave O'Brien. They did nine features for PRC, co-starred as "The Texas Rangers." Those pictured marked the end—in 1945—of Tex Ritter's "B" westerns career; it had encompassed sixty feature films.

It was a period of transition for the cowboy star. He began to tour extensively, to record more frequently, and to keep his eyes open for "the right thing" in television. Then in 1952, the Russian-born composer, Dimitri Tiomkin, came to Tex with a song that was going to be the theme of a movie titled *High Noon*, starring Gary Cooper and Grace Kelly. Ritter wasn't asked to be in the picture; he was simply to sing the title song for the sound track. It was a unique hit, both as a motion picture song and as a record for Tex. It won an Oscar for Tiomkin, and Tex sang *High Noon* during the 1953 Academy Award ceremonies, the first ones to be televised nationally.

That same year Ritter began a "barn dance" series on NBC radio. *Town Hall Party* originated from Compton, California, and featured such West Coast country names as Tex Williams, Joe and Rose Maphis, Cliffie Stone, Johnny Bond, Merle Travis, and Freddie Hart. A portion of the broadcast was telecast on Channel 11 in Los Angeles (later, filmed segments of the show were distributed in syndication under the title of *Ranch Party*).

But somehow, the major television break did not come. Tex continued to tour, and he went into partnership with his close friend, Johnny Bond, in a song publishing venture they called Vidor Publications, Inc. Bond appeared in several of Ritter's motion pictures, he was the writer of the western classic, *Cimarron*, and he was later to become Tex's biographer.

In 1961, Ritter became one of the rotating hosts on a live NBC-TV show out of Springfield, Missouri. *Five Star Jubilee* also used the talents of Jimmy Wakely, Rex Allen, Carl Smith, and Snooky Lanson as hosts. It was on the air only one season.

More and more, Tex was turning his attention to Nashville, which was growing rapidly as the nation's country music center. He became active in the Country Music Association, and he served two terms as president of the organization in 1963 and 1964. In that latter year he was elected to the Country Music Hall of Fame.

By 1965 the decision had been made to move from the West Coast to Nashville. WSM radio offered him a two-pronged deal: a hosting assignment on their widely heard, all night show, and a regular spot on the *Grand Ole Opry,* where his latest hit, *I Dreamed of a Hillbilly Heaven*, was a great favorite.

Ritter plunged into Nashville activities enthusiastically—perhaps too enthusiastically. In 1970, at the urging of many of his friends, he ran for the United States Senate. An avowed conservative, Tex didn't have the support of the Tennessee Republican party organization. That went to William Brock. In the August primary, Brock defeated the country music star by a margin of four to one.

The defeat was bad enough, but Tex, certain of the "rightness" of his political philosophy, had committed a lot of his own money to the costly campaign. Earlier, in a half-joking manner, he had said that if he lost, "I'll be singing *The Boll Weevil* for the rest of my life just to pay for the campaign." As it turned out, that was very close to fact.

While the political loss was disheartening to him, he remained the same easygoing, likeable man. And his career continued. In the latter part of 1973 a single record, *The Americans*, was released by Capitol to strong reviews. And a three-record album, *An American Legend,* was prepared for distribution. He also went on with his personal appearance schedule.

On January 2, 1974, he was getting ready to leave for Philadelphia for a three-day stint at the Bijou Cafe, a dinner theater. A telephone call informed him that one of his band members had been jailed for failure to provide child support.

With his eldest son, Tommy, Ritter immediately left his home and went to the jail to provide bail for the musician. As the release papers were being prepared, Tex sat in a chair in the lock-up office, joking with the police officers. Suddenly, he grabbed at his chest and slumped over. He died instantly of a heart attack.

The words spoken some nine years earlier when he was inducted into the Country Music Hall of Fame flooded back: ". . . when you need him, he is always there."

Woodward Maurice Ritter, born Murvaul, Texas, January 12, 1905; died Nashville, Tennessee, January 2, 1974.
Married, Dorothy Fay Southworth, 1941: (Two sons: Thomas Matthew, Jonathan Southworth.)

There are those who cross over the bridge and mix their music, but I personally have no desire to do this. Country music is good. It is humble and simple and honest and relaxed. It is a way of life. I like it, the people like it, and I'll stick to it.

6

Ernest Tubb

Elected to the Country Music Hall of Fame: 1965

Fact: No country music entertainer has been on the road more than has Ernest Tubb.

Every state in the continental United States and every city in those states have been played by Tubb and his Texas Troubadours, and that includes nearly every town, borough, village, and hamlet, and a good many foreign countries. Tubb annually works in excess of two hundred days a year on tour, covering 150,000 miles and performing in every known country music venue: fairs, parks, clubs, schoolhouses, concert halls, theaters, motels.

Illustrative of Ernest's travels was his schedule from October 23 through November 13, 1981. He played Kingfisher, Oklahoma; Nathrop and Fort Collins, Colorado; Oakley and San Leandro, California; Albany and Eugene, Oregon; Spokane, Washington; Boise, Idaho; Great Falls, Montana; Salt Lake City, Utah; Alpine and Evansville, Wyoming; New Salem, North Dakota; Cable, Wisconsin; and Topeka and Parsons, Kansas.

In addition, Tubb manages to play the Grand Ole Opry more than a lot of the acts on the roster. And why? "What else would I do?" he asked. "There's nothing I love more than singing for a live audience."

E.T. (his myriad friends call him "E.T.") readily admits that he wanted to be a singer because of Jimmie Rodgers. He was born near Crisp, Texas, in rural Ellis County, south of Dallas, the youngest of five children. That was cotton country, and his father was the overseer of a 300-acre cotton farm. His mother was one-fourth Cherokee Indian.

Music was in his life from the beginning; his mother played the piano and organ. When he was growing up in Crisp, and later in Benjamin, Texas, he was called "Wash" by his contemporaries. He had one ambition—he wanted to be a cowboy movie star. Then at thirteen, he heard his first Jimmie Rodgers blue-yodeling record. That sound was to change, and dominate, his life. Having the latest Rodgers record became almost an obsession with him. A brother, Calvin R. Tubb, Jr., recalled that "Ernest saved his nickles and dimes to buy them."

Tubb himself reminisced: "I just wanted to sing like Jimmie, and I didn't really have any idea of making a living with my singing when I first started out."

Starting out was not easy. His parents had separated when he was twelve, and his teen years were spent moving around Texas living with various family members. Schooling was virtually ignored; later he figured that he had had only seventeen months of formal schooling. "When I realized what I had missed," he said, "I began educating myself."

In 1933, when he was nineteen, he worked on a road construction crew near Benjamin and met a guitar player named Merwyn "Buff" Buffington, who was impressed with young Tubb's singing and urged him to learn to play the guitar. Ernest bought a secondhand instrument for $5.50, and Buff was his first teacher; E.T. was so intent on learning to play it that sometimes his fingers bled. Late in '33 he was in San Antonio working on WPA construction projects at various military installations, a job he held only long enough to seek out employment at a San Antonio drugstore. His salary was ten dollars a week. Nevertheless, he married in May of 1934 to Lois Elaine Cook; a son, Justin, was born in August of 1935. His drugstore salary was raised to $12.50 a week.

In San Antonio, he again met Buff Buffington, who was playing on radio station KONO with the Castleman Brothers, Joe and Jim. Tubb sang with them several times and managed to wrangle his own fifteen-minute show, at 5:30 A.M., twice a week. While he was playing at KONO, he contacted the widow of Jimmie Rodgers, who was still living in San Antonio. She was astounded by his knowledge of her husband's records. Carrie Rodgers offered to help him.

"She told me," Ernest said, "that she had been getting up early to listen to me on the air and that she liked the way I sang Jimmie's songs. She told me I had 'heart' in my singing and that she was impressed by my sincerity."

Those were not idle words. Mrs. Rodgers contacted the executives of RCA Records and arranged for Tubb to have a recording session at the Texas Hotel in San Antonio in late October of 1936. Mrs. Rodgers lent the skinny young man Jimmie's guitar (she later gave it to him), and he cut four songs in that first session: *The Last Thoughts of Jimmie Rodgers*, *The Passing of Jimmie Rodgers*, *The TB Is Whipping Me*, and *Since That Black Cat Crossed My Path*. RCA released them, but with little enthusiasm. Four more songs recorded in a second session in '37 were not released until Tubb had become a nationally known star in 1942.

E.T. continued to struggle. There were small radio jobs on a number of stations, dollar-a-night engagements in honky-tonks, two-dollar-a-night appearances at drive-in movies, and even a period when he sold mattresses, making free singing appearances to promote the product.

In 1940, he turned to Mrs. Rodgers again for help and guidance. "Decca Records was a new company," Ernest recollects, "but they had Bing Crosby, and I figured if they were that smart, they must be all right." Mrs. Rodgers recommended E.T. to Decca and, on April 4, 1940, he recorded four songs for Decca's Dave Kapp at the Rice Hotel in Houston: *Blue-Eyed Elaine*, *I'll Get Along Somehow*, *You Broke a Heart*, and *I'll Never Cry Over You*. Kapp was enthusiastic and offered Tubb an either/or deal; either a flat twenty-five dollars per song or a contract with royalties. Ernest, following the advice of Mrs. Rodgers, signed the royalties contract.

E.T. considered 1940 to be the full-time professional start of his career. After the Decca recording debut, he went to radio station KGKO in Fort Worth and was the on-the-air spokesman for Universal Mills, makers of Gold Chain Flour. Billed as the Gold Chain Troubadour, he earned seventy-five dollars a week from the sponsor.

In the fall of 1941, stardom hit. Tubb's seventh Decca record was released: *Walking the Floor Over You*. It all happened pretty quickly after that. He appeared in three Hollywood films, met the top-drawer agent, J.L. (Joe) Frank, who became his manager, and made his first appearance on the *Grand Ole Opry* in December of 1942, where he sang his big hit song and was called back for three encores. A month later he moved to Nashville—permanently.

Tubb became a leader in the country music community. For one thing, he campaigned to have the word *country* substituted for *hillbilly*, and he pressured Decca Records on that subject. Decca, in turn, used its muscle with the music trade publications until they finally capitulated. For another, Tubb was one of the first country music stars to conduct a formal recording session in Nashville. Paul Cohen, the top producer at Decca, recorded Red Foley in WSM's Studio "B" in 1945, and later that year did the same with Tubb. Those two sessions are regarded as the beginning of the Nashville recording industry.

E.T. was also the first country music star to headline a show at New York City's prestigious Carnegie Hall in 1947, hosting a package show that included Minnie Pearl, George D. Hay (the "voice" of the *Grand Ole Opry*), Rosalie Allen, the harmony team of Radio Dot and Smokey Swann, and the Short Brothers, Jimmie and Leon.

While Tubb has always been careful to keep his act in the strictly country vein, he is not above innovation. When juke box operators complained that the acoustical guitars on his early records could not be heard when business got a bit boisterous in the bars and honky-tonks, he became a leader in the use of electric guitars in a country band, adding "body" to the sound. And in 1948, he went to the West Coast to record a duet single with the Andrew Sisters: *Biting My Fingernails* and *Don't Rob Another Man's Castle*. It's important to note that the Andrew Sisters did *his* material; he didn't do theirs.

E.T. had a simple rule: He would do anything to further country music. Thus, he was able to suppress any personal pridefulness he might have felt and record duets with other major stars. Most notable were the records he cut with Red Foley (eighteen in all, including *Goodnight Irene*, *Love Bug Itch*, and *Too Old to Cut the Mustard*) and Loretta Lynn (*Mr. and Mrs. Used-To-Be*, *Our Hearts Are Holding Hands*, *Sweet Thang*, and *Who's Gonna Take the Garbage Out?*).

That desire to promote country music also took Ernest into the retail record business with his now famous Record Shop. *The Midnight Jamboree*, which is heard each week live from the Record Shop following the *Grand Ole Opry*, has been an important early starting point for a lot of acts, among them the Everly Brothers and Bobby Helms.

He has always been available to help others. Jack Greene came out of the Texas Troubadours band. Tubb says he "kicked him out of the nest." Some kick! In 1967, the first year for the Country Music Association awards, Greene was voted the Male Vocalist of the Year, won the Single of the Year with *There Goes My Everything*, which also won Album of the Year, while Dallas Frazier, writer of *There Goes My Everything*, picked up the Song of the Year award. Cal Smith was another Tubb band member who was urged to go out on his own. E.T. helped him to get a recording contract, and in 1974 Cal's recording of Don Wayne's *Country Bumpkin* was responsible for winning Single of the Year and Song of the Year honors.

It's difficult, in anything less than a volume, to sum up Ernest Tubb's career. He has had more hits than most other performers can dream about: *Married Man Blues, My Mother Is Lonely, The Right Train to Heaven, Tennessee Border No. 2, No Help Wanted, A Dear John Letter, Hey, Mister Bluebird, (Take Me Back and) Try Me One More Time, There's a Little Bit of Everything in Texas, Filipino Baby, Rainbow at Midnight, Warm Red Wine, Driving Nails in My Coffin, Waltz Across Texas, Half a Mind, Slippin' Around, (Remember Me) I'm the One Who Loves You*, and on and on.

Perhaps what stands out about Tubb is his innate modesty, operating hand-in-glove with a fierce pride in what he does.

Quote: "I don't read music and I'd fight the man who tried to teach me. I don't care whether I hit the right note or not. I'm not looking for perfection of delivery—thousands of singers have that. I'm looking for individuality. I phrase the way I want to; I sing the way I feel like singing at the moment."

Quote: "Whatever success I've had, I owe to Mrs. Jimmie Rodgers."

Quote (on the occasion of his induction into the Country Music Hall of Fame in 1965): "I don't deserve it. But I'm sure glad somebody thought of it."

When Ernest Tubb takes his final bows in the hundreds of personal appearances he makes each year, he flips over his guitar to reveal a legend printed on the back in bold letters. It says "THANKS." Some think of that as corny. To E.T. it's just a recognition of a reality: The people who paid to see him perform are the people who made him a star.

And he's grateful.

Ernest Dale Tubb, born Crisp, Texas, February 9, 1914.
Married, Lois Elaine Cook, 1934. (Three children: Justin, Rodger Dale, Violet Elaine.) Divorced.
Married, Olene Adams, 1949. (Five children: Erlene Dale, Olene Gayle, Ernest Dale, Jr., Larry Dean, Karen Delene.) Divorced.

This may make the purists mad, but I figure for every purist I lose, I gain five other fans who like country music the modern way.

7
Eddy Arnold

Elected to the Country Music Hall of Fame: 1966

He started as "the Tennessee Plowboy." A decade and a half later *Time* magazine was calling him "the Country Como." In accomplishing that transition, Eddy Arnold's trend-setting move to pop country was so pervasive that it changed the look and sound of much of country music.

In a 1967 NBC News documentary, *Music From the Land,* Arnold said: "Country music is the 'new pop,' and today you can take it anywhere." Then, in tuxedo and black tie, he strolled out onto the stage to sing with the Memphis Symphony Orchestra. By that year, however, he had already been elected to the Country Music Hall of Fame at the comparatively young age of forty-eight, with the wording on his plaque—"He has been a powerful influence in setting musical tastes"—sidestepping the principal point of his influence.

Like it or not (and there were some in the country music community who did not), Eddy Arnold had taken country music out of the honky-tonks and had moved it into the supper clubs. He had, indeed, made it pop and had sold millions upon millions of records along the way. His example was not lost on the generation of young country singers who followed him.

Yet, Eddy's beginnings were not unlike the beginnings of a host of country performers who had gone before him. He *was* a plowboy, in fact; poor, fatherless at an early age, the family farm lost in a foreclosure sale, a start in show business in unsavory dives at fifty cents a night. Somehow, however, the smooth baritone of the young singer was different; from the first it was lacking in country idiom.

Eddy himself wondered about his voice, and offered a hesitant explanation: ". . . I was never a real hillbilly singer of the nasal kind; I never had a twang in my voice. That's what always puzzled me about other country singers, 'cause nobody ever came from farther back in the country than I did. I guess it's just kind of the way you think. I don't know, but I think my family had something to do with it. My family was a proud family—poor but proud—and they considered themselves good people; so I guess they watched how we talked."

Steve Sholes, the RCA Records executive who helped to guide Eddy's career, had another viewpoint. "He just naturally sings right," Sholes told an interviewer. "It's an unusual quality. Caruso had it and so has Bing Crosby, but they're the only ones I can think of besides Eddy."

Arnold was born in 1918 on a farm in Henderson, Chester County, Tennessee, about one hundred forty miles from Nashville. He was the youngest of four children. His father was a big man, a stern disciplinarian; his mother was "a quiet little woman" who sang around the house. Young Eddy was encouraged when he began to show some inclination toward music. "My hero was Gene Autry then," he recalled. "I must have sent twenty dollars to Sears for his records. And Bing Crosby! Those two people were *it* for me."

His musical education, if the word *education* is not wrongly used in this context, began on a Sears Roebuck Silvertone guitar borrowed from a girl cousin. He taught himself to play, and one of the first tunes he could pick out was *Sweet Bunch of Daisies*, a song his mother loved to sing. "I'd steal off by myself and start strummin' and singin'. I was beginning to discover what mattered deeply to me. I liked to sing. I *needed* to sing."

In 1929 his father died after a protracted illness. The date was May 15, Eddy's eleventh birthday. By the fall of that year, everything had collapsed. He stood with his family and watched an auctioneer sell the farm, the livestock, the implements—everything—to satisfy creditors. The Arnolds became sharecroppers on their own farm. By the time he was seventeen Eddy had decided to seek a better life—as a singer.

The year was 1935. The place was Jackson, Tennessee. The act was Eddy Arnold and Speedy McNatt, a young fiddler Eddy had known for some time. They played on radio station WTJS in Jackson and at any little club or beer joint they could. Money was scarce, and Eddy took a job with a funeral director, driving an ambulance. He slept at the funeral home and was paid twenty-five cents every time he took the ambulance out to pick up a body. If he helped out at a funeral as a pallbearer, he earned fifty cents more.

But Arnold and McNatt moved on, first to Memphis and then to St. Louis, where Arnold's married sister lived and who was good for an occasional free meal. "Many nights during 1938 and 1939," Eddy remembered, "Speedy and I played clubs for fifty cents, or a dollar, or a dollar and a half a night, and sometimes just for tips."

The first big break came in 1940, when Pee Wee King gave Arnold a job with his Golden West Cowboys. This was a *real* country music band, with an important regular spot on the *Grand Ole Opry*. Eddy toured with King and, while in Louisville, he met a young girl who worked behind the soda fountain at Woolworth's. Sally Gayhart was her name. In November of 1941 they were married.

Once he got to Nashville with King, Eddy was not to leave. But his ambitions extended beyond playing and singing with the Golden West Cowboys. Screwing up his courage one day in 1943, he went to Harry Stone, the WSM boss, and asked for his own program on the radio station. He was somewhat surprised when Stone agreed. As so often happens, Stone's decision was akin to prying the first olive out of the bottle. It lead to a regular solo spot on the *Grand Ole Opry*. And in that same year, Fred Forster, a prominent Chicago music publisher, recommended Eddy to Frank Walker of RCA Victor, and Walker—without even an audition—offered Arnold a recording contract.

Just about the time the contract arrived in the mail, however, the musicians union went on strike against the record companies, and Eddy's recording debut was postponed for fifteen months. His first record, on the RCA Bluebird label, was *Mommy, Please Stay Home With Me,* backed with *Mother's Prayer*. It was recorded in December of 1944, released early in 1945, and was a reasonably good seller.

By that time, the Tennessee Plowboy also had a personal manager: one Tom Parker, later to be that Colonel Tom Parker who guided Elvis Presley to fame. Everything was going well. Eddy has said to many interviewers that 1946 was his golden year. He had his first big record hit with *That's How Much I Love You;* Parker arranged for Eddy to host a *Grand Ole Opry* segment for the Ralston Purina Company, and that was followed by Purina sponsoring a fifteen-minute daily show on the Mutual Radio Network, for which *Cattle Call* was the theme song.

There was a parade of hits: *I'll Hold You in My Heart 'Til I Can Hold You in My Arms, It's a Sin, What Is Life Without Love?, Bouquet of Roses, Anytime, Don't Rob Another Man's Castle, A Heart Full of Love, Just a Little*

Lovin' Will Go a Long Way, Texarkana Baby, Then I Turned and Slowly Walked Away, I'm Throwing Rice at the Girl I Love. He was the hottest property in country music.

In what was an inevitable move, there was a tearful farewell on the Grand Ole Opry stage and he moved on to other things—Las Vegas bookings, an appearance on *The Milton Berle Show*, then the most important variety show on network television; and two motion pictures, *Feudin' Rhythm* and *Hoedown*, hurriedly produced "B" formula films. "I've got those prints," he says, "but they are so bad I wouldn't want to pull them out. It seems odd to me that those pictures didn't kill my career on the spot."

No career can stay at a fever pitch forever, and Arnold's didn't. Between 1955 and 1963 he stayed home a lot; the old fire of ambition just didn't seem to be there. Then, too, his two children were in the growing up years, and he wanted to be with them more. Whatever the reason, one career seemed to have ended. Another one was still before him.

Enter Gerald Purcell. The year was 1964; Tom Parker had gone on to Elvis, and Purcell became Eddy's personal manager. The New Yorker had a different vision of Eddy Arnold, based on the mobility of the American population. "Country music's gone to the city," he told the singing star. "It's following the country people, and they're going all over the world." Purcell's ideas were in step with what Eddy himself had been contemplating: lusher arrangements and a more modern, "citified" sound to be associated with country music.

An experiment was launched—an April, 1965, concert tour to Cleveland, Cincinnati, Philadelphia, Chicago, Toledo, and Dayton, with young Roger Miller as an opening act. It was a critical success, and Arnold's second career was launched. The tour was accompanied by a series of new hit records: *What's He Doing in My World?* (a gold record and a gold album), *Make the World Go Away, I Want To Go With You, Misty Blue, Turn the World Around the Other Way*.

In 1966, Eddy appeared on *The Ed Sullivan Show*, the premier variety show on television; that was the year, too, that he was one of four new members of the Country Music Hall of Fame. He was a guest star on *The Perry Como Show*, a guest host of Johnny Carson's *Tonight* show, and the host of *The Summer Kraft Music Hall*. There were TV specials with Danny Kaye, Danny Thomas, Red Skelton, and Dean Martin. And there was Carnegie Hall, too.

Time magazine's review of his Carnegie Hall concert was lavish: "Backed by a 17-piece orchestra, he sang about hump-back mules, lonesome hearts and them old cotton fields back home in a mellifluous baritone that poured out just as warm and creamy as milk fresh out of the barn cow. Mostly, the songs were samplings of his biggest hits—*Anytime, Bouquet of Roses*—flavored with a touch of falsetto and yodel-like loops that carried that special stamp of the hill country. Trading on a broad, half-moon smile and an ultra-relaxed manner that could charm the warts off of a hog's back, he drew a standing ovation and a stampede of well-wishers."

Perhaps the best illustration of his new career came in the fall of 1967 when the first Country Music awards ceremony was conducted in the Nashville Municipal Auditorium. Arnold was voted Entertainer of the Year, but he wasn't there to accept the award. At that very hour he was performing before a sell-out dinner audience at the Cocoanut Grove nightclub in Los Angeles.

The Tennessee Plowboy had indeed plowed new ground in country music. And in doing so, he sold more than seventy-five million records. He became wealthy, too, with numerous lucrative real estate investments in the Nashville area. He remembered, when he began earning money as a singer, the humiliation of seeing his family's farm sold out from under them, and his early dollars went into land.

There is pride in Eddy Arnold about what he has done. "I'm an ambitious person. I'm an egotist. There is nothing wrong with ego. I think we all want to feel like we are productive." And that pride is salted with realism. "This is a business; it's no lark. I've got a good accountant, a good lawyer, a good manager, a good minister, and I listen to them."

Richard Edward Arnold, born Henderson, Tennessee, May 15, 1918. Married, Sally Gayhart, 1941. (Two children: Jo Ann, Richard Edward, Jr.)

I was alone and broke and scared when I first came to Nashville. Heck, even the street cars scared me. Four people standing together looked like a mob.

8

James R. Denny

Elected to the Country Music Hall of Fame: 1966

Legends are not built on infallibility. Instead, they are molded from the certainty of human error. Infallibility might be a fine trait to contemplate, but the recalling of human error is the meat of legend. And sometimes, a lot more fun.

It was 1954. A shy young singer out of Tupelo, Mississippi, who had been driving a truck for forty-five dollars a week, had just recorded a single for Sun Records in Memphis. On one side was Bill Monroe's *Blue Moon of Kentucky;* on the other side was *That's All Right.* At the instigation of Hank Snow, the young man made his debut on Nashville's *Grand Ole Opry,* singing both sides of his only record. At the conclusion of the performance, Jim Denny, the talent boss at the Opry, told Elvis Presley that he ought to go back to driving the truck. It is said that Elvis wept all the way back to Memphis.

Twelve years later, Denny was elected to the Country Music Hall of Fame because he was recognized as one of the finest talent promoters in the music business. His mistake on Presley (and was it really an error in the context of

61

country music?) merely served to point up the hundreds of correct decisions he had made on other talent matters.

James R. Denny was the first non-performer, the first "behind-the-scenes" man named to the Hall of Fame. He didn't sing and he didn't play an instrument and he didn't write songs. But the Hall of Fame electors were sure he belonged there. And so did the dozens of performers whose careers he had influenced as a broadcaster, a talent booker, and a music publisher.

Denny was born in 1911 in Buffalo Valley, in the remote Tennessee hill country hard by the Cumberland Plateau. His family, the story is told, invested unwisely in mules during World War I years and was financially destitute. At the age of eleven, young Jim was sent to an aunt in Nashville, put on a bus with forty cents as his total capital.

The city frightened him at first, but there was a toughness in him that allowed him to earn a living on its streets. He was at one and the same time a newspaper hawker in downtown Nashville and a twelve-dollar-a-week telegram delivery boy for Western Union. His education was not a classroom thing; he learned about life in the seamier corners of the city.

At sixteen, he got a job in the mail room at the National Life and Accident Insurance Company. National Life (then and now) owned radio station WSM, and WSM boasted the two-year-old *Grand Ole Opry*. Denny saw a lot of mail from the fans pouring through his mail room. He saw, too, an opportunity. He began to work his way up in the company—first from the mail room to the filing room. He took business courses at Watkins Institute in Nashville and moved up some more—from filing to accounting to actuarial. He set up the mechanical accounting and record system for National Life and became a department head.

Simultaneously, to earn a few extra dollars, he was at the Grand Ole Opry every weekend. There he took telephone messages, ran errands, ushered, sold tickets, and even filled in as a bouncer when the occasion required it. He made himself "useful" at the Opry.

During World War II he took over the operation of the Opry concessions. By 1951, he had become the indispensible man at the Grand Ole Opry and was named its manager. It was Denny who put real muscle in the Artists Service Bureau. Because the Opry was the primary pool of country music talent in Nashville, in those days the Artists Service Bureau was a virtual monopoly; the Opry imprimatur was almost a necessity to get good bookings on the road.

Jim Denny had become a powerful man in Nashville. He knew every promoter in the nation, and when someone wanted something in Nashville, it was Jim Denny they called.

The Music Reporter said of him: "Part of his success lay in his ability to understand artists, temperament and all."

Understanding was not always easy. It was Denny who, with some misgivings, brought Hank Williams to the Grand Ole Opry in June of 1949. And it was Denny, with deep regret, who had to fire Williams for drunkenness in the latter part of 1952.

In 1953, Denny went into the music publishing business. There were two BMI-affiliated companies: Driftwood, which was co-owned with Carl Smith and Troy Martin; and Cedarwood, a partnership with Webb Pierce (later Denny and Pierce were also partners in the ownership of three radio stations in Georgia). A third publishing company, Jim Denny Music, was set up as an ASCAP affiliate.

The first Cedarwood song recorded was titled *Say, Big Boy,* by Goldie Hill on Columbia Records.

Denny's outside music publishing activities began to worry the WSM radio executives; his companies were viewed as a conflict of interest with Denny's broadcasting activities with the Grand Ole Opry. WSM, in a blanket policy decision, ordered its employees to divest themselves of all outside interests in the music industry. To Jim Denny his choice was clear; in the mid-fifties he left the radio station. Later he would say his dismissal by WSM—for so he considered it—was the biggest break in his life.

George D. Hay, "The Solemn Old Judge" of the Opry, sent him a note when he left: "You did a big job for WSM, and only a few know the problems you solved."

Denny's first act after leaving the Opry was the organization of the Jim Denny Artists Bureau, Inc. The Opry talent, aware of Jim's widespread booking contacts, flocked to his agency, as did others not on the Opry roster. An early brochure of the Denny booking agency listed Webb Pierce, Minnie Pearl, Ray Price, Carl Smith, Kitty Wells, Johnny and Jack, Hank Snow, Jimmy Dean, Little Jimmy Dickens, Hawkshaw Hawkins, Jean Shepard, George Morgan, Jimmy C. Newman, Stonewall Jackson, Grandpa Jones, Lefty Frizzell, Marvin Rainwater, Carl Perkins, Porter Wagoner, Roger Miller, the Willis Brothers, Red Sovine, Archie Campbell, Norma Jean, Bill Monroe, Carl Belew, Justin Tubb, Claude Gray, Bill Phillips, Carl Butler, Del Wood, Whitey Ford ("the Duke of Paducah"), Dottie West, ventriloquist Alec Houston, Cousin Jody, Connie Hall, the Bluegrass Gentlemen, and a "young upcoming female vocalist," Deloris Smiley. In later years, Smiley became a well-known Nashville booking agent in her own right.

At first the Denny publishing and booking offices were on Seventh Avenue North in downtown Nashville. But as business expanded, he moved the offices to Sixteenth Avenue South (now Music Square East), which was to become the heart of what is now known as "Music Row."

In 1955, Jim Denny was named Man of the Year in country music by *Billboard* magazine. He was clearly the top booker of country music talent in the United States; his agency handled approximately fifty acts in two thousand booking engagements annually. One of his coups was the establishment of a road show package for the Philip Morris Tobacco Company, which ran for sixteen consecutive months and also included a weekly network radio show.

The job grew into eighteen-hour days, seven days a week. He decided he needed help with the booking agency. Two of his acts, Webb Pierce and Red Sovine, recommended a man who had handled their personal management, W.E. (Lucky) Moeller. From 1934 to 1943, Moeller had been in the banking business. Then, seeking more diversity in life, he went into talent management, and for a time was the manager of Bob Wills, the "King of Western Swing." He had also managed the Trianon Ballroom in Oklahoma City and briefly had managed young Brenda Lee. Moeller came to Nashville in 1957, and the booking agency became Denny-Moeller Talent.

On the music publishing side of things, Denny merged the two BMI companies under the single umbrella of Cedarwood, which represented such writers as Wayne Walker, Mel Tillis, Marijohn Wilken, Danny Dill, Cindy Walker, John D. Loudermilk, Roy Botkin, Fred Burch, Carl Perkins, and others. Hits were plentiful: *I Don't Care, More and More, Are You Sincere?, Waterloo, Emotions, Little Boy Sad, Tobacco Road, Long Black Veil, Detroit City, Dream On, Little Dreamer, Hello Out There*.

In the early sixties, Jim Denny became ill; the diagnosis was cancer. He died in August of 1963 in Nashville's St. Thomas Hospital. He was only fifty-two.

The talent booking part of his country music empire passed to Lucky Moeller. The family retained Cedarwood Music, with a son, Bill, as president; another son, John, as vice-president, and Denny's widow, Dolly, as treasurer.

The tributes to Denny were many. One newspaper editorial called him: ". . . one of the dynamic forces that propelled the industry to phenomenal heights." His one-time partner, Lucky Moeller, commented: "No one will ever know how much this great man has done for country music. . . ." *Music Reporter* said "his stature loomed across the country music field like a colossus."

But he was not infallible.

He once told Hank Williams to forget *Jambalaya*. And he tried to persuade Jimmy Dean not to record *Big Bad John*.

And, then, there was his initial evaluation of Elvis Presley.
The stuff of country music legend.

James Rea Denny, born Buffalo Valley, Tennessee, February 28, 1911; died Nashville, Tennessee, August 27, 1963.
(Three children by a previous marriage: James William, John Everett, Linda Gayle.)
Married, Dolly Dearman, 1959.

We never use the word 'hillbilly' because it was coined in derision . . . Furthermore, there is no such animal. Country people have a definite dignity of their own and a native shrewdness which enables them to hold their own in any company . . .

9

George D. Hay

Elected to the Country Music Hall of Fame: 1966

eorge D. Hay started as a newspaperman, a chronicler of the human comedy, and it was his deep interest in the study of people that brought him to country music. He was only a young man—in his mid-twenties—when the Memphis *Commercial-Appeal* sent him to Mammoth Spring, Arkansas, in the foothills of the Ozarks, to cover the funeral of a Marine hero of World War I. What he experienced was to change his life.

"I sauntered around the town," he would write later, "at the edge of which, hard by the Missouri line, there lived a truck farmer in an old railroad car. He had seven or eight children and his wife seemed to be very tired with the tremendous job of caring for them. We chatted for a few minutes and the man went to his place of abode and brought forth a fiddle and a bow. He invited me to attend a 'hoedown' that neighbors were going to put on that night until 'the crack of dawn' in a log cabin about a mile up a muddy road. He and two other old-time musicians furnished the earthy rhythm. No one in the world has ever had more fun than those Ozark mountaineers did that night. It stuck with me until the idea became 'Grand Ole Opry' seven or eight years later. It is as fundamental as sunshine and rain, snow and wind and the light of the moon peeping through the trees. Some folks like it and some dislike it very much, but it'll be there long after you and I have passed out of this picture for the next one. . . .''

The *Commercial-Appeal* owned a radio station, WMC, and Hay saw the potential of the new medium. He became an announcer on the station, a somewhat flamboyant one, and he identified his appearances by blowing an old wooden railroad whistle he called *Hushpuckena*, the name of a very little town in northern Mississippi. Just why he singled out that name is not really clear, but young Hay had a distinct flair for show business. (In a similar vein was the selection of the title, "The Solemn Old Judge," for himself. There was a joke around the Grand Old Opry that Hay was neither solemn, nor old, nor a judge. But "The Solemn Old Judge" was the title of a column he had written during his newspaper days.)

In any event, George Hay moved from WMC, Memphis, to radio station WLS in Chicago in 1924, to become chief announcer. One of his duties was to announce a new program put on the schedule by station manager Edgar L. Bill. It was called the *WLS Barn Dance*, which would later evolve into the *National Barn Dance* on network radio. The program was perfect for Hay, who hearkened back to his night with the Ozark musicians in Mammoth Spring, Arkansas. His railroad whistle, *Hushpuckena*, was part of the program, and he took it with him in early November of 1925 when he moved to Nashville to become program manager at radio station WSM.

There he was to make broadcasting history. The date was November 28, 1925. The name of the program was the *WSM Barn Dance*, probably for no other reason than it was a convenient title. The first performer was an eighty-year-old champion fiddler named Uncle Jimmy Thompson, accompanied on the piano by his niece, Eva Thompson Jones. Hay seated the old man in front of a round carbon microphone, and the program began. By the end of the third number, telegrams were arriving in the studio with requests for specific songs.

Uncle Jimmy fiddled for a solid hour, when George Hay suggested that perhaps the program ought to come to an end. "Why, shucks, a man don't get warmed up in an hour," the old man complained. "I just won an eight-day fiddling contest down in Dallas, Texas, and here's my blue ribbon to prove it."

The *WSM Barn Dance* was an immediate success. Others quickly came forward who wanted to be part of it. Old-time string bands were popular: the Possum Hunters, the Gully Jumpers, the Fruit Jar Drinkers, the Crook Brothers, and a very good string band called the Dixieliners, consisting of fiddler Arthur Smith and Sam and Kirk McGee on guitar and banjo. The McGee Brothers and the Possum Hunters were among the first members of the show to record. Sam McGee joked about it: "They recorded us because we were outstanding in the field. And that's where they found us—out standing in the field."

December 10, 1927, was another historic day for the WSM program and for all of country music. That was the day that the name "Grand Ole Opry" was first used. George Hay, who coined the name in an ad-libbed remark, wrote about it later, explaining that WSM carried the high-brow NBC network program, *The Music Appreciation Hour*, conducted by Dr. Walter Damrosch, just before *Barn Dance* went on the air.

"We must confess that the change in pace and quality was immense," Hay said. "But that is part of America, fine lace and homespun cloth.

"The monitor in our Studio B was turned on, so that we would have a rough idea of the time which was fast approaching. At about five minutes before eight, your reporter called for silence in the studio. Out of the loudspeaker came the very correct, but accented voice of Dr. Damrosch and his words were something like this: 'While most artists realize that there is no place in the classics for realism, nevertheless I am going to break one of my rules and present a composition by a young composer from Ioway, who sent us his latest number, which depicts the onrush of a locomotive . . .'

"After which announcement the good doctor directed the symphony orchestra through a number which carried many 'shooshes' depicting an engine trying to come to a full stop. Then he closed the program with his usual sign-off.

"Our control operator gave us the signal which indicated we were on the air . . . We paid our respects to Dr. Damrosch and said on the air something like this: 'Friends, the program which just came to a close was devoted to the classics. Dr. Damrosch told us that it was generally agreed that there is no place in the classics for realism . . . However, from here on out for the next three hours, we will present nothing but realism . . . It will be down to earth for the earthy.

"'In respectful contrast to Dr. Damrosch's presentation of the number which depicts the onrush of the locomotive, we will call on one of our performers, Deford Bailey, with his harmonica, to give us the country version of his *Pan American Blues*.' Whereupon Deford Bailey, a wizard with the harmonica, played the number. At the close of it, your reporter said: 'For the past hour we have been listening to music taken largely from Grand Opera, but from now on we will present the *Grand Ole Opry*.' The name has stuck . . . It seems to fit our shindig, hoedown, barn dance, or 'rookus.'"

George Hay, the announcer on the Opry from its start in 1925 until he retired in the middle fifties, was never the final authority on the program, but his influence on the content of the show was considerable. He had two favor-ite phrases that he used over and over again: "Keep it down to earth" and "Keep it close to the ground." He could never forget the impact that night in the log cabin in Mammoth Spring had had on him, and sometimes his determi-nation to "keep it close to the ground" flew in the face of inevitable change.

It's questionable, for example, whether Roy Acuff would have gotten on the Grand Ole Opry as soon as he did if Judge Hay had been the final authority. Roy had approached Hay several times for a chance to appear, only to be told that the program had sufficient personnel. Acuff finally went around him, ap-pealing to agent Joe Frank for help. Frank contacted David Stone, then head of the WSM Artists Service Bureau, who arranged for Roy's first appearance on the Opry. Acuff was different from the string bands that then dominated the program; he had a country band, but the emphasis was on the singer, not on string band instrumental numbers.

Then there was a night in the early forties when Sam McGee, a veteran member of the cast, wanted to play an electrified Spanish guitar on the pro-gram. Hay objected, and McGee backed off.

And, of course, there was the now famous argument over the use of drums on the Grand Ole Opry stage. When Pee Wee King came onto the show with his Golden West Cowboys he introduced a drummer into the band. Judge Hay was not happy, and King said that he was told not to mention their use on the air. After two or three Opry shows with the drums, King had to get rid of them. Sometime later, Bob Wills and his band played the Opry, and legend has it the drums were hidden behind a curtain. They weren't.

George Hay, of course, was fiercely proud of the show and would do any-thing to promote it. He went to Hollywood to play himself in a Republic Pic-tures "B" movie titled *Grand Ole Opry*, which also featured Uncle Dave Macon and Roy Acuff. And he went to New York City to appear as the Solemn Old Judge when Ernest Tubb made history at Carnegie Hall.

Of all the performers who appeared on the Grand Ole Opry during the first twenty-five years, perhaps Uncle Dave Macon was George Hay's favorite. They fit together like bread and butter. The freewheeling, high kicking, old-timey banjo player admired "Hay's inquiring mind, friendliness, and com-mand of the language." And Hay's admiration for Uncle Dave was shown through his consistently lavish introductions of the old man. An example: "And now, friends, we present Uncle Dave Macon, the Dixie Dewdrop, with his plug hat, gold teeth, chin whiskers, gates-ajar collar, and that million-dollar Tennessee smile! Let 'er go, Uncle Dave!"

Hay's career with the Grand Ole Opry extended through all of its homes but the last (and current) one. He watched it grow as it moved from the studios of WSM to the Hillsboro Theater, to the Dixie Tabernacle, to the War Memorial Auditorium, and then to the Ryman Auditorium, the "Mother Church of Country Music."

Every broadcast over which Judge Hay presided opened with the plaintive tone of the railroad whistle and closed with a colorful piece of nonsense that became George Hay's trademark:

> *That's all for now friends . . .*
> *Because the tall pines pine*
> *And the pawpaws pause*
> *And the bumble bees bumble all around,*
> *The grasshoppers hop*
> *And the eavesdroppers drop*
> *While, gently, the ole cow slips away . . .*
> *George D. Hay saying, so long for now!*

In the spring of 1968, the son of an Attica, Indiana, jeweler who had become one of the nation's most important pioneer broadcasters, died in Virginia Beach, Virginia, far removed from his beloved Grand Ole Opry. Grant Turner, a veteran Opry announcer (himself to be honored in the Hall of Fame thirteen years later), delivered the eulogy for Hay in the Ryman Auditorium.

"The songs we sing on this Grand Ole Opry stage will have a special meaning tonight," he said, "because the men and women of the Opry stand in respect at the passing of a wise counselor and good friend, George D. Hay. George Hay not only created the Opry out of the fabric of his imagination, he nurtured and protected it during the years.

"Country music was his profession, hobby, and first love. He lived to see the Grand Ole Opry become an object of national pride and international interest. George Hay's love for this music from the land was surpassed only by his affection for the people who listened to, played, or sang it. Tonight, we'd like to return some of that love.

"He called himself the Solemn Old Judge. If he was solemn, it was only in the face of those who sought to change or corrupt the purity of the barn-dance ballads he sought to preserve. We, the performers and friends of the Grand Ole Opry, salute the memory of one whose influence is felt on the stage of the Opry tonight . . . the Solemn Old Judge, George D. Hay."

George Dewey Hay, born Attica, Indiana, November 9, 1895; died Virginia Beach, Virginia, May 8, 1968.
Married, Lena Jamison, 1917. (Two daughters: Margaret, Cornelia.) Divorced.

*It ain't what you got, it's what you put out; and, boys, I can
deliver.*

10
Uncle Dave Macon

Elected to the Country Music Hall of Fame: 1966

Picture this: On stage is a round-faced old man, a little goatee showing over a winged collar, a mouthful of gold teeth flashing from a wide grin. He wears a foulard tie, elastic sleeve bands, pinstriped trousers, vest, watch fob, and a black plug hat. He strikes a few introductory chords on a banjo, the feet start to dance, and he shouts "Come clean now!" The banjo leaves his hands, sails up into the air, and back to his hands again. "Gotta get behind the plow!" Then, in a clocklike motion, the banjo—as he continues to play a tune all the while—goes under one leg, then the other, then behind him, back to the front, up in the air again, with more verses of the song. And through it all the stomping dance continues. When he finishes, the audience roars its approval.

That was Uncle Dave Macon—showman, entertainer, and the first individual star of the Grand Ole Opry. The selection he performed was titled *Uncle Dave Handles a Banjo Like a Monkey Handles a Peanut*, and it was a show finale like no other in country music. It was the energetic output of a man who didn't decide on a show business career until he was fifty. It is perhaps too easy to eulogize the departed, to assign to them a stature not deserved. But not Dave Macon. He was the genuine article—one of a kind.

He was born at Smart Station, Tennessee, in 1870, at a time when the South was struggling through the bitter Reconstruction period. Not far away, seven years earlier, blue-clad and gray-clad armies had clashed on the Stones River battlefield during the Civil War. His father, John Macon, had been a captain in the Confederate Army; he tried now to scratch out a living as a farmer in the hilly country that was perhaps best known for its sorghum molasses. It was not an easy time.

Young David was thirteen when his father decided to try a new venture. He moved the family to Nashville, where the captain became the manager of the old Broadway Hotel, a favorite stopping-over place for the traveling show people who came through the city. One of the shows to stop at the hotel, during a two-week engagement, was Sam McFlin's Circus with twenty-four men and four ladies in the troupe. Dave got free passes for the show.

Much later, he would write (in the third person, as he often talked about himself): "Uncle Dave, being honest, always wanted to give 'honor to whom honor is due.' So, it was in the Fall of 1885 that he first met Mr. Joel Davidson, a native of Davidson County, Tenn., who was then a noted commedian [sic] and banjoist in the concert of Sam McFlin's Circus show then showing in Nashville on the corner of 8th Ave. and Broadway, at that time an open field. So it was Joel Davidson who proved to be the spirit that touched the mainspring of the talent that inspired Uncle Dave to make his wishes known to his dear old Mother, and she gave him the money to purchase his first banjo."

Dave attended the old Hume-Fogg school in Nashville, and remembered it lovingly: ". . . it was in this first school in that city that my beloved teacher, Miss Julie Burton, aroused in me an ambition to be neat, to learn my lessons well and, above all, be careful with my writing. And though today I am past 62 yrs. old [he wrote this in 1933], I never write a letter but what her dear face filled with tender instructions comes up before me, urging me to do my best . . . Her good influences have followed me through life."

The young Macon was sixteen when his father died suddenly. His mother, unable to cope with the city alone, moved the family back to the farm. They settled near Readyville, on the banks of the Stones River in Cannon County. The banjo went with him, and Dave played it whenever he had time off from his farm work.

In 1897 he married Mary Matilda Richardson; they were to become the parents of seven sons. At the age of thirty-one, in 1901, he started the Macon Midway Mule and Transportation Company, a freight hauling business between Woodbury, the county seat of Cannon County, and Murfreesboro, the county seat of Rutherford County. The trip took two days; the first leg was eight and a quarter miles from Murfreesboro to Kittrell, the second leg was ten and three quarters miles from Kittrell to Woodbury. Perhaps the most profitable cargo was Jack Daniels No. 7, carried at a fee of twenty-five cents a gallon.

Dave Macon became a familiar figure on those trips, sitting on the wagon, four mules in front of him, playing the banjo and singing his songs. For nearly twenty years the mule and wagon transportation company prospered, until a rival trucking company took his customers. Uncle Dave never could adapt to modern technology, especially the internal combustion engine. He never learned to drive a car. And in one of his songs he would declare: "I'd rather ride a wagon and go to heaven/Than to hell in an automobile." In yet another song he was to say:

> You can talk about your evangelists,
> You can talk about Mister Ford, too;
> But Henry is a-shaking more hell out of folks
> Than all of the evangelists do.

The freight business ended, Uncle Dave faced a turning point in his life. The year was 1920; he was fifty years old. He recalled in a letter to George D. Hay (writing again in the third person) what happened to him then: "Early in the Summer of 1920, while in the Ozark Mountains of Ark. for the benefit of his health . . . he gave himself up almost entirely to his favorite pasttime, that of playing and singing on his banjo afternoons and evenings for the pleasure of the tourists stopping at his hotel. One gentleman came to Uncle Dave . . . and said 'Uncle Dave you saved my life.' The answer was 'How, my friend?' He replied, 'I was so blue and down and out I did not care for life any longer. But by seeing you at your age act out [sic] as well as playing and singing on your banjo at the same time, my spirits just rose and refreshed my whole soul and body and has given me hope to go on with life's duties.'"

Thus encouraged, Dave Macon looked to a career in show business. And it was quick in coming. In his own words: "All of my life I had played and sung for fun. My neighbors always asked me to play at picnics and special occasions. Finally, one very self-important farmer approached me and asked me to play at a party he was planning. I was very busy and a bit tired, so I thought I would stop him. I told him I would play at his party for fifteen dollars. He said 'Okay, it's a deal.' It was a large affair, and in the crowd was a talent scout for Loew's Theatres. My act seemed to go over very well. When I had finished, the theatre man offered to book me at a leading theatre in Birmingham, Alabama, at several hundred dollars a week. They held me over for many weeks and booked me throughout the country. I was in show business and I have been ever since."

Uncle Dave Macon was the complete entertainer. His vaudeville shows were gems; his recording career—with such outstanding sidemen as fiddlers Sid Harkreader and Mazy Todd, and the brother team of Sam and Kirk McGee—was a prolific one; and his radio career, starting on the *WSM Barn Dance* in December of 1925, was unlike any other.

Basically, he was a country balladeer, but his repertoire was as broad as any performer's. He had such comedy songs as *Keep My Skillet Good and Greasy* (his first record for the Aeolian Vocalion company), *Old Maid's Last Hope (A Burglar Song)*, *(She Was Always) Chewing Gum*, *Bile Them Cabbages Down*, *All-Go-Hungry Hash House*, *I Tickled Nancy*, *Ain't It a Shame to Keep Your Honey Out in the Rain?*, *Kissin' on the Sly*, *The Cross-Eyed Butcher and the Cackling Hen*, *She's Got Money, Too*.

And there were gospel songs: *One More River to Cross*, *Thank God for Everything*, *Bear Me Away on Your Snowy Wings*, *Shall We Gather at the River*, *When the Roll Is Called Up Yonder*, *In the Sweet Bye and Bye*, *Nearer My God to Thee*, *Sweet Hour of Prayer*.

And topical songs: *The Bible's True* (on the subject of evolution), *Governor Al Smith* (Democratic politics), *Farm Relief* (the plight of poor farmers), and *Wreck of the Tennessee Gravy Train* (commenting on the embezzlement of state highway construction funds).

And even pop country songs, such as George Morgan's *Candy Kisses* and Eddy Arnold's *I'll Hold You in My Heart 'Til I Can Hold You in My Arms*.

A vast quantity of Uncle Dave Macon's records survive him, but his repertoire of unrecorded songs was just as large. Unhappily, there is only one visual record of his performing technique, a 1940 Republic Pictures film, titled *Grand Ole Opry*, in which he played and sang *Take Me Back to My Old Carolina Home*. In that film he jumps up from his chair, does a clog around his banjo, and fans it with his plug hat. His fifth son, Dorris, who accompanied his father on the guitar for many years, appears in the film with him.

Happily, dozens of Uncle Dave Macon stories have been preserved; for example, the story of one of his early recording trips to New York City. A city fellow approached him and said: "Where are you from, hayseed?"

With his usual smile, Uncle Dave answered: "Tennessee."

"A lot of queer people come from Tennessee, don't they?" the New Yorker suggested.

"Maybe so, son," Macon said with a wink, "but they don't come in bunches like they do here."

Another story from that same era recalls a visit Uncle Dave made to a hotel barbershop. He asked for a trim and a shoeshine; the bill was $7.50. "Hmmm," said Uncle Dave, "that's cheaper than I expected." But in his expense records he noted: "$7.50. Robbed in a barbershop."

Minnie Pearl remembered touring with Uncle Dave. "He used to carry a black satchel with him on those tours," she said. "In it was a pillow, a nightcap, his bottle of Jack Daniels bourbon, and a checkered bib. He was quite a ladies' man, who proved to me that some men never cease to believe themselves irresistible, no matter how old they are. We would often sit in the back of the tent while others were performing, and Uncle Dave would talk of religion. He complained about preachers departing from the Bible. He could quote at great length from Scripture and use it to solve all the problems of the world. Uncle Dave loved Jack Daniels. He would usually take a toddy at night. Many people thought he'd be drinking all the time, but he didn't need it for that wonderful burst of energy. He was a born showman."

Another touring story comes from Bill Monroe, who booked Uncle Dave for his tent shows. When the audience was good, Macon would tell Monroe, "The old man can still draw 'em in." But if the audience was small, he'd say to the bluegrass performer, "You can't pull 'em like you used to, Mr. Bill."

That kind of pride manifested itself at the Grand Ole Opry when, in the late forties, Earl Scruggs made his debut on the Opry stage. People had been telling the old man—who billed himself as "The World's Greatest Banjo Player"—of the skill of the young Scruggs, exclaiming about Earl's revolutionary three-finger banjo technique. When Scruggs began to play, Macon stood in the wings of the Ryman Auditorium watching him for a few moments. Then he turned and stalked away. "He ain't one damned bit funny," Uncle Dave grumbled.

Roy Acuff remembered when he and Uncle Dave went to Hollywood for the *Grand Ole Opry* movie assignment. Roy and the Smoky Mountain Boys were going to drive to Los Angeles, but Uncle Dave elected to go by train. Several days before Roy left, Macon came to him with a big wooden box. "Roy Boy," he said, "I've got a ham that I'd like for you to take out there so I'll have some good country ham to eat in California." Acuff agreed.

"I put it in my car," Roy said, "and started off with it. We soon found that the border guards were checking everything at each state line. I guess they were looking for fruit flies or whiskey or something. Well, anyway, everywhere we stopped, we'd have to undo that ham box, knock the slats off, and let them examine the ham. We finally got it out there and Uncle Dave had ham all the time he was working on the picture. Then, just before we started back, he came to me and said, 'Roy Boy, would you mind taking the box back with you? I want to use it as a hen's nest.' So we lugged the box back with us."

Uncle Dave Macon made his last public appearance on Saturday, March 1, 1952. Ironically, in making that appearance on the Opry stage at the Ryman Auditorium, he was only a few yards removed from the one-time location of the Broadway Hotel, where he first met banjoist Joel Davidson, who stirred a young boy's spirit. The young boy was now nearly eighty-two.

He contracted a throat ailment shortly after that Opry appearance, entered a hospital in Murfreesboro, and died three weeks later.

His Grand Ole Opry friends erected a monument to him on a hillside just outside Woodbury, Tennessee, overlooking U.S. 70, the road on which Uncle Dave used to drive his mule-drawn freight wagons. A banjo is carved on the stone, with a likeness of Macon, and the title of one of his favorite hymns: *How Beautiful Heaven Must Be*.

But Uncle Dave Macon was his own memorial. In a letter he wrote to George D. Hay, he said: "Uncle Dave, not yet being satisfied with what he now does, is looking forward to television that he might add one more attraction to his radio programs."

That letter was dated May 23, 1933!

David Harrison Macon, born Smart Station, Tennessee, October 7, 1870; died Murfreesboro, Tennessee, March 22, 1952.

Married, Mary Matilda Richardson, 1897. (Seven sons, including Dorris, who performed with him for many years.)

I was born and raised on folk music, the kind that is sincere and comes straight from the heart . . . simple songs that tell a story. They are the easiest of all to sing, too, because you actually feel them.

11

Red Foley

Elected to the Country Music Hall of Fame: 1967

In September 18, 1968—it was a Wednesday night—Red Foley was appearing in Fort Wayne, Indiana. As part of that appearance he was proclaimed an honorary Allen County deputy sheriff. But the show didn't go well that night. Foley told the large audience that he felt weary, and that he hoped the fans wouldn't mind if he closed a bit early. Then he sang *Peace in the Valley*.

It was, fittingly somehow, the last song he ever sang. He went back to his motel and died in his sleep during the early morning hours. He was only fifty-eight. An autopsy revealed that the cause of death was acute pulmonary edema—excessive fluid in the lungs.

A year earlier, Foley had been inducted into the Country Music Hall of Fame; he said it was one of the proudest moments in his life. In October of 1968, when it came time for another Hall of Fame induction, Foley's son-in-law, Pat Boone, appeared on the Country Music Association awards telecast and movingly sang that same song, *Peace in the Valley*, in tribute to one of the most versatile performers in any field.

Red's plaque in the Hall of Fame notes that versatility: ". . . He could make you pop your fingers to *Chattanoogie Shoe Shine Boy*, choke back a tear with *Old Shep*, or look to your God with *Peace in the Valley*." He was known as a singer's singer. "Red had a beautiful voice," Roy Acuff has said of him, "as good a voice as anyone that sang country music." And he was a star on three of the most important country music broadcast shows: *National Barn Dance* and *Grand Ole Opry* on network radio and *Ozark Jubilee* on network television.

Foley was born the son of a Berea, Kentucky, storekeeper in 1910. His birthplace was a little log cabin between Berea and Blue Lick in the east central part of the state. Stories of his youth are akin to a "B" movie plot. Before he was old enough to go to school, his father took in an old guitar in barter, and young Red learned to play it, using his thumb instead of a pick. When he went to school, it is said, he had a teacher who used a hickory stick on those who didn't sing loudly enough during the music periods in class.

Although he was exposed to music from his earliest days (his father was a left-handed fiddler), it was sports that filled his dreams as he grew. Even then Kentucky schools were basketball oriented, and he used to practice by nailing a barrel hoop to the side of a corncrib and using an inflated hog bladder filled with buckshot as a basketball. In high school, Foley proved to be a good basketball player, and he excelled in track and field as well: 100- and 220-yard dashes, pole vault, shot put, and broad jump.

While he was in high school, his parents decided to give him singing lessons. A voice teacher was hired—for two short weeks. It's not clear whether young Foley rebelled against the voice training, or whether there was no more money to continue. The latter is probably true, because the teacher did urge him to enter the Atwater-Kent singing contests (Atwater-Kent manufactured radios), an important competition in those days to seek out talented youngsters for college scholarships.

Red won the local, district, and regional contests in which he sang, qualifying him for the state competition in Louisville. He was seventeen. What happened then was detailed by writer Paul Bryant in *The Mountain Broadcast and Prairie Recorder*. Bryant said Foley, somewhat shy in those days, was overwhelmed by the big audience and forgot the words to the song he was to sing, *Hold Thou My Hand, Dear Lord*.

The lad walked over to his accompanist-teacher and whispered: "What's the next word?" The teacher prompted him and he started over. On the second verse, he again forgot the words, and again started over. He finally finished the song and won third place in the prestigious contest.

Bryant quoted the judge as having told Red: "Young man, that was one of the greatest examples of unconscious showmanship any of us have ever witnessed . . . Your voice is good—yes, but you were awarded one of the prizes on the strength of your grit. Don't ever forget that when the going gets tough."

If his story *had* been a "B" movie plot, Foley would have moved on from that experience directly to show business stardom. But it wasn't like that at all. He enrolled at Georgetown College. It was there that a talent scout for the *WLS Barn Dance* in Chicago found him and convinced him to join the show.

There was no big money in those deals; opportunity offered was looked upon as more important than cash. His parents gave him the princely sum of seventy-five dollars for the trip and, apparently, also gave him warnings about the ways of life in the big city. "I limped around Chicago for several days," Foley recalled, "with my shoes full of five- and one-dollar bills. I was afraid to get it changed into bigger bills. Finally, it got so painful that I took it out and pinned it inside my shirt pocket and kept my vest tightly buttoned. No one ever got to that money but me, but my feet still hurt when I think about that experience."

WLS Chicago was where the "barn dance" radio shows started, in April of 1924. George D. Hay, who was later to develop the rival *Grand Ole Opry* on WSM in Nashville, was the *Barn Dance's* first announcer. By the time Foley got there, the station had been sold by the Sears Roebuck Company to *The Prairie Farmer* newspaper, and the show had been renamed the *National Barn Dance*. One of his initial stints on the show was to do short comedy bits with a girl singer named Lulu Belle, later to team with Skyland Scotty Wiseman in the famous Lulu Belle and Scotty duo.

Bradley Kincaid, billed as "The Kentucky Mountain Boy with His Houn' Dog Guitar," was the star of the WLS show when Foley came on the scene in 1930. Gene Autry also was there. Red's career developed slowly. A mid-thirties printed program for the *National Barn Dance* showed that Foley was a member of John Lair's Cumberland Ridge Runners ("Old-Time Fiddling and Kentucky Mountain Songs"), along with Linda Parker, "The Sunbonnet Girl"; Slim Miller; Karl Davis; Harty Taylor; and Clayton McMichen. Others on the program were the Prairie Ramblers; the Maple City Four; Grace Wilson, the "Bringing Home the Bacon Girl"; George Goebel, "The Little Cowboy"; and Ralph Waldo Emerson, WLS staff organist with his "Little Haywire Organ."

Tragedy struck Foley in those formative years. His wife, the former Pauline Cox, died during the birth of their first daughter, Betty. But Chicago was where Foley stayed. He made numerous personal appearances on the WLS road shows, and he cut some records for the Sears Roebuck Conqueror label. He also remarried in 1933; his new wife was Eva Overstake, a member of a sister trio on WLS, The Little Maids.

In 1939, Foley went back to Kentucky with John Lair to help to organize the *Renfro Valley Barn Dance*, another important pioneer country music radio show. It, too, developed a host of stars, including Homer and Jethro, Martha Lou Carson, Old Joe Clark, and Whitey Ford, the Duke of Paducah. Red stayed at *Renfro Valley* for nearly three years and then returned to WLS.

The *National Barn Dance* had prospered. It was on the network as the *WLS-NBC Alka-Seltzer Barn Dance*, and Foley was an important part of it. His return to Chicago led to a recording contract with Decca, and he got his own network show, *Avalon Time*, with a former burlesque comic, Red Skelton, as the co-star.

In 1944, Foley had his first major hit on Decca, *Smoke on the Water*, a wartime song that promised victory in the end to the Allied forces. It went to the number one position on the country music charts.

The following year he was involved, with Decca record producer Paul Cohen, in what country music historian Bill C. Malone has called the beginning of the modern era of Nashville recording. It was either in March or April of 1945 (the exact date is in doubt) that Cohen took Foley into Studio B at WSM radio for a recording session that was to put Nashville on the road to becoming a major recording center. In September of that same year, Cohen also recorded Ernest Tubb in Studio B.

In 1946, the *Grand Ole Opry* beckoned Foley. He was brought to Nashville to host the prime-time Saturday night Opry spot on the NBC radio network. "I guess I never was more scared," Red remembered, "than I was the night I replaced Roy Acuff on the network part of the Opry. The people thought I was a Chicago slicker who had come to pass himself off as a country boy and bump Roy out of his job."

That attitude soon passed, however, and the weekly network exposure enhanced his recording career. The hits came fast: *New Jole Blonde, Our Lady of Fatima, Birmingham Bounce, Old Shep, Cincinnati Dancing Pig, Tennessee Border*. In 1950, he had four major hits, including the number one, million-selling *Chattanoogie Shoe Shine Boy; Good Night, Irene* (a duet with Ernest Tubb); the gospel tune, *Steal Away*, with the Jordanaires; and another gospel best-seller, *Just a Closer Walk With Thee*.

In 1951, his recording of *Peace in the Valley* became the first gospel record ever to sell a million copies. Eventually, *Steal Away* and *Just a Closer Walk With Thee* would also reach million-seller status. Foley would become the number one sacred song performer for five consecutive years.

Decca Records signed Foley to an unprecedented lifetime contract, and not just because his gospel records were best sellers. He was a genuine crossover star. At one time he had records on three different charts simultaneously: *One by One* (a duet with Kitty Wells) on the country chart, *Don't Let the Stars Get in Your Eyes* on the pop chart, and *Peace in the Valley* on the gospel chart. On another occasion his recording of *Hearts of Stone* made the charts in three categories—country, pop, and R&B (rhythm and blues).

Red spent eight years on the *Grand Ole Opry* and then left to try his hand at television. In 1954, he moved to Springfield, Missouri, to host *Ozark Jubilee*, which had begun as a radio show on KWTO. When the program was on the ABC television network in 1957 and 1958, with Foley at its head, it was renamed *Country Music Jubilee*. In any event, the *Jubilee* became a showcase for a child singer named Brenda Lee; Foley had discovered her on an Augusta, Georgia, radio station. Jim Reeves also had valuable national exposure on the Springfield, Missouri, TV show.

In the 1962-63 television season, Foley was an actor in a network series with Fess Parker—*Mr. Smith Goes to Washington*. And in January of 1968, Foley added Las Vegas to his varied career. He had done it all.

Perhaps he wrote his own epitaph when he said: "Just remember that when you take the last breath and go to the great beyond, all of your belongings, all your earthly possessions will then belong to someone else. But everything that you have been will be yours forever."

Clyde Julian Foley, born Berea, Kentucky, July 17, 1910; died Fort Wayne, Indiana, September 19, 1968.
Married three times: Pauline Cox, deceased; Eva Overstake, deceased; Sallie Sweet. (Four daughters: Betty, Shirley Lee, Jennie Lou, Julie Ann.)

Gene Autry was the only man who could call my husband 'hillbilly' and get away with it. He'd hit anybody else who did.

—Mrs. Marie Frank

12

J. L. (Joe) Frank

Elected to the Country Music Hall of Fame: 1967

Joe Frank was called the "Flo Ziegfeld of the Hillbillies." He was also known as a notorious soft touch. That combination of expertise as a promoter/showman and his inability to say no to performers in need made his life a paradox. He was a star maker of the first rank; yet, when he died suddenly at the age of fifty-two, he was nearly broke.

No one with show business aspirations was turned away. "If he liked you," his widow recalled, "whether you could sing or not—if you could just hum— well, he'd say: 'I'll build you up if that's what you want. Prove it to me—that you can do it.' He never fired a person . . . he built them and he brought them in. I fed more. I dressed more. I kept them in my house. He loaned money on his insurance until it was nothing. That proves love and loyalty."

When Joe Frank was inducted into the Country Music Hall of Fame, posthumously, one sentence on his plaque summed it up: "This unselfish, compassionate man was one of the industry's most loved members."

If he was a soft touch, he was also a consummate showman. Elsewhere in the Hall of Fame are the names of the stars in whose careers he played a major role: Roy Acuff, Ernest Tubb, Eddy Arnold, Gene Autry, Pee Wee King, Minnie Pearl, and Kitty Wells.

Frank was a Southerner and proud of it. Born in Rossal, Alabama, in 1900, just across the state line from Tennessee, Joe was orphaned when he was seven. That's when his father died; he had lost his mother when he was only two. Relatives in Aspen Hill, Tennessee, raised him. In his midteens he went to Birmingham to work in the steel mills; later he was a coal miner in Illinois.

In 1923, he made his way to Chicago, where he became a bellhop at the fashionable Edgewater Beach Hotel. And it was then that he met Marie Winkler, the young widow (and mother of five) of a well-known concert pianist.

"I was on a horse in a bridle path," Marie remembered, "and I fell off and he helped me. There was something—I don't know—he just appealed to me and I appealed to him. And we just started seeing each other."

By the time they were married in 1925, Marie had persuaded him to give the entertainment business a try. Through her first marriage she had acquired some experience, and Joe and Marie Frank became an inseparable team. One of their first clients was the vaudeville duo of Jim and Marion Jordan, later to gain network radio fame as Fibber McGee and Molly.

At that time, the *WLS Barn Dance* in Chicago had a large pool of talent, and the Franks began working with some of the acts. Enter Gene Autry. "I was just a green kid from Oklahoma," Autry said, "when I went over to the WLS studios. I met Joe Frank at the door of the studios. I told Joe my ambition was to be a radio singer. It wasn't until two weeks later that I knew that was the best acquaintance I could have made in Chicago."

Frank placed Autry on the *WLS Barn Dance* and simultaneously began to book him in theatres in the Midwest to take advantage of his radio exposure. But it wasn't easy at first. An illustration of that is found in *The Country Music Story*, by Robert Shelton and Burt Goldblatt: "During a personal appearance . . . in 1932 at the Tivoli Theater in Danville, Illinois, Autry wrote on his dressing room door, 'Gene Autry, America's Biggest Flop.' The door was later framed under glass in the theater's lobby."

In the same period, Joe Frank got a letter from the Myers Theatre Operating Company ("Photo Plays—Road Attractions—Vaudeville") in Janesville, Wisconsin: "Replying to your letter of April 24th, wish to advise that under present conditions it is impossible to pay you $100.00 for Gene Autry in the Rex Theatre in Beloit. We are unable to understand why this act is worth $100.00 now whereas we paid you $75.00 for Mr. Autry's appearance in this theatre just a few months ago. Business has certainly not improved since then. We will give you $75.00 for this act in Beloit or, if you prefer, we will give you 25% of our Sunday receipts for the act. We know of no fairer deal than this for all concerned." Frank accepted the flat guarantee.

Very little of what was happening in the music business escaped Frank's notice. In 1934, he contacted a singer and musician named Frank King. "I was in an accordion shop in Milwaukee," King said, "and there was a phone call from Mr. J.L. Frank. And they were looking for an accordion player to work for Gene Autry at the time. And they had heard one of my radio shows and they said, 'Well, let's get this boy, he sounds like a nice, likeable boy.' So I joined the Autry group [on a tour]."

Frank's diligence also turned up another piece of talent important to Autry's career, a young entertainer named Smiley Burnette. "My husband was in Indiana when he heard Smiley," Marie Frank reminisced. "He liked his voice and he liked his accordion playing. But his father was a preacher, and he specified [no performing] . . . where drink was sold. And that's how we got Smiley. And then we put him with Gene."

The Autry-Burnette team, of course, lasted through Autry's long film career. Years later, Smiley inscribed a photograph to Joe: "To J.L. in appreciation for diggin' me out of the hills."

By 1935, the Franks had made their decision to concentrate entirely on the growing country music business, and they moved their base of operations to Louisville, Kentucky. There they managed the careers of Bob Atcher, the Callahan Brothers, Cousin Emmy, and Curley Fox. And it was in Louisville that Frank King, now called "Pee Wee," joined the family when he married Joe Frank's stepdaughter, Lydia.

More and more, the country music booking business was taking Joe Frank to Nashville, where the Grand Ole Opry was dominating the burgeoning industry. In 1939, the Franks moved to Nashville. One of the first acts he was to place on the Opry was Pee Wee King and his Golden West Cowboys.

And then there was the Roy Acuff episode. Acuff, a Knoxville act, had tried to get on the Opry but was frustrated by the refusal of George D. Hay. Roy turned to Joe Frank for help.

Elizabeth Schlappi, Acuff's biographer, wrote of the incident. It was February, 1938: "Frank talked with David Stone, head of WSM's Artists Service Bureau, and it was arranged that Roy and his band could have a short audition on the show the following Saturday night because Arthur Smith, the main Opry fiddler, was going to be away . . . Waiting backstage in the Opry's Dixie Tabernacle, Roy was terribly nervous and scared. Just as he was being introduced . . . Frank tried to loosen him up by asking, 'Roy, is Mickey Mouse a dog or a cat?' Apparently Frank's efforts had little immediate effect, because Roy later admitted, 'I did an awful job of fiddlin'. I played back of the bridge about as much as I played in front of it.'"

Nevertheless, Joe Frank got Roy Acuff on the Grand Ole Opry. And he was to do the same for Ernest Tubb. Constance Keith, who was the head of Acuff's fan club in those days, touted Frank onto Tubb, and Frank arranged to schedule an Opry appearance for the Texas singer in December of 1942. That was the night he sang *Walking the Floor Over You* and got three encores.

Free-lance writer Townsend Miller reported: "Frank became Tubb's manager that night, 'with just a handshake.' He initiated the famous series of Tubb songbooks and remained his manager until 1947. 'Joe Frank had a great sense for country music talent,' says Tubb, 'and I credit him for having a great deal to do with building the popularity of the Grand Ole Opry.'"

Pee Wee King says it was Frank who persuaded the Opry authorities to charge admission for the radio show. "The Opry was at the Dixie Tabernacle on Fatherland in those days," King said, "and Joe told the National Life people that they ought to charge for the show. 'If you give it away,' he told them, 'people are going to be wondering why you're giving it away. If it's free is it worth anything?' And they listened to him."

The Frank home in Nashville became a gathering place for country music entertainers, not all of them successful. Joe was an enthusiastic gardener and many of the vegetables he raised went to feeding performers, some of whom lived with the Franks when they had nowhere else to sleep. He even clothed some of them, and more than one went away from the Frank home with the "borrowed" money that enabled them to buy gas to get them to their next engagement.

Joe Frank gradually built one of the largest country music booking agencies in the world. Pee Wee King told how it worked: "Joe would put together package shows, big shows that took the country acts out of the schoolhouses and put them into the larger auditoriums. In addition to himself he had Tom Parker, and Oscar (The Baron) Davis, and Frankie More fronting various units. At one time, for example, Davis would have Minnie Pearl and Pee Wee King as a package; at another time, Tom Parker would have Eddy Arnold and maybe Johnny and Jack and Kitty Wells as a package. And Joe kept shifting them around, as the bookings dictated."

King laughed. "I really don't know how he did it. His office was in his hat and his secretary was in his pocket."

Back in 1945, newspaper columnist Henry Vance called Frank "the booking bazooka. Possibly he'll have six shows going in one week, scattered all the way from Louisville, Kentucky to Miami, Florida." Vance quoted Frank as saying he didn't know the reason for his success, "but there's money in the box office to prove it."

One of Joe Frank's most successful booking ideas was conceived during World War II, when he originated the Grand Ole Opry Camel Caravan tours, with Ford Rush as the master of ceremonies. It played service camps all over the nation.

Frank was also a songwriter of sorts, having been responsible for *Chapel on the Hill, My Main Trial Is Yet to Come*, and *Sundown and Sorrow*. "He didn't play an instrument or read music," Mrs. Frank said, "but he could hum—he'd kind of give you the idea."

In May of 1952, Joe Frank went to Detroit to arrange some bookings for the Pee Wee King group and became ill with a strep throat infection. He told friends not to inform Marie, because he didn't want his wife to worry. He died of a massive heart attack in his sleep, in a Detroit hotel room.

Cash Box magazine said of him at that time: "His were the efforts and ideas which combined cowboy boots and country songs, the visions which gave the world a major entertainment figure—The Singing Cowboy—whose efforts have been felt since the motion picture industry made its first awkward steps from infancy to puberty."

His son-in-law, Pee Wee King, said: "His love of the business is what motivated him."

Marie Frank put it simply: "Everybody loved J.L. And he knew his business."

And in the week following his death, Mrs. Frank received a letter from cowboy star "Hoot" Gibson. "I just learned of your losing J.L.," he wrote. "At a time like this, the lyrics are hard to write."

Joseph Lee Frank, born Rossal, Alabama, April 15, 1900; died Detroit, Michigan, May 4, 1952.
Married, Marie Winkler, 1925.

If I, a lowly singer, dry one tear or soothe one humble heart in pain, then my homely verse to God is dear, and not one stanza has been sung in vain.

—Reeves Monument Inscription
Carthage, Texas

13

Jim Reeves

Elected to the Country Music Hall of Fame: 1967

A summer storm whipped the Nashville area. Air traffic controllers at Berry Field received the call from the pilot of a single engine Beechcraft: ten miles out, in the vicinity of Brentwood, flying into heavy rain. Seconds later the plane's blip disappeared from the radar screen. The date was Friday, July 31, 1964.

It was the *beginning* of a story like none other in the entertainment world.

Country music singer Jim Reeves was at the controls of that plane. Pianist Dean Manuel was his passenger. The small aircraft crashed onto the tangled, heavily wooded "Old Baldy" hill. It would be nearly two days before the wreckage was found and the bodies identified.

Eleven years earlier Reeves' first hit—*Mexican Joe*—had been released. It made him a national star, and there followed *Bimbo, My Lips Are Sealed, Am I Losing You?, Four Walls, Anna Marie,* the classic *He'll Have to Go, The Blizzard, Welcome to My World, Love Is No Excuse* (a duet with Dottie West). He sold millions of records in just over a decade.

The fact is, Jim Reeves' posthumous recording career has been longer

93

and greater than when he was living. There have been nearly three dozen single releases since his death; the first seven of those went to number one on the national charts. More than thirty LP albums have been released since that tragic July day; all of them have charted.

Reeves was a Texan, born in Panola County, from whence had come Tex Ritter. He was a farm boy, raised on land along the Sabine River; his family raised cotton, rice, and watermelons. There's one story that says he swapped a bushel basket of pears for his first six-string guitar, with three missing strings. As happened not infrequently in the thirties, young Jim was captivated by the recordings of Jimmie Rodgers.

His family encouraged his interest in music. At the age of ten, before his voice changed, he had his own fifteen-minute radio program on a station in Shreveport, Louisiana, just across the state line from his home.

As he grew up, however, his primary concern was baseball. He was a big, strong youngster, and he was a right-handed pitcher of sufficient ability to earn an athletic scholarship to the University of Texas. When he graduated from high school in Carthage, Texas, he was six feet two and weighed 185 pounds. The scholarship and the side money he earned as a part-time performer sustained him during his college days.

Then came what he thought was his big break. He was signed to a professional baseball contract by the St. Louis Cardinals, at that time the operators of the best farm system in the minors. He was assigned to the Lynchburg, Virginia, club; in his second year he severely injured a leg while sliding into second base. Doctors told him his baseball career was ended.

Reeves returned to Texas, taking a job as a disc jockey at radio station KGRI in Henderson (later he'd buy the station). In that interim period, he also married Mary White, of Tenaha, Texas, whom he had met at a dance in Marshall during his college days.

During his entire period in Henderson—five years—he was singing on small dates whenever possible. Then, in 1953, another opportunity opened up for him. He went to radio station KWKH in Shreveport, Louisiana, where he became the master of ceremonies (singing occasionally) of the *Louisiana Hayride* show. In that same year his second record, on the rather obscure Abbott label, was released. It was *Mexican Joe*, and it was a hit. *Bimbo* followed shortly thereafter.

To test the waters, Jim took a leave of absence from the *Louisiana Hayride* and undertook a nationwide tour. It, too, was a success. The venture quickly led to a recording contract with RCA Victor, a summer replacement stint for Red Foley on the televised *Ozark Jubilee*, and an invitation, in the fall of 1955, to join the Grand Ole Opry.

In 1957, *Four Walls* was a major hit. His soothing, velvety voice was heard everywhere. One of his best records, as a matter of fact, was titled *A Touch of Velvet*. His crossover style gave him hits with *Guilty, Blue Canadian Rockies, Tahiti, Heartbreak in Silhouette, Golden Memories and Silver Tears, I Could Cry, I'll Follow You, Where Does a Broken Heart Go?*, and dozens more.

In 1960, *He'll Have to Go* was released; it sold more than three million copies. Trade publications named him the number one male artist in country music. Reeves and his wife, Mary, became virtually a mini-conglomerate: publishing, broadcasting, major concert tours. At the height of his popularity he was on the road so much that his times at home in Madison, Tennessee, were limited to about ninety days a year.

Reeves also had a vast popularity base overseas—in England, Germany, Norway, and, strangely, South Africa. He was practically a national idol in South Africa; he was mobbed by crowds in that country, playing to tens of thousands on his tours there. To solidify his base in South Africa, he recorded a number of records in Afrikaans, learning the lyrics phonetically.

(It's an interesting·sidelight of his South African experiences, that he met there a young Australian musician, Bill Walker, who was working as an A&R man for RCA Victor. Reeves offered him a job in the States; Walker accepted. On the day that Jim's plane crashed, Walker arrived in New York City to begin his new career. Bill was later to become the musical conductor for Eddy Arnold, and then Johnny Cash.)

In South Africa Reeves made his first and only motion picture—*Kimberly Jim*, advertised as a "robust, action adventure, starring Jim Reeves as a guitar-strumming gambler from Dixie seeking his fortune in the South African diamond rush." The film further endeared the Texan to the South Africans, because the songs he sang in it were written by South African composers: *Born to Be Lucky, A Stranger's Just a Friend, Dolly With the Dimpled Knees, I Grew Up*, and *Diamonds in the Sand*. A second movie script was being prepared by the South African producers when he was killed.

His death did nothing to diminish his popularity, either in the United States or overseas. The charts were full of his songs in the latter half of the sixties: *This Is It, Is It Really Over?, Snow Flake, Distant Drums, Blue Side of Lonesome, I Won't Come in While He's There, I Heard a Heart Break Last Night, The Storm, Trying to Forget, That's When I See the Blues, When You Are Gone, When Two Worlds Collide*. The phenomenon continued into the seventies: *Nobody's Fool, Angels Don't Lie, Why Do I Love You?, You're Free to Go, Missing You, The Tie That Binds*, and more.

As the seventies ended and the eighties began, Jim Reeves was still putting records on the charts. Two of them were Top Ten hits, duets with a young country singer named Deborah Allen: *Don't Let Me Cross Over* and *Oh, How I Miss You Tonight*.

Reeves' posthumous success was not—and is not—a fluke. The appeal of Jim's voice was real enough. But there were two other facts to be considered. His widow, Mary Reeves Davis, had kept careful tabs on his unreleased material. A small portion of that had been recorded by RCA and had already been planned for release when he was killed. But there were other recordings: some "demo" tapes Jim had made, with only his guitar, of songs that were cataloged by his publishing companies, and a series of electrical transcriptions (ET's) that had not been made originally for commercial release. Those included big discs made for the Armed Forces radio, or as promotional shows for a variety of sponsors. Ordinarily, those discs are destroyed after their initial use; Mary had retained them. The other fact was that recording techniques had advanced to such a state that those unreleased songs could be re-engineered. Background singers could be added; so could entire orchestras. In the case of the Deborah Allen duets, Reeves "sang" with another vocalist fifteen years after his death. He also had a successful, engineered duet with Hall of Famer Patsy Cline.

None of this would have made any difference, however, if Jim Reeves' unique voice and easy singing style had not been so universally accepted. One suspects that he has remained a recording star because the singing voice was not "dated." Thus, albums are still being merchandised and singles are still being released.

In Carthage, Texas, Jim's grave is marked by a life-size statue on a fourteen-ton granite base. There is a constant flow of Reeves fans to the grave site; it is never without flowers left by someone from someplace. Fan clubs are still active. Some fans still write for autographed pictures. Each year, on Jim's birthday and on the date of his death, some country music radio stations still do tribute programs. There is even an occasional call from a booker in some small, out-of-the-way place, asking the prices for a Jim Reeves personal appearance.

In 1981, Mary Reeves Davis opened the Jim Reeves Museum in the Nashville area, not far from the Grand Ole Opry. The fans immediately flocked there.

In truth, there are some who cannot accept the fact of Jim Reeves' death, who insist that he still lives. But Jim *did* die in that airplane crash.

It is the velvet voice that lives on records and albums—and the voice remains as "Gentleman Jim" Reeves' lasting monument.

James Travis Reeves, born Galloway, Texas, August 20, 1924; died
Nashville, Tennessee, July 31, 1964.
Married, Mary White, 1947.

Writers must be careful that they do not lose their attitude and their ear for the problems of the day; they must keep their feeling for the great themes of country music, the great story ideas which are implicit in the song material—ideas which a Tin Pan Alley writer would discard, but which nevertheless has great appeal to the common man.

14
Stephen H. Sholes

Elected to the Country Music Hall of Fame: 1967

Steve Sholes was a big man in country music—in stature and in influence. He was a burly "city" man with an unerring ear for what was good in country music. He never lived in Nashville, or in any other place that could be even remotely classified as country, but his decision to commit a major record company—RCA—to permanence in Nashville did much to solidify the community as Music City, U.S.A.

And Sholes was a constant warning voice that country music should not lose its identity. In an interview with *Billboard* magazine in the mid-sixties, Sholes said: "As New York and Hollywood personalities and executives descend upon Nashville, it behooves Nashville to remain 'unhip'—that is, to avoid losing the attitudes and points of view which have made country music the great culture that it is. I do not mean to indicate that Nashville is going Broadway—but the danger is increasingly present, and it is proper at this time to sound a warning.

"The country field's contribution to the world of music will continue strong as long as there are writer talents such as Boudleaux and Felice Bryant, Har-

Ian Howard, Hank Cochran, Don Robertson, John Loudermilk, Don Gibson, Cindy Walker, Willie Nelson, and others of that stamp.

"Writers continue to drift into the Nashville music business complex either in person, or via the mail. They come from Mississippi, Arkansas and other areas where the roots of the indigenous American culture persist . . . It is necessary to develop these writers. . . . Much of the future depends on them.

"Nashville and the country field could 'blow it all' if they became an annex of New York and the Brill Building."

The Brill Building, of course, was—and is—the heart of the Tin Pan Alley songwriter in New York City, and Sholes was intimately familiar with it. He understood that going too far into pop with country music would homogenize it so much that it would not be country anymore.

Steve Sholes grew up in the recording business. Born in Washington, D.C., in 1911, he was the son of an employee of the old Victor Talking Machine Company. The family moved to New Jersey when he was just a boy, and he grew up in the metropolitan environs of New Jersey and New York. While he was still a Camden high school student, Sholes worked as a part-time messenger boy for RCA. When he graduated from Rutgers University in 1935, he went to work full time for the recording company.

His first A&R work at RCA was with such jazz greats as Sidney Bechet, Jelly Roll Morton, and Mezz Mezzrow. When World War II came along, Sholes served in the Army and produced the inexpensive "V-discs" of the wartime years, with artists ranging from Piatigorsky to the Original Dixieland Jazz Band. That also included the last recordings made by Fats Waller.

In 1945, RCA named Sholes as Studio and Custom manager and appointed him as manager of both country and western and rhythm and blues A&R. He had already had a brush with country music in 1939, when his superior, Frank Walker, sent him on the road to Atlanta and Charlotte for field recording sessions.

Eli Oberstein had been one of the early RCA recording men in the area of country music, cutting songs by white country singers and black, Cajun, and Mexican musicians for regional sales. Walker followed Oberstein, riding horses "into the woods to find people who were individualistic in their singing and could project the true country flavor." Walker recorded such acts as Clayton McMichen, Gid Tanner, and Charlie Poole, and Steve Sholes followed in the footsteps of Oberstein and Walker. He succeeded Walker at RCA as World War II came to an end.

Sholes saw the potential of Nashville as a recording center. In 1946 he did his first recordings at the old Brown Brothers studio at Fourth and Union

Streets. "After the first recording trip to Nashville," Sholes told an interviewer, "I agitated for us to build a studio there."

One of the things that was responsible for Sholes' enthusiasm was his visit to the Grand Ole Opry in that same year. "I had never seen it, and when I got down there and saw the Grand Ole Opry—and I remember distinctly it was the night Roy Acuff was leaving the Opry and Red Foley was taking over as the star; so it was quite an eventful night—when I saw everything that was going on I thought this is the place we ought to be recording. It seemed to be the center of everything . . . "

At first there was just a temporary studio, with portable equipment and an imported engineer. And that studio, country music journalist Robert Shelton reported, was shared with a Presbyterian church: "An ardent church member found an empty vodka in the studio after a session and said this proved to him the outsiders were Communists!"

Eventually, of course, RCA built a large permanent studio complex on Seventeenth Avenue South, now known as Music Square West. "We spearheaded the move [toward making Nashville a recording center] to the extent that we were the first company to establish a permanent office and permanent employees, including an engineer," Sholes said.

While he made frequent visits to Nashville, Sholes ran the Nashville operation out of New York. And that didn't always work. Sholes told the story about how he tried to straighten out the meter in some of Eddy Arnold's early songs. He finally gave up and told Arnold, "Eddy, forget what I said and go back and sing it the way you did in the first place."

Sholes needed a good right arm in Nashville and, through a gradual evolution, that became Chet Atkins. The young guitarist had been playing in Springfield, Missouri, where he cut a guitar solo on a transcription. It was titled *Canned Heat*. RCA pressed it, and one of Sholes' friends in Chicago heard it and sent it on to New York.

"When I got this thing called *Canned Heat*," Sholes recalled, "I was so knocked out by the finger-style guitar that Chet played, and I'd never heard before, that I thought I'd like to take a chance with this guitar player. I started to try and track him down. By the time I found him, he was in Denver."

Steve signed Atkins by mail and then released the record as a single. "*Canned Heat* was a complete flop," Sholes laughed. But that was the beginning of a long Atkins association with Sholes and with RCA; Chet eventually became the vice-president in charge of the Nashville operation.

Even though Sholes never headquartered in Nashville, and even though he spent some years as head of the RCA division on the West Coast, he maintained a close tie with the city. He was a founding member of the Country

Music Association and was one of its first chairmen of the board. With Roy Horton, Sholes headed the money-raising committee for the building of the Country Music Hall of Fame.

He was well aware of the growth of Nashville as a music center. "Once the Nashville scene became important," he said, "the better musicians migrated to Nashville. Through a process of natural selection, the best and most accomplished musicians became the ones that were used on more and more recording dates. And the artists who previously used to record with their road bands began to record with the studio musicians who were the cream of the crop.

"And the more recording that went on, the better some of those musicians became. And that accounted for a very rapid increase in ability of the musicians appearing on country records. As far as the arranging and the more sophisticated sound . . . that [was] an attempt, and a successful one, to broaden the market for country records. I don't think if we kept the old original sound, we'd been able to sell country records and country albums in the quantities we sell today."

Sholes, of course, knew the old original sound. But he also knew that it caused RCA, and other companies, to release records for specific territories; regional releases were common. The broadened appeal of country music came from what was to become known as the "Nashville sound." Sholes didn't invent it, but he did nourish it.

That nourishment, he thought later, came too slowly. "If I'd really known definitely what could be done with country music—I only guessed and dreamed then—I might have moved a little faster. It's the one distinctive kind of recording sound that I think has been developed in this country."

Steve Sholes was a genuine enthusiast for country music, and he was in a position to act on that enthusiasm. He was involved in the John Edwards Memorial Foundation, a nonprofit research organization dedicated to preserving the history of country music; he was active in the early National Academy of Recording Arts and Sciences, in addition to his involvement in the CMA and the Country Music Foundation. He had a simple rule for such participation: "If I lend my name to a cause then I will try actively to do something for that cause."

The "cause" was always country music. It is said that he coined the phrase "country and western" as far back as 1943, when the phrase fitted the product then being produced. Later he supported the move to call it simply "country," because, again, the term was more appropriate to the times.

In April of 1968, on a trip to Nashville to attend a meeting of the Country Music Foundation, Sholes rented a car at the Nashville airport and was driving to Music Row when he suffered a fatal heart attack. Four days later, hundreds of people from the country music community crowded into the Country Music Hall of Fame for a memorial service.

"Each of us here today," the Reverend John Bozeman, Jr., told the mourners, "associated in some way with the Nashville recording industry, has been directly or indirectly affected by the life of this great man whose pioneering efforts were influential in winning for this metropolis the coveted title, *Music City, U.S.A.* And many of you here now enjoy an honored place on the roster of country and western stardom, because at some point back in your career, Steve Sholes had faith in your abilities and potential as an artist and stood up for your right to develop that potential. . . .

"And as an expression of appreciation for his dedication to the world of country music, last October Steve was named to the Country Music Hall of Fame. And only a few weeks ago he had the thrill of seeing his newly hung portrait enshrined alongside the other country music pioneers honored here. . . .

"The good that he has accomplished within the recording industry here will live on long after he is gone, and the ethical principles upon which he transacted business will continue to inspire us to keep Music City's name forever above the level of reproach. . . ."

Sholes might have been uncomfortable with such a lavish eulogy. While he was serious about his business, he never took himself seriously. Although he was a major recording company executive, his young daughters never seemed impressed with what he did—until cowboy star Roy Rogers came to New York to play Madison Square Garden.

The three girls were fascinated by Rogers' dog, Bullet. After the performance Sholes was able to take them backstage, where they could meet Roy Rogers and actually pet Bullet.

"From then on," Steve laughed, "I had some respect at home—I knew the man who owned Bullet!"

Stephen Henry Sholes, born Washington, D.C., February 12, 1911; died Nashville, Tennessee, April 22, 1968.
Married, Katherine Craft, 1940. (Three daughters: Lelia Karen, Katharine Leslie, Kimberly.)

*. . . If you've got some mules that ain't fed enough or well
taken care of and treated right, and you try to make 'em
plow cotton, why, they'll get about five or six acres a day
done. But if you take them same mules and feed 'em and
treat 'em fine and switch a harness on 'em and put 'em to a
plow, they'll step out and plow ten to twelve acres a day.
Musicians are just the same way as them mules.*

15

Bob Wills

Elected to the Country Music Hall of Fame: 1968

Friday, October 18, 1968, was a nervous time at the old Ryman Auditorium in Nashville. For the first time the Country Music Association awards ceremonies, in their second year, were to be televised as part of the prestigious *Kraft Music Hall* series on NBC. It would not be broadcast "live"; network programmers simply weren't sure about the advisability of going live with a group of country music performers they didn't know or understand. And, indeed, it proved to be fortunate that the show was being videotaped for a later airing.

Near to the end of the program was the announcement of the newest member of the Country Music Hall of Fame. Tex Ritter and Roy Acuff were introduced as the presenters, and when they revealed the name of Bob Wills, the seat he had been assigned in the front row of the audience was empty. He was gone. *Stop tape!* A search was undertaken, and Wills was found backstage, chatting with old friends, unaware of what was happening. When the show was finally resumed, the King of Western Swing strode out of the wings, raised high his white Stetson, revealing a bald pate, and said with a grin: "I don't usually take my hat off to nobody. But I sure do to you folks." There was a standing ovation.

It's not surprising that Wills came to Nashville not expecting to receive the Hall of Fame honors. He was the distinct dark horse; the other nominees were Chet Atkins, Gene Autry, Jimmie Davis, and Minnie Pearl. All would be named to the Hall of Fame in later years, but that night in October of 1968 belonged to Bob Wills, who was not considered as part of the country music establishment. He was unique, no question of that.

His father, Johnnie, was a champion fiddler in the area around Kosse, Texas, where Bob was born in 1905 on a small cotton and corn farm nestled between the Brazos and Trinity rivers. On both sides of his family there were musicians. Bob was one of ten children, and there was a story that on the day he was born his father looked at him and exclaimed: "I'll make a fiddler out of you, son." Even though the story may be apocryphal, that's exactly what happened.

Bob was nine years old, we are told, when he was listening to a thirty-five-year-old cousin who was trying to fiddle a tune and was botching it. The confident youngster wagered that he could play it better and in less time. He won the bet. At ten, he was playing guitar and mandolin accompaniment for his father's fiddling at dances in the area. There was one night when his father, taken suddenly drunk, could not show up for a dance engagement, so young Bob filled in for him, playing the six selections he knew at that time.

Those were hard times for the Wills family. At sixteen, with only a few cents in his pocket, Bob hopped a freight and left home, to wander across Texas seeking work. He would be a cotton picker, a shoe shine boy, a barber, a carpenter, a telephone line surveyor, a zinc smelter, an insurance man, a rooming house manager, a blackface minstrel show performer, and even a lay preacher-evangelist. But all the while, his fiddle was with him.

Isolating his show business career from all of the rest, it can be said that Bob Wills began his professional career in the summer of 1929 (he was twenty-four) when he started what he called the Wills Fiddle Band. There was Bob on the fiddle and one Herman Arnspiger on guitar. They played at house dances in the Fort Worth area. In November of that year they went to Dallas to record for Brunswick Records: *Wills Breakdown* and *Gulf Coast Blues*. The latter was a song by the outstanding blues singer, Bessie Smith.

The blues idiom was significant to Wills, as it was to Jimmie Rodgers and Hank Williams in their careers. Wills, however, would combine his traditional fiddle tunes with black jazz and blues to develop a new style of popular music. He recorded *Gulf Coast Blues* because Bessie Smith was one of his favorites. In any event, it cannot be said that his initial recording venture was a success; Brunswick never released the record.

But the Wills Fiddle Band grew. In 1930 Milton Brown was added as a vocalist; a short while later Milton's brother, Durwood, joined the group on guitar, and "Sleepy" Johnson became the fifth member with his rhythm tenor banjo. That group played on at least three Fort Worth stations: KTAT, KFJZ, and WBAP.

It was on KFJZ, in January of 1931, that the group began to prosper. The Burrus Mill and Elevator Company, run by a colorful character named W. Lee ("Pass the Biscuits, Pappy!") O'Daniel, sponsored the Wills band, and they renamed themselves the Light Crust Doughboys. O'Daniel was announcer, manager, and leading fan of the band. They were moved to WBAP, then to WOAI, San Antonio, and KPRC, Houston, and eventually onto what was known as the Southwest Quality Network, which also took their music into Oklahoma. It was the most popular radio show in the area.

Early in 1932, they recorded again, this time for Victor Records, cutting *Nancy Jane* and *Sunbonnet Sue*. Even though the record was released, it was not a success. And it was about that time that a rift started with Pappy O'Daniel, who wanted the Light Crust Doughboys to stop playing for dances. Singer Milton Brown quit over the decision and started his own band. Wills, trying to keep the unit together, hired a new singer named Tommy Duncan, after auditioning sixty-seven vocalists.

O'Daniel and Wills continued to argue, partly over band personnel matters and partly because Bob was drinking and would sometimes miss broadcasts. In August of 1933, O'Daniel fired him. (O'Daniel continued in the business, however, and would later ride to the Texas governorship and to the United States Senate, using the popularity of his own Light Crust Doughboys as the cornerstone of his campaigns.)

Wills, with some of the original Light Crust Doughboys following him, moved to Waco, and Bob Wills and the Playboys came into being. The ill feelings of O'Daniel followed him, however. Pappy and Burrus Mills brought a ten-thousand-dollar lawsuit against Wills to prevent him from advertising his band as "formerly the Light Crust Doughboys." Wills won the suit and moved to Oklahoma City for a better spot on radio station WKY. Again, the bitter O'Daniel interceded. He got the Wills band fired from the station by promising to sponsor his own Light Crust Doughboys on WKY.

That drove Bob and his group, now called the *Texas* Playboys, to Tulsa for a program on KVOO. Once more, O'Daniel tried to have Wills' show canceled, but without success. Bob bought his own radio time and re-sold it to

General Mills to advertise a new product called Play Boy Flour. Bob Wills and his brother, Johnnie Lee, would stay at KVOO for the next twenty-four years.

What followed, in September of 1935, was the stuff of country music legend. Bob Wills and the Texas Playboys went to Dallas for another Brunswick Records session; this time there were thirteen musicians in the band. It was, in reality, the group that started western swing. Bob was on violin, of course; Johnnie Lee Wills on banjo, Son Lansford on bass, Herman Arnspiger on guitar, Leon McAuliffe on steel guitar, Jesse Ashlock on violin, Everett Stover on trumpet, Zeb McNally on saxophone and clarinet, Art Haines on trombone and violin, Sleepy Johnson on guitar and tenor banjo, Alton Stricklin on piano, Smokey Dacus on drums, and Tommy Duncan as vocalist.

Several things about that band should be noted: The use of horns flew in the face of country music tradition; so did the use of drums. It may be that Dacus was the very first country music drummer. The other startling difference, of course, was the style of music. Douglas B. Green, the respected country music journalist, has written that western swing is "a combination of mountain fiddle, big band drums and reeds, prairie lullabies, black blues, mariachi brass, and cowboy singing." Some predicted that the combination would never work. There's one story that the musicians union in Tulsa initially refused to accept the Wills players for membership on the basis that what they played wasn't music and, therefore, they weren't musicians.

Bob Wills and the Texas Playboys defied all of the skeptics and critics. The Wills style, accompanied by his shouted "Ah haa!" and other outbursts of enthusiasm for various instrumental solos, spread like wildfire. They drew standing-room-only crowds from Cain's Academy in Tulsa to Venice Pier in California. In some ballrooms they outdrew the big name swing bands of the day. A New York writer, J.R. Goddard, perhaps best captured the flavor of that era: "Imagine a Saturday night at a dance hall in Norman or Muskogee, Oklahoma. There might be 1,200 people jammed in the hall, some of whom drove 150 miles for the dance. Some were hard-shell Baptists, oil workers, and mule farmers. Most of Bob Wills' fans were poor working-class. They were just coming out of the Depression, out of the worst kind of rural isolation, just beginning to get electricity in their homes. Wills . . . had bought a bus to take his band around, a bus with a big longhorn steer head on the front. The people had never seen anything quite like that. Wills could provide a visual style as well as a musical style. He was sort of a folk hero, but a reachable hero . . . Those dances had incessant music. You could hear the feet stomping on the old wooden floor. Up near the bandstand were fifty or sixty people standing, hollering, trying to give Wills cigars. There was a down-home grandmother, wearing a thirty-dollar set of false teeth. They had a strong need to get in contact with him . . . ."

There's no question that Bob Wills was larger than life. He was a tough little man, who chomped on cigars, drank too much, and loved too much. He was five times married and divorced between 1935 and 1942. And he had many bands, several as large as twenty-two pieces. It's believed that in his long career he hired more than six hundred musicians. He introduced more than five hundred songs, and had a repertoire of some thirty-six hundred songs. He made movies, and he sold more than twenty million records.

He had dozens of hits, including *Spanish Two-Step, Steel Guitar Rag, Trouble in Mind, Right or Wrong, Get Along Home Cindy, Maiden's Prayer, Take Me Back to Tulsa, My Life's Been a Pleasure, Please Don't Leave Me, Home in San Antone, Miss Molly, You're From Texas, Roly Poly,* and, of course, *San Antonio Rose.*

San Antonio Rose was the number one selling record in 1939; Bing Crosby also had a major hit with it. A sequel, *New San Antonio Rose,* was the number one country-western record in 1940. There are many versions about how Bob Wills came to write *San Antonio Rose,* a song allegedly created by simply "turning around" *Spanish Two-Step.* One version says he wrote the hit song in forty-five seconds, another says two minutes, still another claims it was four minutes. Whatever the truth may be, *San Antonio Rose* has become a country music classic and has sold, in its various interpretations, more than eight million records. It is still being recorded and will remain a lasting tribute to the man his family called "Jim Rob" and his close friends called "Hot Shot."

When Bob Wills came to Nashville in October of 1968 to be inducted into the Country Music Hall of Fame, he was not a well man; the rigors of more than fifty years on the road, and the toll of his own excesses, were beginning to tell on him. In February of 1969, however, he had a recording session, in March he had a successful California tour, and on May 30 of that year he appeared before the Texas legislature to receive special honors from the State of Texas.

The next day he suffered a stroke; it was thought he would not live. But the indomitable spirit was still there, even though recovery was slow—even partial recovery. As 1973 approached, he set three goals for himself. One goal was to play again at a dance. That was accomplished in the spring of '73 when Hoyle Nix invited him to appear at a Saturday night dance at Big Spring, Texas. On that night he held the fiddle in his good left hand and had Nix bow it. Then Wills took the microphone and sang a Bessie Smith song, *Down Hearted Blues.*

Later in 1973, his second goal was accomplished. He traveled to Nashville to accept a special award from the American Society of Composers, Authors and Publishers. As his wife brought him into the room in a wheelchair, the orchestra played *San Antonio Rose* and the other songwriters gave him a standing ovation. The ASCAP citation honored him "for his long productive and creative association with country music and his unequaled leadership as a musician and a man."

His third goal was still before him—to record again. That was set for Dallas on December 3 and 4. Dallas was where he had first recorded in 1929. The album session, for United Artists, was to be a reunion of sorts for various members of the many Playboys bands. One non-Playboy was Merle Haggard, who sought Wills' permission to sit in on the session. Bob Wills had been one of his heroes, and he had already recorded a tribute album in 1970 titled *The Best Damned Fiddle Player in the World*.

Thus, Haggard was included in the final Wills recording session. Bob showed up on the first day, spent a few hours in the morning with his former colleagues, and returned to his Fort Worth home. That evening he suffered another stroke during the night. Nevertheless, the musicians finished the album the next day; twenty-seven songs that capsulized the career of the King of Western Swing.

Bob lingered on, mostly in a coma, for seventeen months more, dying on May 13, 1975.

The concluding album, when finally released, was titled *For the Last Time*.

Fortunately, there will be no "last time" for the Bob Wills sound, nor for the likes of *San Antonio Rose*, nor for the theme song that was so familiar to millions of Americans:

> *Howdy, everybody, from near and far*
> *You want to know just who we are?*
> *We're the Texas Playboys from the Lone Star State . . .*
>
> *Ah haa!*

James Robert Wills, born Kosse, Texas, March 6, 1905; died Fort Worth, Texas, May 13, 1975.
Married, Edna Posey, 1926. (One daughter: Robbie Jo.) Divorced.
Married, Ruth McMaster, 1936. Divorced.
Married, Mary Helen Brown, 1938. Divorced, remarried, and divorced again—all in 1939.
Married, Mary Louise Parker, 1939. (One daughter: Rosetta). Divorced.
Married, Betty Anderson, 1942. (Four children: James Robert II, Carolyn, Diane, Cindy.)

I was the first of the singing cowboys. Maybe not the best,
but that doesn't matter if you're first.

16

Gene Autry

Elected to the Country Music Hall of Fame: 1969

Gene Autry was an original

That he was an outstanding country music singer in his early days and that he became the first of the "singing cowboys" are important facts to music historians. But he was more than that; more important than his music, really, was the fact that he was a moral force.

In his one hundred feature films, and in his subsequent television series, Autry was larger than life as the white-hatted "good guy," the heroic figure astride his horse, Champion, who overcame the "bad guys" with his inherent goodness. Good triumphing over evil—a basic concept that fell into dis-repute in the sixties and seventies—was a lesson not lost on the millions of American youngsters who cheered him on Saturday mornings in motion picture houses across the nation.

And when Autry left the screen, and those who followed him (Tex Ritter, Roy Rogers, Rex Allen, et al) faded from the zenith of their popularity, the country lost something dear, perhaps never to regain it.

Born in 1907 in Tioga, Texas, due north of Dallas and less than forty

113

miles from the Red River that separates Texas from Oklahoma, Autry was the son of a horse trader and livestock dealer. His grandfather, the Reverend William Autry, was pastor at the Indian Creek Baptist Church, where young Gene first raised his voice in song. His mother taught him to play the guitar he bought at the age of eleven—a dollar down, fifty cents a week. Autry was raised on a cattle ranch near Tioga, and, while he was still a youngster, the Autrys moved to Oklahoma, where his father ran a ranch near the little town of Achille. The boy often drove cattle to the railroad for shipment.

While still in high school, he spent some time with the Fields Brothers Marvelous Medicine Show and sang at small clubs near his home, passing a plate for tips (a fifty-cent "take" was a good night). There was even a time when he was enamored with the saxophone, but that soon passed.

With every performer, there is a benchmark moment that seems to set a pattern for life. With seventeen-year-old Gene Autry, newly graduated from high school, it came in 1928 at Sapulpa, Oklahoma, where he was working as a relief telegrapher on the St. Louis and Frisco Railroad. Will Rogers, the famous cowboy humorist, was visiting a sister nearby and had to go into the depot to write his newspaper column to his syndicate. Noting that the telegrapher had a guitar, Rogers asked the young man to play. Gene sang *They Plowed the Old Trail Under*, and then Rogers joined in on *Casey Jones*.

There are several versions of what was said that night, but whatever the specific dialogue, Will Rogers encouraged the teen-ager to pursue a musical career. Aided by a free railroad pass and buoyed by the advice from Rogers, Autry took off for New York City. He was unsuccessful on that first trip, but he did meet Johnny and Frankie Marvin, a popular country duo in the big city at that time, who were to play a role later in his life.

In 1929, having lost his job on the railroad, he returned to New York and recorded his first songs for Victor (there were other recordings made under several pseudonyms for Okeh, Columbia, Grey Gull, and Gennett labels). The best of that period was a good-selling record of *I Left My Gal in the Mountains* and the Jimmie Rodgers' *Blue Yodel No. 5*. Victor Records billed him as "Oklahoma's Singing Cowboy."

That early success landed him a job on the important 50,000-watt radio station, KVOO, in Tulsa. It also brought him to the attention of Arthur Satherley, the peripatetic Englishman who was a talent scout and producer for the American Record Company. It was apparent that Satherley was drawn to Autry because Gene's style in those days was almost a carbon copy of Jimmie Rodgers. Rodgers, of course, was selling hundreds of thousands of records for Victor, and Satherley needed something to compete. ARC distributed records under numerous labels, including Perfect, Oriole, Banner, Melotone, and Romeo, selling them in the W.T. Grant and Kress chain stores.

In 1930, agent Joe Frank got Autry on the *WLS Barn Dance* radio show in Chicago. It was a vastly significant move for him, because WLS was owned by the Sears Roebuck Company (WLS means "World's Largest Store"). Not only was he a regular on the *Barn Dance*, but he also starred on his own show, *Conqueror Record Time*, on WLS. Early in that period, Gene recorded *That Silver-Haired Daddy of Mine* with songwriter-singer Jimmy Long, who had actually been Autry's boss on the railroad. The plaintive hillbilly ballad was a smash hit, eventually selling well over a million copies.

Sears Roebuck, in the meantime, was delightfully aware of Autry's unique appeal. Sears was selling millions of his records, thousands of his song-books, and one of the most lucrative of the catalog items was the Gene Autry "Roundup" guitar, at $9.95 each. By 1934, Gene was being called the "best known cowboy in the United States." It may have been an exaggeration, but he was very popular. There were other record hits: *Moonlight and Skies, The Death of Jimmie Rodgers, There's an Empty Cot in the Bunkhouse Tonight*, and *The Last Roundup*. And Joe Frank was keeping him busy on radio and on tours.

It was a foregone conclusion that Hollywood would beckon. The American Record Company, which controlled Autry's recording output, was part of an entertainment complex run by one Herbert J. Yates. Yates was also the boss of Consolidated Film Industries, which financed smaller motion picture companies, including one called Mascot, later to be merged into Republic Pictures. Yates and Mascot producer Nat Levine, in an attempt to answer growing complaints of the National League of Decency about increasing violence in western films, elected to replace some of the gunslinging with music. What they needed was a "singing cowboy," and record producer Art Satherley had been recommending that fellow named Gene Autry.

As a test he was given a featured singing role in a 1934 Ken Maynard western, *In Old Santa Fe*. Audience reaction was enthusiastic. Yates and Levine rushed Autry in as the star of a twelve-episode western/science fiction serial titled *The Phantom Empire*. That, too, was successful.

In 1935, then, Autry, made his first feature, *Tumbling Tumbleweeds*, playing himself, as he was to do in every picture he made. By 1937, he was the number one western star in Hollywood. And the hit songs spewed forth: *Tumbling Tumbleweeds, Nobody's Darlin' But Mine* (recorded as a duet with Jimmie Davis), *Mexicali Rose, There's a Gold Mine in the Sky, When It's Springtime in the Rockies, Back in the Saddle Again, South of the Border, You Are My Sunshine, It Makes No Difference Now, Tweedle-O-Twill*.

The money spewed forth as well, as Autry started his own music publishing company to handle the songs he was co-writing with Fred Rose, Ray Whitley, Jimmy Wakely, and his old New York friend, Johnny Marvin. Johnny's brother, Frankie, was a member of Autry's band, appearing in his motion pictures and in the elaborate road shows Gene mounted to cash in on his stunning popularity as a movie star. Autry also fronted a highly successful rodeo, and in 1939 he began a CBS radio show, *Melody Ranch*, sponsored by Wrigley's Gum and destined for a seventeen-year run.

Gene Autry was a big name overseas as well. There was a 1939 personal appearance schedule in Dublin, Ireland, that drew three-quarters of a million fans. He had fan clubs in Europe, Australia, and South Africa.

In November of 1941, the residents of Berwyn, Oklahoma, voted to change the name of their town to Gene Autry, Oklahoma. It remains that today, under the postal zip code of 73436.

Within a month of the name-changing ceremonies at the little Oklahoma community came the Japanese attack on Pearl Harbor and the entry of the United States into World War II. Autry enlisted at the age of thirty-five; he was sworn into the Army Air Corps, initially as a tech sergeant, on a 1942 episode of *Melody Ranch* radio show. Within a short time he was a flight commander and pilot with the Air Transport Command, ferrying planes and supplies to India, Burma, and North Africa.

Returning from the service, Autry found that things had changed in Hollywood. Roy Rogers was the top singing cowboy in the business, and frankly, relationships at Republic Studios became a bit strained. He commented on that period: "I wanted to have control over my own pictures . . . I made five [more] pictures at Republic and then went over to Columbia and set my own corporation up."

Autry was also delving into other substantial ventures—ownership of hotels, radio and television stations, record companies, investments in oil and real estate. He became a very wealthy man. Smiley Burnette, his comic sidekick in many of his films, joked that "Gene's hat made more money than I did."

He also began a TV production company, Flying A Productions, and made ninety-one of his own starring shows. He produced among others, the successful *Annie Oakley* series. In 1953 he made his final feature film, *Last of the Pony Riders*. An apt title, indeed.

After the war he had five gold records: *Here Comes Santa Claus, Frosty the Snowman, Peter Cottontail*, and the 1950 and 1969 versions of *Rudolph the Red Nosed Reindeer*. Gene's recordings of the song sold more than five million copies, and it's still selling. Ironically, none of those tunes had anything directly to do with country music or with Autry's cowboy image.

Rudolph, as a matter of fact, was almost turned down. Tin Pan Alley songwriter Johnny Marks wrote the song in 1949, and no one seemed to want to record it. Marks had taken it to Perry Como and RCA Records and was dismissed. Several other singers also turned it down. Finally, as almost an afterthought, Marks approached Autry. The cowboy said no, but his wife, Ina, liked the song and persuaded Gene to record it. Even then he put it on the "B" side of a Christmas release. The song on the other side, *If It Doesn't Snow on Christmas*, was supposed to be the hit. (Autry had the first hit with *Rudolph*, but not the only one. More than four hundred versions of the song have been recorded, in just about every language, and the sales figures have topped 115 million.)

Of all the post-war activities of Gene Autry, the one on which he expended the most effort—and, without question, the most money—has been the California Angels major league baseball team.

"I've been a frustrated ball player all my life," he said when he started the expansion team. "I played in high school and was good enough to play some semi-pro."

That was the only thing even remotely "semi-pro" about Gene Autry's career.

Orvon Gene Autry, born Tioga, Texas, September 29, 1907.
Married Ina Spivey, 1932. Deceased.
Married, Jacqueline Ellam, 1981.

LOOK! Victor Artist A.P. Carter and the Carter Family will give a Musical Program at Roseland Theater, on Thursday, August 1. The Program is Morally Good. Admission 15 and 25 Cents.

—Advertising Poster

17
Original Carter Family

Elected to the Country Music Hall of Fame: 1970

On the last day of July, 1927—a Sunday—a Model A Ford left the tiny Clinch Mountain community of Maces Spring, Virginia, to embark on a twenty-five-mile drive over rough dirt roads to the town of Bristol, sitting astride the Virginia-Tennessee border. At the wheel was a tall, stern-faced man named "Doc" Carter, and with him in the car was his wife, Sara, who held their suckling baby son, Joe; an eight-year-old daughter, Gladys; and Doc's sister-in-law, Maybelle, who was seven months pregnant. Musical instruments filled the remaining space in the small car.

They were responding to a newspaper announcement placed by Ralph Peer, an itinerant recording pioneer who worked for the Victor Talking Machine Company. On August 1 and 2, Doc, Sara, and Maybelle cut six songs on Peer's portable equipment that had been set up in a makeshift studio on the Tennessee side of Bristol's State Street. (Two days later, on August 4, Peer also recorded a yodeler who had come into Bristol from Asheville, North Carolina. His name was Jimmie Rodgers.)

Years later, Sara Carter capsuled that experience in a letter to the noted

119

Australian discographer, John Edwards: ". . . So there was an ad come out in the Bristol, Va.-Tenn., paper for all talent to come to Bristol to try out on records. So we three decided to go. We made three records. *Single Girl, Married Girl* tipped it off. The Carter Family and Jimmie Rodgers made a hit out of the talent that went." If ever there was an understatement in the history of country music, that last statement was it.

Few artists have had the influence on country music that can be attributed to the Carter Family. In fourteen years they recorded nearly three hundred songs, and from August of 1927 until October of 1941, when the original Carter unit did its final recording, they retained the pureness of their sound: tight harmony singing with trend-setting instrumentation.

"Carter songs" remain a staple of country music to this day: *Bury Me Under the Weeping Willow, I'm Thinking Tonight of My Blue Eyes, My Clinch Mountain Home, Foggy Mountain Top, Lulu Wall, Sweet Fern, Worried Man Blues, Wabash Cannonball, Lonesome Valley, Keep on the Sunny Side, Cowboy Jack, Will the Circle Be Unbroken?, Coal Miner's Blues, Wildwood Flower, Gathering Flowers from the Hillside, Jimmie Brown the Newsboy, Poor Orphan Child, The Lover's Farewell*, and more.

To properly understand the Carter Family you have to break the group down to its individual components.

Alvin Pleasant Carter, the musical family's patriarch, was born in 1891, one of nine children in a family that could trace its roots in Scott County, Virginia, back to 1784. In that year there was built a Carter's Fort, a way station of sorts on the Wilderness Road that led to North Carolina and Kentucky. There was music in Alvin's family, but it was largely church-oriented; Alvin, a sister named Vergie, and two uncles, formed a quartet that sang in many churches in the area around Maces Spring.

A.P. played the fiddle, but not really very well. And the stern religious beliefs of the family prohibited him from playing what were considered worldly dance jigs.

By the time he was a young adult, A.P. was making a living as a fruit tree salesman. On one of his selling trips to Copper Creek, Virginia, Alvin met Sara Dougherty, seven years his junior. She, too, came from a musical family, and when he first met her, legend has it, she was playing the autoharp and singing a song titled *Engine 143*.

Whatever the truth of that, A.P. and Sara were married in June of 1915 and settled down at Maces Spring, where they began singing and playing together. It's known that the Alvin-Sara duo auditioned for Brunswick Records in the twenties, singing *Poor Orphan Boy* and *Log Cabin by the Sea*. But

Brunswick sought primarily square dance tunes, and the recording company wanted to bill A.P. as "Fiddlin' Doc." The offer was rejected.

In 1926, the former Maybelle Addington joined the family circle when she married A.P.'s brother, Ezra. She, too, came from a family with a rich musical heritage and was an accomplished guitar, autoharp, and banjo player. It wasn't long before A.P., Sara, and Maybelle combined their talents, with Sara singing lead; Maybelle, alto harmony; and A.P., bass.

There followed, then, the famous trip to Bristol, to record for Victor's Ralph Peer. What distinguished the Carter Family act was their tight, precise vocalizing and the superb guitar work of Maybelle (A.P. did not play an instrument on the recordings). There is considerable doubt that the Carter Family would have prospered as it did without Maybelle's unique guitar techniques.

In the most simple terms, Maybelle played melody on the bass strings, while maintaining the rhythm with chords on the treble strings. It was a style that had not been heard before, and it was to become known as the "Carter lick."

Another key ingredient of the Carter Family success was A.P.'s seemingly unerring sense in selecting the right material. He has been listed as the composer of many songs that had other sources, or were widely known public domain songs. Ralph Peer had a lot to do with putting A.P. Carter's name on many of those songs, copyrighting them through Peer's Southern Music Publishing Company.

Perhaps the most succinct explanation of A.P.'s song gathering comes from a British country music researcher, John Atkins, writing in the University of Illinois Press' *Stars of Country Music*. "Today A.P. Carter may be . . . looked upon in some circles," Atkins said, "as a pillager and pirateer of traditional folksongs . . . but this charge can arise only because of his position as leader of a popular recording group. Had Carter been academically oriented rather than entertainer oriented, he would now undoubtedly be regarded, along with the Lomaxes, as a great collector of folksongs. Carter's motivation for collecting songs was not to preserve them in print in a scholarly project, but purely to provide a source of original material—in terms of what was on phonograph records—for his group to record. The end product, however, is exactly the same, as both attitudes have the effect of preserving the songs for future generations. A.P. Carter thus firmly deserves a place in the annals of the collectors as well as the entertainers."

Just a few examples will illustrate Atkins' point.

Wildwood Flower goes back to a nineteenth century tune originally titled *The Pale Amaranthus*.

No one believes that A.P. actually wrote *Wabash Cannonball*, although it is copyrighted under his name in the Peer-Southern catalog.

The tune on *I'm Thinking Tonight of My Blue Eyes* has been a widely used public domain tune that also found its way to Roy Acuff's *The Great Speckled Bird*, Hank Thompson's *Wild Side of Life*, and Kitty Wells' *It Wasn't God Who Made Honky Tonk Angels*.

Even what might be considered the Carter Family's theme song, *Keep on the Sunny Side*, had been originally copyrighted in 1899.

In spite of the fact that the Carter Family was immensely popular in the thirties, they did not take advantage of it by touring widely for personal appearances. Much of what they did "live" was in schoolhouses, churches, and small rural theaters, for admission prices that rarely exceeded twenty-five cents.

Ralph Peer, who was something of an unofficial booking agent for the Carters, brought them together with his other major act, Jimmie Rodgers, in a recording session in Louisville, Kentucky, in 1931. Rodgers was already very ill, and it took them seven days to put down eleven songs, including several in which Sara yodeled in harmony with Rodgers. There were also two substantial Sara-Jimmie duets: an original Carson Robison tune, *Why, There's a Tear in My Eye* and *The Wonderful City*, which was the only sacred song ever recorded by the Singing Brakeman.

A.P. and Sara separated in 1932, and eventually were divorced, but the Carter Family continued as a musical unit. In 1935 they switched their recording efforts, however briefly, to the American Record Corporation, and from 1936 through 1938 they recorded for Decca.

In '38, the Carter Family was lured to the super-powered X-stations along the Texas border, "wildcat" stations with transmitters across the border in Mexico, operating at 100,000 to 150,000 watts (and sometimes more) and capable of blanketing most of the United States, especially during nighttime hours. The Carters worked primarily at XERA, situated just across the border from Del Rio. That was the station operated by the colorful Dr. J.R. Brinkley, who used the station to sell his various medical remedies and his infamous goat-gland operation, said to restore sexual potency to men.

There are stories that the stations were so powerful that the Carter Family could be heard on the barbed wire fences of Texas. But, in reality, the twice daily X-station programs extended the popularity of the Carter Family beyond the South for the first time. Those programs also introduced the second generation Carters. A.P.'s daughter, Janette, was heard on XERA, as were the three young daughters of Maybelle: Helen, June, and Anita.

(As reprehensible as the X-stations may have been—they were designed to circumvent U.S.-Canadian communications laws—they did a great deal to promote country music in the thirties. Nearly one hundred percent of the programming was country music, and such acts as Mainer's Mountaineers, the Callahan Brothers, the Delmore Brothers, the Pickard Family, and Cowboy Slim Rinehart, built reputations through the X-stations. All of them were run by North Americans. One across from Laredo, XENT, was owned by Norman Baker, a con man who used the station to sell spurious cancer cures. Another near Reynosa, XEAW, was owned by Carr Collins, who became a millionaire by selling a purgative called Crazy Water Crystals. Crazy Water Crystals, by the way, sponsored many country music acts on small stations around the country, selling the patent medicine for a dollar a box, postage paid.)

It was during the X-station period, in 1939, that Sara remarried, exchanging vows with one of A.P.'s cousins, Coy Bayes, in Brackettsville, Texas.

As much as the nearly three-year stint on the X-station extended the influence of the Carter Family, it also served, negatively, to keep them from recording commercially. It wasn't until the latter part of 1940 that they recorded twenty songs for Columbia Records in Chicago. A year later, on October 14, 1941, they cut their final records for Victor in New York City. Thirteen songs were put down at that time. Less than two years later, while they were working at radio station WBT in Charlotte, North Carolina, the original Carter Family was disbanded.

Sara retired to California; A.P. went back to Maces Spring and started a country store. Maybelle, however, had no thoughts of retirement. With her three daughters she began to work the *Old Dominion Barn Dance* radio show in Richmond, Virginia, and soon moved to the more prestigious *Grand Ole Opry* in Nashville. She made new recording deals with Victor and Columbia.

In 1952, A.P. himself decided to make a comeback, banding together with his former wife, Sara, and with two of his children, Janette and Joe, and recording for the small Acme label in Bristol, Tennessee. Musicologists say that the vocals were fine, but that the instrumentation left a lot to be desired. Acme's lack of distribution doomed the project to failure.

In 1967, Maybelle and Sara were reunited in an appearance at the Newport Jazz Festival, and in that same year they recorded a strong album in Nashville, *An Historic Reunion*, for Columbia. Joe Carter played bass on the session. With numerous re-issues of their older masters, the Carter Family was being revived across the nation, and folksingers in the late fifties and early sixties were rediscovering the unique Carter sound.

A.P. died in November of 1960, and Sara returned again to retirement. A.P.'s monument at Maces Spring features a gold record and the words: "Keep on the sunny side."

Maybelle, now known to the young folksingers as "Mother Maybelle," continued. In the late sixties, the Carter Family (meaning Maybelle and her three daughters) became associated with Johnny Cash, and Maybelle had another resurgence of national recognition on network television. Cash married June Carter in 1968.

As the seventies began, the original Carter Family was elected to the Country Music Hall of Fame (some said the honor was long overdue). And in 1971, Maybelle appeared on an ambitious three-LP album with the Nitty Gritty Dirt Band, a young country-rock group of excellent musicians. The highlight of that was the old Carter song, *Will the Circle Be Unbroken?* The album drew lavish reviews.

Maybelle Carter died in October of 1978; her sister-in-law, Sara, followed her in death just a few months later, in 1979. The original Carter Family was gone, but the tradition remains. Helen, June, and Anita continue as active performers, and Mother Maybelle's grandchildren are also carrying on: Helen's sons, David, Kevin, and Danny Jones; June's daughters, Carlene and Rosey; Anita's daughter, Laurie Davis; and the only child of the union of Johnny Cash and June Carter, John Carter Cash, has made his debut on network television.

At the foot of Clinch Mountain in Virginia the spirit of A.P. "Doc" Carter is kept alive by his children, Janette and Joe. In 1975, in a spur of the moment decision, Janette decided to establish the annual Carter Memorial Festival and Craft Show at Hiltons, Virginia, which is the newer name for Maces Spring. She and Joe undertook to refurbish A.P.'s old grocery store and turn it into a simple museum of Carter family memorabilia.

The festival is held for three days each August, but now there is music almost every weekend—old-timey music, with buck dancing, and the players limited to acoustical instruments. There's one exception. When Johnny Cash comes to play from time to time, he's allowed to use his electrified instruments. "After all," Janette explained, "John was plugged in before he joined the Carter family."

Janette, the middle of the three children, remembered her father as a performer: "He was above average on stage. He was a better singer than most, and in a program or anything you've got to get the audience's attention, they've got to be interested in you or to like you. He had that appeal about him. On stage Maybelle and Mommy (Sara) never did talk but very little. Daddy always done most of the talkin'. But back then women didn't speak out in public."

The divorce of her parents was recalled with emotion. "It always hurt me," Janette said, "because I felt Daddy didn't have anybody. I always felt maybe that I'd let him down. I guess the reason I do all this is maybe he'll understand that I'm tryin' to do now what I couldn't do then."

Alvin Pleasant Delaney Carter, born Maces Spring, Virginia, December 15, 1891; died November 7, 1960.
Married, Sara Dougherty, 1915. (Three children: Gladys, Janette, Joe.)
Divorced. (Sara remarried, 1939, to Coy Bayes.)

Sara Dougherty Carter Bayes, born Flat Woods, Virginia, July 21, 1898; died January 8, 1979.

Maybelle Addington Carter, born Copper Creek, Virginia, May 10, 1909; died Nashville, Tennessee, October 23, 1978.
Married, Ezra J. Carter, 1926. (Three daughters: Helen, June, Anita.)

If a man listening will let it, bluegrass will transmit right into your heart. If you love music and you listen close, it will come right into you. If that fiddle's cutting good and they're playing pretty harmonies, it will make cold chills run over me and I've heard it many times. If you really love bluegrass music it will dig in a long ways.

18

Bill Monroe

Elected to the Country Music Hall of Fame: 1970

There is a growing tendency to overanalyze country music, to try to explain it in scholarly terms, often with bewildering obfuscation. And no element of country music has been more analyzed than has bluegrass. Yet, it is the pure *simplicity* of it, accompanied by superb musicianship, that has drawn the audience to bluegrass.

Perhaps it is Bill Monroe, the Father of Bluegrass Music, who explains it best: "To me bluegrass is really THE country music. It was meant for country people."

In a way, it's strange that bluegrass gained its most loyal support in urban areas at a time when the trend in country music was to its popularization. Pop country and bluegrass prospered side by side. And it took a proud man (and a stubborn one) like Bill Monroe to buck the pop tide.

Few country performers have had the solid grounding that William Smith Monroe got at a very early age; his was an intense musical heritage. And, indeed, he was instilled with a pride in family; he is a direct descendant of the fifth President of the United States. Bill, the youngest of eight children, was born in the Jerusalem Ridge section near Rosine, Kentucky. His father, a farmer and a saw mill operator, was fifty-four years old at the time; his mother was forty-one. His brother, Charlie, was the closest to him in age, and yet Charlie was eight years older. Bill had very poor vision as a youngster, and that caused him to be left out of a lot of activities with children of his own age. He was a lonesome lad, and painfully shy; he'd hide in the barn when visitors came to their farm.

What rescued him was the music that came from his mother's side of the family. Malissa Monroe sang the old-time ballads around the house; she also played the harmonica, accordion, and fiddle. And then there was Bill's uncle, Pendleton Vandiver, the "Uncle Pen" about whom Bill would write an important song years later. "When I first can remember him," Bill told an interviewer, "he'd bring his fiddle and he'd stay a night or so, and after supper, why, we'd get him to fiddle. We didn't have no guitar or anything, we'd just all gang up around him and listen to him fiddle—maybe an hour, hour and a half. My father would call bedtime then."

There was always singing around the house, but the shy youngster found it difficult to join in. His singing was done in the fields: ". . . I used to go out in the field maybe a quarter of a mile from where any of 'em was at, so they couldn't hear me. I was seeing if I could sing numbers like *Joe Clark* and that kind of stuff like some of the old ones in the family could do."

Bill's brothers were musicians. His first recollection of their music was when he was about three years old. Charlie played the guitar; Birch the fiddle. As Bill got a little older, about ten, he started to play the mandolin and guitar. He selected the mandolin because no one else in the family played it. By the time he was eleven, both of Bill's parents had died, and he went to live with his Uncle Pen. That's when his real musical education began.

"Maybe if I hadn't heard him," Monroe mused in later years, "I'd never have learned anything about music at all. Learning his numbers gave me something to start on. . . . When I was about twelve, thirteen years old, we used to ride mules and go play for square dances around the country. Any place that would want us, why, they'd send word to come and we'd make a little money out of it—never over five dollars a night and most of the time a couple of dollars a night. [Uncle Pen] always give me as much as he got."

Then, too, there was a second important element in young Monroe's musical education, an association with a black coal loader named Arnold Shultz, a guitarist and fiddler. Bill was given the opportunity to play guitar backing to Shultz's fiddle at local dances, and something new was added to his musical awareness—the blues. [Arnold] was a real musician," Monroe reminisced, "and I thought it was an honor to get to play with him. . . . There's no colored man could play the blues with him, nobody in the world could play blues with that man."

By the time he was eighteen, Bill Monroe was an accomplished musician. It was then, in the summer of 1929, that he went to Whiting, Indiana, to join his brothers, Birch and Charlie, who had industrial jobs there. Young Bill got a job washing and loading barrels in an oil refinery. In their spare time, the Monroes played as a trio at square dances and house parties. They also performed six shows a week on a Gary, Indiana, radio station. Take-home pay: eleven dollars a week.

In 1934, the "big break" came—the offer of a full-time performing job for Texas Crystals, the patent-medicine purgative. Birch elected not to continue, but Charlie and Bill began a duet act (guitar and mandolin) they called the Monroe Brothers. They went first to a ninety-day engagement on a radio station in Shenandoah, Iowa, then spent six months on the radio in Omaha, Nebraska. Next, Texas Crystals sent them to the Carolinas, where they did daily shows in Greenville, South Carolina, and Charlotte, North Carolina. From 1936 to 1938, they also did radio shows for the rival Crazy Water Crystals.

While they were in Charlotte, in February of 1936, the Monroe Brothers first recorded for Victor Records. Their best seller was *What Would You Give in Exchange*, but they also had success with *My Long Journey Home, Nine Pound Hammer Is Too Heavy, On Some Foggy Mountain Top*, and *New River Train*.

In 1938 the brothers decided to go their separate ways. Bill went to Little Rock, Arkansas, for a job at KARK radio, where he formed his first band, called the Kentuckians. It didn't go too well, so he headed for Atlanta and some work there on a popular radio show, *Crossroad Follies*. In Atlanta he formed the first Blue Grass Boys band. For the record, that band consisted of Monroe on mandolin, Cleo Davis on guitar and vocal lead, and Art Wooten on fiddle. They played in Asheville, North Carolina, where John Miller, a jug player, was added. Then it was on to Greenville, where the jug player was replaced by a string bass player, Amos Garin.

They polished the act, and· in October of 1939, Bill Monroe and the Blue Grass Boys auditioned for the *Grand Ole Opry* in Nashville. They were hired, and Opry announcer George D. Hay told Monroe: "If you ever leave the Opry, it'll be because you've fired yourself." The next Saturday night they debuted with *Muleskinner Blues*, and they never left.

Obviously, the Blue Grass Boys personnel has changed much over the years, but perhaps the classic bluegrass group was put together by Monroe in December of 1945, when a twenty-year-old Carolina banjo player named Earl Scruggs joined them. His driving, three-finger banjo style was to become a standard for all bluegrass units of the future. Others in the Monroe band of that era were Lester Flatt on guitar, Chubby Wise on fiddle, Howard Watts (a.k.a. Cedric Rainwater) on bass, and Monroe on mandolin and vocal lead with his high and true mountain tenor.

For three years—a long time considering the "revolving door" person-nel changes in country music bands—*that* Blue Grass Boys band made history. Musicologists contend there never was a better five-piece band in existence. Some of the songs they played are used by all bluegrass groups today: *Will You Be Loving Another Man, Sweetheart You Done Me Wrong, The Wicked Path of Sin, I'm Going Back to Old Kentucky, Toy Heart, My Rose of Old Kentucky,* and, of course, Monroe's *Blue Moon of Kentucky.*

Flatt and Scruggs left the Monroe band in the spring of 1948 to form their own substantial bluegrass group, the Foggy Mountain Boys. At that time it may have seemed that the heart had been taken out of the Blue Grass Boys, but Monroe was confident in his leadership of the bluegrass genre. In retro-spect, the list of the graduates of Monroe bands reads like a "Who's Who" of bluegrass: Flatt, Scruggs, Mac Wiseman, Don Reno, Jimmy Martin, Carter Stanley, Gordon Terry, Sonny Osborne, Chubby Wise, Dave "Stringbean" Akeman, Vassar Clements, and others.

And the hits were just as numerous as the musicians: *Memories of Mother and Dad, When the Golden Leaves Begin to Fall, My Little Georgia Rose, Memories of You, Uncle Pen, I'm on My Way to My Old Home, Letter from My Darling, In Despair, Rawhide, Wheel Hoss, Pike County Breakdown, Panhandle Country.* Plus a number of moving gospel songs, including *Lord, Build Me a Cabin in Glory; A Voice From on High; I'll Meet You in Church Sunday Morning; River of Death; I'm Working on a Building;* and *Walking in Jerusalem.*

In the sixties, Bill Monroe was "re-discovered" as the Father of Blue-grass. He made his first college appearance at the University of Chicago in February of 1963, and played his first New York City concert date in that same month. In July of that year he was paired with the virtuoso Doc Watson on the opening night of the Newport Jazz Festival, introduced by the governor of Rhode Island.

Folk festivals proliferated, with the prototype festival being the *First Annual Blue Grass Music Festival* at Fincastle, Virginia, put together by Carlton Haney and Ralph Rinzler. There seemed to be folk festivals everywhere, some successful, some disastrous financial wrecks. And Bill Monroe had his own at a country music park he owns in Bean Blossom, Indiana.

In October of 1979, one of his proudest moments came when he ap-peared on the stage of the historic Ford's Theatre in Washington, D.C., in a televised concert for the President of the United States. Jimmy Carter sat beaming in the audience as Monroe and the Blue Grass Boys performed *Blue Moon of Kentucky*.

Summing up Bill Monroe is not simple. He's a complex man with a complex talent. "Inside stories" about him abound; not stories told by Monroe, because he maintains a taciturn, no-nonsense attitude about himself.

One story that has been heard backstage at the Grand Ole Opry is about the early days when he was touring with his own tent show. It was a cash business, and Monroe would return home with the money in several shopping bags. One of his associates, worried about all that loose cash just sitting around, persuaded him to put it into a bank. When it came time to go on the road again, Bill instructed the associate to get some money out of the bank for traveling expenses. "How much, Bill?" he was asked. "Oh," Monroe was supposed to have answered, "about two bags."

One of those who knows him best is Ralph Rinzler, a city-boy musician who has become a respected American folk music authority (and who traveled with Monroe for several years as his manager): ". . . his regal bearing, pride almost to the point of arrogance, terse expression and profound musical dynamism have given rise to countless tales among the few who know him and the many who admire him. His vocal range has set a standard that produced the . . . jest: 'That was so high it would take Bill Monroe to sing bass to it.' His virtuoso compositions for mandolin and other bluegrass lead instruments are standard fare for city and country musicians alike.

"Bill Monroe is a musician's musician. His respect for his own music is, according to Mike Seeger, like the attitude that a concert artist has for his work . . . [He] continues to carry on his function as a leader and an inspiration to other musicians—not as a commercial faddist, but as the profound artist and creator that he is."

But does even that knowledgeable evaluation fully explain Bill Monroe? Perhaps not.

It might be easier for the layman to understand Monroe and the purity of his country music when it is known that he owns and works a 280-acre farm near Goodlettsville, Tennessee. And even today he does his farming with a horse and a plow.

Old values—they mean a lot to him.

William Smith Monroe, born Rosine, Kentucky, September 13, 1911.
Married, Caroline Brown, 1935. (Two children: Melissa, James.)

I was known as one of the strictest men in this business. I don't believe in doing anything unless you put into it what you expected to get out of it.

19

Arthur E. Satherley

Elected to the Country Music Hall of Fame: 1971

He was twenty-four when he came to the United States from Britain, and he used to say he came looking for cowboys and Indians. Art Satherley certainly found some cowboys, and even saw a few Indians, but the young Englishman's most important discovery about America was that it had a vast, untapped reservoir of folk music—"people" music that had a real commercial value.

Satherley was one of those immigrants who was at the right place at the right time, and he became one of the leading pioneer recording entrepreneurs. He wasn't the only one who sought out the indigenous American music and first put it on phonograph records—Ralph Peer, Eli Oberstein, and Frank Waller were key among the recording pioneers—but he was certainly one of the more colorful, and he was at it longer than most. Indeed, it is that longevity (he was ninety-three in 1982 and living in a California nursing home) that has contributed to some of the legend that has built up around the man known as "Uncle Art" Satherley.

He was born in 1889 in Bristol, England, "in the county of Somerset, considered a most beautiful part of England," and was well educated. He paraded before Queen Victoria as a Cub Scout and was a young member of the North Somerset Yeomanry. And he was ambitious. Opportunity, it seemed to him, was greater in the United States.

"In 1913," Satherley said, "I came on a steamer, the S.S. *Royal George*, which was sunk during World War I . . . I had studied the then forty-eight states and knew of their greatness."

Shortly after arriving in this country, Satherley made his way to Grafton, Wisconsin, a town of six hundred, where he got a job with the Wisconsin Chair Company. His salary was $60.00 a month, "29.50 for my board and room, leaving me over $30.00 for whatever I wanted to spend it on."

One of Satherley's early jobs at the chair company was to go into the woods with lumbering crews and grade the timber to be cut. It wasn't long after he got there that the fledgling Edison Phonograph Company contracted with the Wisconsin Chair Company to make wooden cabinets for its early record players. And by 1916, the chair company was sold to Edison.

Art made the most of the opportunity that presented itself. He became one of several secretaries to Edison himself. "Many a note I've signed," he recalled, "with my little ol' name under the great Thomas Edison."

The new industry was ripe for an ambitious young man, and Satherley also learned to make—actually manufacture—records. He experimented with different kinds of substances for the recording surface. "I still have records that I made myself," he told an interviewer in 1971. "But after I learned to make them, I wanted to sell them."

Edison was making records for a number of early recording companies—Puritan, Famous, Paramount, and others. About 1919, with a co-worker named Laibley, Satherley began to seek out acts that he might record.

"The music then was all Broadway stuff," he reminisced. "If a song hadn't been written by the coffee-and-cakes boys in New York, it wasn't supposed to be a song. They didn't figure anybody else was smart enough to know anything about [the kind of] music people would buy."

Satherley reasoned, however, that there was a ready market for what were to be called "race records"—music by black artists. "We found we could get ads for nearly nothing in a black paper called the *Chicago Defender*, and other places where no recordings were being advertised. And it happened like a bomb. Those black people heard their own dialect being sung for the first time on recordings. For the first time, in other words, they could hear themselves."

So, Art was the first to record Blind Lemon Jefferson, the elder Josh White, and the legendary female singer, Ma Rainey.

Encouraged by the success of his "race records," Satherley sought a broader field in which to work. Folk music challenged him, and he started to travel widely with his portable recording equipment, looking for talent. Some of his early country records were released on the old Paramount label.

The young record industry was churning wildly at the time. Labels were begun and dropped; companies were merged and folded almost daily. One of the stronger companies, however, was the Plaza Music Company, started in 1923. It took control of two labels, Banner and Regal, which had been owned by the Emerson Phonograph Company. Regal was a budget label, selling records for fifty cents, as opposed to the eighty-five-cent price tag on most other records.

In any event, in 1928 Satherley moved to Plaza Music and continued his talent searches across the country. Within a year, Plaza Music merged with Cameo-Pathe and the Scranton Button Company, operator of a record-pressing plant, and the new company was called the American Record Corporation. The owner was an entrepreneur named Herbert J. Yates, who was also associated with what was called Consolidated Film Industries, Inc. It's important to note that ARC released Oriole records for the McCrory stores, Romeo records for the S.H. Kress stores, and the Conqueror label for the vast Sears Roebuck retail complex.

Satherley became vice-president and general sales manager for ARC. At that time, ARC and RCA Victor were the two most powerful record companies in the nation.

His ARC job brought him in contact with a young radio singer in Chicago named Gene Autry. Late in 1929, Autry had made a trip to New York and had made several records for labels which included Victor, Grey Gull, Columbia, Cova, Okeh, and Gennett. Several of those recordings were released under pseudonyms, but one for Columbia carrying Autry's name was reasonably successful: *I Left My Girl in the Mountains*, backed by Jimmie Rodgers' *Blue Yodel No. 5*.

Soon afterwards, Autry met Art Satherley and signed a contract with ARC. Country music historian Douglas B. Green has written: "Satherley was to play a large part in Autry's film and record success in the ensuing years, but in the beginning he apparently signed Autry because of [his] stylistic similarity to Jimmie Rodgers, who was one of Victor's biggest sellers at the time. In other words, ARC may well have been hoping to cash in on this then-popular sound. Autry's session for ARC in October of 1931 was, characteristically, a mixture of sentimental tunes and blues, but it also contained one of the most popular country songs of the 1930s, a ballad firmly rooted in the Appalachian tradition called *That Silver-Haired Daddy of Mine*, a plaintive lament of a penitent son's love for his aging father. The song, a duet with Jimmy Long, sold half a million records almost immediately and established Gene Autry as an extremely popular country entertainer."

Satherley recalled that "for some time there, Autry was outselling everybody, pop artists and all—nobody could touch him. So I went to Herbert J. Yates, of Republic Studios, and told Mr. Yates that Autry would be a film star because of his popularity."

Apparently, Yates was skeptical, and Satherley said he told the moviemaker that he'd take Autry to Paramount. "And Mr. Yates said, 'You can't—you're on my payroll.' And I said, 'Well, you can take me off if you want.' Cocky, you know."

Satherley's campaign did get Autry his initial motion picture opportunity. In later years, however, the two men became estranged. Art said it was because Autry denied Satherley's stories that Autry was hired for thirty dollars a month in Chicago. Whatever the reason for the break-up, Satherley was bitter in his comments in 1971 during an interview with Nashville newspaperman Jack Hurst. Art was eighty-two years old at the time.

Example: "He [Autry] didn't know how to comb his hair or press his pants in those days—because I had to show him."

Example: "If Gene Autry had not come to a recording man who had distribution of the sort I had with Sears Roebuck, he'd still be a telegrapher."

In that same interview, Uncle Art told Hurst that it was in the old Gayoso Hotel in Memphis, in a room he had rented, that Roy Acuff made his first phonograph record. Acuff's biographer, Elizabeth Schlappi, pointed out in her 1978 book that Roy's first recording session was in 1936 in Chicago and, while it was for ARC, it was handled by A&R man William R. Calaway. And there was a second session with Calaway in 1937 in Birmingham, Alabama.

Schlappi reported: "Relations between Roy and Calaway and the American Record Corporation declined rapidly. At this point Roy was beginning to feel that the ARC and Calaway were treating him dishonestly, and that the rights to some of his songs—including *An Old Three Room Shack*—had slipped through his hands. As a result the band quit recording. . . ."

In 1938, the Columbia Broadcasting System purchased the capital stock of ARC from Consolidated Film Industries, and Columbia Records was born. Satherley stayed on as Columbia's A&R man.

Biographer Schlappi picks up the story: "Satherley didn't discover Roy, as many have thought, but he was A&R man for all Roy's Columbia sessions. In this capacity he did help Roy develop professionally, although not to the degree for which he is given credit.

"In October of 1938, Satherley came to Roy and asked him to renew his contract with Columbia (formerly ARC), promising to personally see that Roy was treated fairly. Roy signed a contract . . . ."

Acuff's first recording session with Satherley was in November of 1938, on portable equipment in Columbia, South Carolina. The Gayoso Hotel recording session which the elderly Uncle Art recalled in the 1971 newspaper interview didn't take place until 1939.

The Satherley-Acuff association was a good one. Art recalled: "He was the easiest man I ever recorded. We once recorded eight sides in an hour and forty-five minutes, and that's a record for the artists I've recorded." Acuff earned the nickname of "One Take Ache."

Elizabeth Schlappi again: "By the very early 1950's the songs and instrumentation of country music became less traditional. Having had tremendous success, Roy resisted this change violently, sticking to non-electrified instruments and the old-time songs. But gradually he, too, began to change. First evidence was in the songs he recorded. Art Satherley wanted him to change his style, so his final Columbia sessions of January, May, and September of 1951 included *Ten Little Numbers* and *Don't Hang Your Dirty Linen on My Line*. Those songs definitely were not Roy's style. Sales went down and a mutual unhappiness developed between Roy and Columbia Records. At the end of 1951, despite the advice of Fred Rose, Roy left Columbia."

Whatever disenchantments may have developed between Satherley and Autry, and later between Satherley and Acuff, one facts remains clear: Uncle Art Satherley guided the recording careers of two of country music's superstars at a time when his guidance was vital to the development of their careers.

And there were others—many others—with whom he worked over the years: Bob Wills, Bill Monroe, Uncle Dave Macon, Bill Carlisle, Spade Cooley, Al Dexter, Curley Fox and Texas Ruby, Johnny Bond, Ted Daffan, Red Foley, Ray Price, Marty Robbins, Jimmy Dickens, Judy Canova; pop artists such as Russ Morgan, Freddy Martin, Rudy Vallee, and Ozzie Nelson; and black stars such as W.C. Handy, Ethel Waters, Fletcher Henderson, Duke Ellington, and Cab Calloway.

There can be no accurate account, but Satherley worked with hundreds of acts over the years and made tens of thousands of recordings.

When Columbia bought out ARC in 1938, Satherley began an association with another Englishman named Don Law. And they became fast friends as well as co-workers. Art never learned to drive a car and "Don Law has probably driven me 300,000 miles," Satherley guessed. "All over the South and Southwest. When I wanted to go fishing we'd stop and go fishing at the first place we found. 'Arthur, you're always right,' he used to tell me—although I'm not so certain he was entirely correct about that."

As Columbia Records grew, and the field work increased, Law and Satherley struck an agreement. They split the southern states between them in their continuing search for new talent; Satherley took everything west of El Paso, Texas, and Law took everything east of the Texas city. That put Nashville in Law's territory, and it would be Law who convinced Columbia of the necessity of opening its own studios in Nashville. The Satherley-Law arrangement continued until Uncle Art retired in 1953. He had been a recording man for three and a half decades.

In October of 1971, Satherley was elected to the Country Music Hall of Fame. He sat down then and recorded some of his thoughts.

Of the England he remembered: ". . . the old farm houses there were covered with thatched roofs and there was no linoleum or rugs—they were stone floors. But they were polished stone. . . . And every night at sundown—they had no electric lights, all candles and oil lamps—we all had a sheepskin rug. And we had to kneel on that for the evening prayers . . . The farmers were not rich. I presume if they had forty acres, it was a big farm. Crops were gathered by scythe, sickle and reaper. In the winter, many of them earned their small wages by cracking stones by the sides of the road to help lower taxes and expenses in road repair. They lived well. They prayed well."

About his clipped British accent: "The use of my language—the flow of my language—that is a part of my success, really. I can always talk myself into a sandwich."

On the way he worked: "I lived and worked according to the situation. There is a place for fun and there is a place for sincerity. When I made sincere records it was a sincere job. When I made laughing records, mister, it had to be spirited . . . When I made dance records, I did the part of the dance to bolster the players and join in the fun."

Of his own life in retirement: ". . . Every Sunday . . . I have two records that I play—one on Sunday morning and one on Sunday evening. One is by Ray Price—*Faith*—and when I play that record I am lifted. I only wish that everyone—many, many more—would play *Faith* by Ray Price, or by any other great artist. And I finish up on Sunday evening—I put on *The Lord's Prayer*.

"In my home, that does me and serves me to give thought every week of where are my friends. And I consider that my life has been a life of play, because my life's work has been play. And I've loved it.

"From whence I came, here I am."

Arthur Edward Satherley, born Bristol, England, October 19, 1889. Married, Harriet Melka. (One daughter: Judy.)

'You Are My Sunshine' is a sacred song. It may not be a sacred song to you, but it's a sacred song to me.

20

Jimmie H. Davis

Elected to the Country Music Hall of Fame: 1972

In 1977, when he was seventy-three, Jimmie Davis told an interviewer: "I would quit this, but I can't find a stopping place."

Stopping place? Anyone who knew Davis could not conceive that he'd even look for one. It boggles the mind to review his career: Street singer, dish washer, lawn mower, musician, songwriter, politician (Public Service Commissioner, Public Safety Commissioner, Governor—twice), movie actor, music industry executive, public relations man, gospel singer, farmer.

It was a career born of poverty—a motivating force that is reflected in many country music lives. But in Davis' case, he preserved the symbol of that poverty, the tiny "shotgun" log cabin in the Jackson Parish of Louisiana where he was born. It stands today, as a memorial of sorts to his success.

He was one of eleven children of a sharecropper, and the little cabin was crowded—very crowded. In addition to his own immediate family, Davis recalls that the cabin often housed a few aunts, uncles, and cousins, and "a hound dog and an old cat with a bunch of kittens."

Music played a major role in his early days. "There wasn't much to do, but we could sing; somebody always had a fiddle or a guitar." He remembers that there were "one or two people" in the little Beech Springs Community who had an organ. "Not a pipe organ, you understand, one you pump. That was one of our favorite pastimes . . . We'd sing the old folk songs, church songs—just anything to sing.

"And there was more church singing then. You got a lot of practice—at least you could do a lot of hollering whether you were in tune or not.

"I finally got a ukelele," he went on, "and tried that a little bit. Then I got an old guitar. But I'm not very good at it. Fact of the business: I just didn't have the patience to try it, but I played a little when I had to."

The need to have an education became clear to Jimmie early in his life. "Nobody around us had ever been to school much. My grandmother, for example, could neither read nor write . . . she didn't know a one from a two . . . My father was a third grader, but I often say I learned more from him than I did from any professor I ever had in any college or university I ever attended. I realized way back there that there are just some things you can't get out of a book.

"At the same time, I saw the need for, and the importance of, a formal education . . . There were no school buses in those days, and my family couldn't spare a mule and wagon for the ride to school, so I walked the two and a half miles to the one-room schoolhouse in Beech Springs each day.

"The situation progressed, of course, as time went along. Beech Springs later became a two-room school, and it even expanded to three rooms for awhile. Then we consolidated a few of the schools around the area, and had Beech Springs High School."

Davis was a member of the first class to graduate from that high school; there were only two others in the class. "I managed to get through it," he said, "then I caught a freight train and went to college. . . ." He enrolled first in the Soule Business College in New Orleans, and then worked his way through Louisiana College in Pineville. It was difficult; there was no money from back home in Jackson Parish. Jimmie washed dishes, mowed lawns, and sang on street corners for the few coins that people would drop into his hat.

The library at the college—he had never seen a library before—was a mystery to him at first; and he didn't know how to use a shower when he first arrived at the school dormitory. But he learned and he persisted, and earned a Bachelor of Arts degree in education at Louisiana College. Next, he went to Louisiana State University for his Master's degree. He sang with the Tiger Four at LSU, which had engagements in Baton Rouge theaters.

"I got a job," Davis said, "teaching in a girls' college (Dodd College in Shreveport)—and I want to tell you that a man that hasn't taught in a girls' college . . . he just hasn't taught, period. They'd ask me more questions! I'd say, 'Don't ask me—ask your Momma.' "

It was in Shreveport that his political career began—*and* his show business career. He got a civil service job as criminal clerk in the Shreveport City Court and simultaneously began to appear regularly on radio station KWKH. His style was reminiscent of Jimmie Rodgers. A Victor record scout heard him and, on September 19, 1929, took Jimmie to Memphis to cut his first records. Four songs were recorded that day, and from 1929 to 1934, Davis recorded sixty-eight sides for Victor.

A 1930 Victor catalog, listing records by Carson Robison, Jimmie Rodgers, the Allen Brothers, Ashley's Melody Makers, and the Floyd County Ramblers, advertised a release by Davis of *My Louisiana Girl*, backed by *My Dixie Sweetheart*. The description of the record was "yodeling with guitars."

He began to write in that period, as well. Peer International published his *Where the Old Red River Flows* in 1931, and *When It's Roundup Time in Heaven* in 1934.

It was in 1934, also, that he switched to the new Decca Records. And it was on Decca, in April of 1935, that he had his first major hit, *Nobody's Darlin' but Mine*. It was so big that Jimmie tried to duplicate it with no less than three sequels: *Answer to Nobody's Darlin'*, *That's Why I'm Nobody's Darlin'*, and *By the Grave of Nobody's Darlin'*.

In 1937, he had another solid-seller record with *I Wish I Had Never Seen Sunshine*, written with Johnnie Roberts. That may have been a portent of another hit yet to come.

Davis' political ambitions were helped by his visibility as a country music star. In 1938, he was elected as Shreveport's Commissioner of Public Safety, a job that in other areas of the country might be called police commissioner. Somehow, he was able to juggle both his career as an entertainer and his career as a politician successfully.

In November of 1938, his recording of Floyd Tillman's classic, *It Makes No Difference Now*, was released by Decca. It may have been bigger for him than *Nobody's Darlin' but Mine*. Tillman, who had been strapped for money, sold his copyright to the song for a few hundred dollars, and when he was able to recapture it when it was renewed in 1966, he shared the copyright with Davis.

Lightning struck for Jimmie Davis in 1939. With Charles Mitchell, who played steel guitar in his band, Jimmie wrote a song titled *You Are My Sunshine*. Oddly, it was not Davis who recorded it first. That honor fell to the Rice Brothers Gang in November of 1939, followed by covers by Bob Atcher, and Bonnie Blue Eyes and by the Pine Ridge Boys. In March of 1940, the Davis version was released on Decca; Gene Autry had an Okeh release in June of 1941, and in that same year Lawrence Welk and Bing Crosby both recorded it. *Billboard* magazine said that the Crosby record was "the taproom and tavern classic of the year."

You Are My Sunshine quickly became one of the most important copyrights in the history of country music. It has been recorded more than three hundred and fifty times, has been translated into a dozen languages, and has sold millions upon millions of copies.

Davis tried to explain the reason for the success of the song: "Anybody who plays anything—if they play guitar, or organ, piano, or anything else—can play that [song]. And if they can harmonize a song, they can harmonize that . . . You don't have to be a professional singer to sing it, you know."

Jimmie made his first motion picture in 1942, in which he sang *You Are My Sunshine*. At the time he was the Louisiana State Public Service Commissioner, a post once held by Huey Long, and he was in Hollywood for a recording session. "We were at Universal Studios," he recalled, "and Trip Work asked if I would like to make a picture. I said, 'Well, I might as well. I've tried just about everything else. When do we start?' . . .

"Man—I didn't even have a cowboy hat. They said, 'We'll get you one.' They rigged me up in two cowboy outfits and a hat—about size nine. I can't see out of that hat to this day. With that hat on, I rode in all those chases. I never did know where I was going. I just kept holding on to the horn of the saddle—and hoping."

That film was titled *Strictly in the Groove*. A year later he made another one, *Frontier Fury*, in which country singer-songwriter Johnny Bond was featured.

Back home in Louisiana, Davis' political career was getting serious. Democratic reformers, meaning the anti-Long politicians, prevailed on the popular Davis to seek the Democratic nomination, which was tantamount to election. It was a crowded field in 1944; eight sought the nomination.

One was the Long-backed candidate, Lewis Morgan. Another was the flamboyant Cajun promoter, Dudley LeBlanc, who was later to gain a national reputation as the inventor and super salesman of a patent medicine called Hadacol.

The Long forces took Davis seriously, especially when he began to campaign with his country music band, which drew large crowds. Opponents accused him of "singing dirty songs," and they pointed to the risque lyrics of some of his early Victor releases: *High Behind Blues*, *Red Nightgown Blues*, and *She's A Hum Dum Dinger From Dingersville*. One 1936 song, *Bed Bug Blues*, was called "depraved vulgarity."

Louisiana political reporter Charles C. Phillips wrote that "his opponents spread rumors that he had been married nine times and they circulated 'fake' photographs of him dancing with Lena Horne, a black singer. At that time, of course, the black vote was non-existent and if his opponents could have convinced the voters that Davis had actually danced with Lena it would have hurt his chances."

Davis ignored the attacks and continued the campaign with *You Are My Sunshine* as his theme. In the primary, he got thirty-five percent of the vote, forcing him into a runoff with the Long-backed Morgan. In that runoff, Jimmie won by a slim 30,000-vote edge.

Being governor, he learned, was a lot tougher than talking about being governor. He once told a colleague that during the entire four years in the governor's mansion he hardly ate a solid meal. In spite of that, however, he continued in show business. In 1947, he was featured in a Monogram film titled *Louisiana*, loosely based on his life story. Margaret Lindsay played his wife.

When he left office in 1948, the Jimmie Davis music was changing. He was angling away from country music and moving strongly to gospel. He did write one well-known country song with Hank Williams in 1951, *(I Heard That) Lonesome Whistle*, but he was concentrating on gospel music. In 1957, he was named the Best Male Sacred Singer of the Year.

By 1960, his friends in Louisiana had convinced him to run for governor again. This time his strongest opposition came from the popular New Orleans mayor, deLesseps A. Morrison, whom he defeated handily in the runoff. Times had changed since he had last been governor. Political writer Phillips again: "There was rioting in New Orleans as forced integration was applied to public schools there. There was strong pressure on Davis to stand up to the federal government. In retrospect there was little he could do against a President who had already used troops to force integration in Little Rock, Ark."

Once more in 1972, Davis was persuaded to run for the governorship. This time he didn't make the runoff and he had no regrets: "Losing was the best thing that ever happened to me."

He continued performing, as he had done even while he was in political office. And he especially continued to sing in the nondenominational Jimmie Davis Tabernacle that friends had built in his honor, on the property on which stands his log cabin birthplace.

The Jimmie Davis legacy to country and gospel music includes a lot of songs: *Sweethearts or Strangers; Columbus Stockade Blues; There's a New Moon Over My Shoulder; Let's Be Sweethearts Again; Shackles and Chains; How Far Is Heaven?; Down by the Riverside; Take My Hand, Precious Lord*, and many more.

The legacy also includes his philosophy about music:

"Art is the transferral of the artist's soul into a tangible expression and art always is greater than the artist. The creation is greater than the creator, because it will live and inspire long after the creator has passed on. To me, music will always be the highest form of art, whether it be grand opera, march, popular or folk.

"Since the dawn of civilization . . . we have relied upon music to express those things that even poetry could not translate. Every emotion known to Man has its counterpart in music, and music is a part of the being of Man almost as much as is breathing . . . And, of all kinds of music, there is none as charming or as pure as folk music. Uncorrupted by scholarship, folk music is the music of the heart of the average man, music of the masses . . .

"The music of the simple people will always be the clearest and most indelible expression of the common lot. It is hard for me to imagine that a man could put down a hymn book and reach for a gun. The language of music is the universal language. It is the medicine of the breaking heart of a lover, the tranquilizer to the infant, and the property of saint and sinner, as well.

"Music has played a greater part in our country than any of us can realize. I am sure it will continue, for if the day should ever come that music, in general, fails to be an integral part of our nation, then we can wrap our arms around it, hold it close to our breasts, take one last, long look, and kiss it good-bye. For the world, as you and I have known it, will have passed forever."

James Houston Davis, born Beech Grove, Louisiana, September 11, 1902.
Married, Alvern Adams, 1936. (One son: James William.) Deceased.
Married, Anna Gordon, 1968.

Technically, there is no such thing as the Nashville sound. It's the musicians. Southern people have a relaxed way of life, a relaxed way of playing.

21

Chet Atkins

Elected to the Country Music Hall of Fame: 1973

Chet Atkins began 1982 as his own man.

For the first time in four decades he was not working for other musicians and singers, he was not producing, he was not guiding the careers of others. The tall, slim, relaxed man with whose efforts a great deal of Music City, U.S.A. was built, was turning a corner in his life.

"I'm playing guitar now," he said, "and that's what I always wanted to do anyway. I think of myself first as a guitarist. I want to be remembered as a guitarist."

To music fans outside of the Nashville establishment, that may have seemed to be a strange statement; they know him as one of the finest guitarists in and out of country music. To his friends and associates in country music there was perfect understanding of what he meant. Atkins, at age fifty-eight, had paid his dues. He sought now, unselfishly, a total commitment to his *own* talent, a commitment he had put aside for so many years while helping others.

Atkins has been called "Mr. Nashville." He certainly was that. A full evaluation of what he meant to Nashville is difficult, but one sideman came close to it: "Chet Atkins saved country music. He made it respectable."

In looking back, it seems impossible that Chet would have been anything but a musician. He was born in 1924 on a small farm at Luttrell, Tennessee, some twenty miles from Knoxville. His father, although he came from a family of old-time mountain fiddlers, was really a classically trained musician who taught piano and voice. His older half-brother, Jim Atkins, was an accomplished jazz guitarist who left home to play with the Fred Waring Orchestra and the Les Paul Trio.

Chet knew of the poverty of living in the rural South in the twenties and thirties, and his growing up days were anything but happy. His father left home when he was just a child, and he was an ill youngster, suffering serious asthma attacks. Then, too, there was the trauma of leaving his Clinch Mountain home to live with his father and stepmother in Georgia. Chet was withdrawn and shy, and what he retreated to was music. When he was only six years old, it is said, he found an old ukulele which he strung with wire off a screen door. Later, he traded an old pistol for a guitar.

But it was as a fiddler that he began his career. At eighteen, after graduating from high school in Georgia, he was hired as a fiddler on radio station WNOX, Knoxville, the starting place for so many country music performers. Playing both fiddle and guitar, he toured with Archie Campbell and Bill Carlisle. "I was more interested in the guitar than the fiddle," he recalled, "and I'd fool around practicing it whenever I could. One time, the radio station boss heard me playing my guitar in the back seat of his car. He told me to throw away the fiddle for good and he'd give me a job playing guitar. That was how I got started."

Getting started was one thing; succeeding was another. He had a succession of jobs on radio shows at WLW in Cincinnati, WPTF in Raleigh, North Carolina, WRVA in Richmond, Virginia, even as far away as KOA in Denver, Colorado. In the mid-forties he went to Nashville to audition for a job in Roy Acuff's Smoky Mountain Boys; he didn't get it. In 1946, he went to Chicago to audition for Red Foley, who was getting ready to join the Grand Ole Opry, and he actually accompanied Foley to Nashville. But it all seemed to be smoke. In 1947, he recorded in Chicago for RCA Victor, both as a singer and instrumentalist. No one seemed to be impressed, and it was back to the security of WNOX in Knoxville to work with Homer and Jethro and, as a touring sideman to play some fiddle with the Carter Family.

Things began to turn around for him as the fifties began. He found himself performing as a studio musician and organizing record sessions for producers Steve Sholes of RCA, Paul Cohen of Decca, and Fred Rose of the burgeoning Acuff-Rose music publishing company. Sholes liked Atkins and was impressed with his musicianship. By 1952, Atkins was the assistant A&R man to Sholes. A year later, RCA released his first solo album, *Chet Atkins' Gallopin' Guitar*. He was becoming known as RCA's man in Nashville, because Sholes was actually headquartered in New York City. In 1955, the two of them recorded Elvis Presley's first RCA release, *Heartbreak Hotel;* in 1956, RCA built its own recording studio in Nashville with Atkins in charge. (To complete the picture of the RCA association, Atkins was named Nashville A&R manager in 1960 and was a vice-president of RCA Records by 1968.)

Thus, Atkins had a power base in Nashville, and he was doing things differently. "Skeeter Davis was a good example," Chet remembered, "of how we were able to bring country to pop. I always thought she had a chance for pop, so we took out the steel guitars and fiddles and made her a little more 'uptown' with her overdubbing of the harmony, and she did very well." Things moved fast. Atkins recalled that the first recorded use of a modern vocal group backing a country singer was behind Ferlin Husky on *Gone*.

People were beginning to talk about the Nashville sound, as Atkins and other producers had available to them new technical advances in recording, and as the demand for country music grew. There were numerous definitions offered of the Nashville sound, but perhaps it is easiest to say that the mountain fiddle became a violin, and that the new arrangements had a loose, easy, even jazzy, beat—contemporary.

However it was defined, the country music business was changing, and Chet Atkins became one of the most important producers in Nashville. He was responsible for the recorded output of Jim Reeves, Eddy Arnold, Don Gibson, Charley Pride, Waylon Jennings, Jerry Reed, Dottie West, Trini Lopez, Al Hirt, Perry Como, and a lot more. He also gave Dolly Parton her start as a recording artist.

His door was always open to promising, young talent. John D. Loudermilk's story is typical. A music student from the University of North Carolina, Loudermilk came to Nashville in 1959, vowing to "give this town one year. If it didn't work, I was ready to go back to Durham and work in my wife's daddy's hardware store." He sought an appointment with Atkins, showed him some of his songs, and Chet gave him a job as an A&R assistant, which simply meant that Loudermilk listened to new material sent in by songwriters. That job enabled Loudermilk to survive that first year in Nashville, and he went on to become one of the leading songwriters in country music, with such hits as *Abilene, Tobacco Road, Joey Stays With Me, Language of Love, A Rose and a Baby Ruth, Sad Movies (Make Me Cry)*, and *Then You Can Tell Me Goodbye*.

Somehow, Atkins managed to pursue his own recording career. He was universally recognized as one of the finest musicians in country music. There were awards from all sources. In *Cash Box* magazine, for example, he was named the outstanding country music instrumentalist for fourteen years in a row. He won *Playboy*'s poll four times as Best Guitarist; he was the Country Music Association Best Instrumentalist three times (and was always nominated), and he won seven Grammy awards from the National Academy of Recording Arts and Sciences.

Among his Grammy awards were albums with three musicians he admired deeply: *The Atkins-Travis Traveling Show*, with Merle Travis, whose guitar style influenced Chet in his earliest playing; *Chester and Lester*, a duet performance with Les Paul, and *Me & Jerry*, with his protégé, Jerry Reed. Atkins is also proud of an album he recorded with Arthur Fiedler and the Boston Pops Orchestra, and another with folk virtuoso Doc Watson, titled *Reflections*.

Perhaps the Chet Atkins story can best be told through his own comments.

On his role in the growth of country music: "It was an accident. I just happened to be in the right place. I knew a good song, and that's all it really takes. Any good musician would have done the same thing. I was just there."

On songwriters: "The song's the thing. You can have the biggest and most expensive studio, the best-sounding musicians, and expert engineers and technicians, but if you don't have the song, the artists can't be expected to have a hit."

On Spanish classical guitarist Andres Segovia, with whom he has studied: "Segovia got kind of mad at me once because he thought I didn't read music . . . I told him I read a little . . . He's sort of a mean old man, you know. He needs to let somebody else blow his horn. He says that he brought the guitar out of obscurity—and he *has* done a great deal for the guitar. But he needs to let someone else say that for him."

On his style: "I'm strictly a melody man. One reason jazz has never been a great success is because it is improvisational, and the public loses the melody. It takes a well-trained ear to enjoy jazz. Music, to be commercial, should have a melodic line somewhere that is appealing, and I try to keep this in mind in all my recordings. I'm a little square, but it helps to be that way, I think."

On young guitarists: "They've taught me. There are some amazing things happening—the schools, the colleges, are turning out great guitarists. It's not like it used to be. With what they can do now, the guitar has really replaced the saxophone."

On composing: "I guess I'd like to have composed more. I did compose a little once. But not much. I might try to again . . . the older you get, the less energy you have for that kind of thing. I really would like to write some beautiful melodies, though."

As 1981 drew to a close, Atkins—perhaps with a thought of writing those beautiful melodies—announced that he was ending his long formal association with RCA to concentrate on his own career as a guitarist. "My goal," he said, "is to always stay hip musically and be respected by my peers. To do that, you need to practice a lot and keep up with music—otherwise you get stale."

It was obvious that staying "hip musically" also caused Atkins to evaluate honestly what had happened to country music over the years. Back in 1974, he was thinking that perhaps the Nashville sound had gone too far. "I hate to see country going uptown because it's the wrong uptown," Chet told an interviewer. "We're about to lose our identity and get all mixed up with other music . . . a music dies when it becomes a parody of itself, which has happened to some extent with rock. Of course, I had a lot to do with changing country, and I apologize. We did it to broaden the appeal, and to keep making records different, to surprise the public."

If mistakes were made, Chet Atkins is capable of correcting them with his music.

William Ivey, the executive director of the Country Music Foundation (which operates the Country Music Hall of Fame and Museum) has written: "He projects the image of a country boy who has never quite grown comfortable with his accomplishments—an image which has certainly helped him maintain warm relationships with the entertainers he has worked with over many years. Atkins remains an attractive and comfortable person to be around, for his ego never jumps out to hurt people . . . He has inspired and influenced generations of American guitarists, and he has created an image of 'rags to riches' success which many will emulate, but few will duplicate."

Chester Burton Atkins, born Luttrell, Tennessee, June 20, 1924.
Married Leona Johnson, 1946. (One daughter: Merle.)

I used to sing or hum with just about every song I'd hear on the radio, and one day I got real brave and walked into the radio station in Winchester when a hillbilly band was being featured. I told the leader: 'If you'll just give me a chance to sing with you, I'll never ask for pay.'

22

Patsy Cline

Elected to the Country Music Hall of Fame: 1973

Her real stardom encompassed only three years.

Yet, Patsy Cline was the first female solo artist to be elected to the Country Music Hall of Fame—before the "Queen of Country Music," Kitty Wells; before the venerable comedienne, Minnie Pearl.

The argument could have been made (and, indeed, some did make it) that Patsy's election was expedient, perhaps even intemperate. But the Hall of Fame electors are country music people, and her brief, mercurial life could have provided the emotional lyrics for a country music ballad. While emotion certainly won the hour in 1973, there is no question several decades after her tragic death that Patsy Cline was—and is (through her existing recordings)—a star of the first magnitude.

Had she lived beyond thirty, there is little doubt that she would have been the dominant female artist in country music. Patsy had a reality, a power, that transcends the counting of years.

She was born Virginia Hensley in Winchester, Virginia, positioned at the head of the fabled Shenandoah Valley. The year was 1932 in the depth of the

155

Great Depression. And, in the show business vernacular of later years, she "paid her dues."

From the beginning, she wanted to be an entertainer. She made her first public appearance at the age of four, winning a tap dancing contest. That was the time of Shirley Temple, and there were dreams in poor families all across the land that, given the opportunity, any little girl could be another Shirley.

With Virginia, however, the emphasis soon switched from dancing to singing. Whenever and wherever she could sing she did—in churches, in clubs, in honky-tonks, on street corners. It was necessary for her, because of family financial needs, to quit school as a teen-ager and go to work as a clerk in Gaunt's Drug Store in Winchester. The singing continued.

"Mother would pick me up at the drugstore after work," she once told a reporter, "and would take me wherever I could get a job. We'd usually get home about three in the morning and a few hours later I was up again getting ready to go to work in the drugstore. And you know something, I loved every minute of it."

That enthusiasm, accompanied by a total lack of shyness, enabled her to contact every name act that came through Winchester, seeking an opportunity to perform. In 1948, Wally Fowler's Oak Ridge Quartet came to town; they were regular performers on Roy Acuff's *Dinner Bell* radio show in Nashville. Patsy sought an audition, got it, and Fowler suggested to Mrs. Hensley that her daughter go to Nashville. He'd get her, he said, an audition with Acuff. They went. Patsy was not yet sixteen.

"When I first came to Nashville, in 1948," she recalled, "I drove in with my mother, sisters, and a few friends of the family. We shared expenses. I didn't even have enough money to rent a hotel room, so the night before we were to audition, we stopped outside town at a picnic site and I spent the night sleeping on a concrete bench."

Acuff heard her, as Fowler had promised, was impressed, and offered her a job on his program. But there wasn't a lot of money in local radio, she had no money to fall back on, and the decision was made to return to Winchester and the drugstore. The reception she had received in Nashville encouraged her, however, and for three years she appeared as a regular vocalist with a local group, Bill Peer and the Melody Playboys.

In 1953, at the age of twenty-one, she married Gerald Cline. Her professional name was established: *Patsy Cline*. As before, she sought out every opportunity to perform, and she had appearances on such regional radio and television shows as the *Louisiana Hayride*, the *Old Dominion Barn Dance*, the *Ozark Jubilee*, and *The Jimmy Dean Show* in Washington, D.C.

The country music community began to notice her. Ernest Tubb, it is said, interceded with William McCall, president of Four Star Records, to get her a recording contract in 1955. Four Star had a distribution deal with Decca, and Decca producer Owen Bradley was approached to help with the new singer. Bradley told country music reporter Jack Hurst that the only thing he knew about Patsy Cline then was that she had a reputation of being "a little hard to get along with."

That wasn't true, he learned. The problem with Patsy, Bradley found soon enough, was that her voice was "too good."

"Patsy had such a beautifully silky voice," he said, "and . . . it was hard to get country radio stations to play her records. So we did things that, if you listen to her old records now, make you say, 'What in the world did you do that for?' We did it to try to rough those records up a little, so that maybe they'd be considered more country."

Her first record, released on the Coral label, was *A Church, A Courtroom, Then Goodbye*, backed with *Honky Tonk Merry-Go-Round*.

The big break came in January of 1957, when she was accepted as a contestant on the important *Arthur Godfrey's Talent Scouts* network television show. There she met Janette Davis, who was a regular singer on the Godfrey television shows, and Janette worked with Patsy to find the right material for her network debut. Patsy wanted to sing *A Poor Man's Roses*, but Janette recommended that she sing *Walkin' After Midnight*, a song by Donn Hecht, of which Patsy had made a demo tape. Hecht had written the song for pop singer Kay Starr, but she didn't like it. In truth, Patsy didn't like it much either, but she decided to accept the advice of Janette Davis.

Walkin' After Midnight brought the studio audience to their feet; Patsy won the Talent Scouts competition. And Decca (not Four Star) released the song immediately. It was a million seller, going to number three on the *Billboard* country music charts. Patsy Cline was a star.

Not everything was rosy, however. Her marriage to Gerald Cline collapsed, she divorced him, and in September of 1957 she married Charlie Dick, a Korean war veteran from Winchester.

After *Walkin' After Midnight*, she recorded *A Poor Man's Roses, Stop the World*, and *Come On In*. But there wasn't much magic in them. Bradley said that one of the problems was that Four Star insisted that she sing songs published by that company, severely limiting her choice of material.

It didn't seem to matter too much, though, because she went into semi-retirement in 1958 and 1959 following the birth of her daughter, Julia.

In 1960, several things happened that brought her back. Her husband,

Charlie, realizing that she needed to perform, prodded her into accepting a spot as a regular on the *Grand Ole Opry* in Nashville. And her contract with Four Star ran out. Decca, and Bradley, immediately signed her and the first record released, of Hank Cochran's *I Fall to Pieces*, became her initial number one on the charts.

The tragic streak in Patsy's life came to the fore. On June 14, 1961, she was critically injured in an automobile accident. During her hospitalization she met a young singer from the Kentucky coal fields named Loretta Lynn. They became fast friends—important friends.

After several months of recuperation, she came back to the Opry stage. She also went back into the recording studio with Owen Bradley. He remembered that it took several weeks to finish the vocal on Willie Nelson's new song, *Crazy*, because some of the notes were too high for her to hit with broken ribs.

Crazy was a major hit. Other hits followed: *She's Got You, Leavin' on Your Mind, Imagine That, So Wrong, When I Get Through With You*, and even the Bob Wills country standard, *Faded Love*. Trade publications named her the top female vocalist in country music, ending more than a decade of dominance by Kitty Wells.

What happened next developed in two poignant scenes.

One unfolded on Thursday, February 28, 1963, and is recorded in Loretta Lynn's best-selling biography, *Coal Miner's Daughter:* "I went over to Patsy's house because she had some tapes she wanted me to hear from a recording session. At that session she cut *Sweet Dreams* . . . I remember that while we listened to the tapes, Patsy embroidered a tablecloth. She did that to relax. Her little boy, Randy, was on a rocking horse, rocking very hard. I was worried that he'd fall off and get hurt, but Patsy said not to worry. That night we made plans to go shopping when she returned from doing a benefit show in Kansas City for some disc jockey . . .

"Just before I left her house about midnight, she said she had something for me. Then she gave me a great big box filled with clothes for me to take home. One thing in that box was a little, red, sexy shorty nightgown. She told me, 'This is the sexiest thing I've ever had. Red is the color men like.' . . .

"I remember that before we said good-by, we'd usually hug each other, but that night I was carrying that huge box. Patsy said, 'Aren't you going to hug me?' I put down the box and hugged her. Then came the last words I would hear from her. She said, 'Little gal, no matter what people say or do, no matter what happens, you and me are gonna stick together.'"

The second scene was reported by Alabama newspaper man Rebel Steiner, Jr.: "Jerry Lee Lewis, Charlie Rich, Lester Flatt and Earl Scruggs, and Tex Rit-

ter were on the bill that Saturday night at Birmingham's Municipal Auditorium. Also on the bill was Patsy Cline.

"The first show was sold out. The second performance was standing
room only. Still, more than five hundred fans were outside wanting tickets.

"Many of them stood in line along Eighth Avenue North on March 2,
1963, to see and hear country music's most popular woman singer.

"For two shows the promoter was paying Patsy Cline $1,000 cash, a hefty
fee then. The crowd grew, and the promoter wanted all the performers to do a
third show. But he wouldn't give them more money.

" 'Well, we'll do it if everyone else does,' Miss Cline replied. So she swag-
gered on stage and sang her traditional first number, *Come On In* . . .

"Helen Holcombe of Alabaster was in the audience that night. She is the
mother of Wendy Holcombe . . . 'I had seen her on the Arthur Godfrey
show and I just always thought she was super great, you know. When I heard
she was coming to Birmingham I just wanted to see her and hear her . . . To,
me, she was just the best . . .'

"Mrs. Holcombe got to meet Patsy Cline backstage, and 'I remember I was
very impressed with her. She was so happy and content with her career and
everything.'"

Patsy went from Birmingham to Kansas City for a benefit concert for the
widow of country music disc jockey, Cactus Jack McCall. Playing the benefit
with her were Billy Walker, Cowboy Copas, Wilma Lee and Stoney Cooper, and
Hawkshaw Hawkins. When the concert was concluded, the Coopers drove to
their next engagement, and Walker left on a commercial flight. Patsy,
Hawkins, and Copas elected to fly back to Nashville in the private plane of
Randy Hughes, Copas' son-in-law. They took off on the evening of Sunday,
March 3.

It was three days later that radio broadcaster Paul Harvey reported to his
network audience: "Three familiar voices are suddenly silent today. And over
an ugly hole on a Tennessee hillside, the heavens softly weep.

"No more mournful ballad was ever sung on the *Grand Ole Opry* than the
one which was hammered out on the nation's newsprinters this morning. The
Nashville country music stars Hawkshaw Hawkins and Cowboy Copas and Patsy
Cline, and their pilot. They'd flown in a one-lung Comanche to Kansas City
for a benefit performance. For the benefit of the widow of a friend who'd been
killed in a car wreck. And they were returning to home base—Nashville,
Tennessee.

"They'd refuelled at Dyersburg. Some severe thunderstorms had been rak-
ing that area along the Tennessee River. At least one commercial airliner
had detoured. Precisely what happened thereafter will be subject to conjecture

forever. And what terror there was toward the end we'll never know. But there was no pain. When they found the plane this morning its engine had entered the earth straight down."

Patsy's body was returned to Winchester, Virginia, for burial. A decade later the tragedy was remembered when she was honored in the Country Music Hall of Fame.

And that, except for the recollections of family and close friends, seemed to close the Patsy Cline chapter in the country music story.

The book was reopened again, however, by the 1980 motion picture based on Loretta Lynn's biography, *Coal Miner's Daughter*. In that film, actress Beverly D'Angelo's gutsy portrayal of Patsy not only won her an Academy Award nomination, but it also brought the colorful singer back to public attention.

There was a full-scale print biography, talk of a biographical film on her, a "re-engineered" album of Patsy's past hits, a revived fan club, the establishment by her family of a Patsy Cline Foundation, and the revelation of plans to establish a museum in her honor.

Yet, it had all been summed up in 1963 when a flat, bronze plaque was placed on her gravesite: *"Death cannot kill what never dies."*

Virginia Patterson Hensley, born Winchester, Virginia, September 8, 1932; died Camden, Tennessee, March 5, 1963.
Married, Gerald Cline, 1953. Divorced.
Married, Charles Dick, 1957. (Two children: Julia, Randy.)

*I'm a fair piano player who had some lucky breaks—and a
whole lot of help from a whole lot of people.*

23

Owen Bradley

Elected to the Country Music Hall of Fame: 1974

What Owen Bradley wrought in Nashville is known around the world as
Music Row. He was the architect of it.

Characteristically, Owen Bradley will deny that.

The veteran chronicler of the Nashville scene, newspaper columnist Red
O'Donnell, wrote that "probably next to the Grand Ole Opry, Bradley has
been the most significant factor in establishing Nashville as an important music
center."

Chet Atkins described Bradley as a "dreamer who is also a doer."

Friendly, talkative, quick to laugh, painfully self-deprecating at times,
Bradley played a role in the careers of uncounted country music performers.
And his own career is a mirror of the growth of musical Nashville.

In a sense, he is a native of the city. Although he was born, in 1915, on a
farm near Westmoreland, Tennessee (that's some fifty miles northeast of Nashville), his family moved to the city when Owen was only seven. His farmer
father—Vernie Fustus Bradley—became a salesman for a tobacco company.

It was in east Nashville, when he was ten or eleven, where Bradley says

163

his interest in music really started. "We had a lot of people from up in the country," he remembered, "that would come down and visit. The *Grand Ole Opry* started about this time and some of these people would like to go and see the *Opry*. [They were] players—they would play guitars and sing and they'd come down and visit with us and they would spend the night. So I got to listening to country music and I started trying to play the harmonica."

An eye injury, in one of those odd twists of fate, started young Owen on a musical career. He had begun a course on the electric steel guitar, and when he suffered the eye injury, which kept him out of school for six months, "I had nothing to do but practice." In that same period, the family acquired a piano. "I drove everybody crazy trying to play it." (Later he would add the trombone and vibraphone to his skills.)

From about the age of sixteen, Bradley began earning a living as a musician; his father thought "I was wasting my time." But in the Depression days, the young man was earning as much as a hundred dollars a week. He laughed: "I couldn't spend over twenty-five dollars to save my life."

It was a fascinating life for a young pop musician in the thirties (he didn't play country music then), especially one like Bradley who sought out every opportunity to work. "You get your biggest kicks when you're young," he said.

Radio work: "I'd try to figure out some way I could be successful and stay home." He began working around Nashville radio stations as a free-lance musician. At one time, he was performing on two stations a day, using an assumed name at one of them.

On the road: Bradley remembered playing in the gambling houses in Cheatham County, northwest of Nashville: a "whole row" of gambling houses, operating seven days a week. "You'd go weeks without seeing the sunshine unless you saw it in the morning on your way home. We'd get there at eight or nine o'clock at night and we'd play until the guy told us we could go home. Sometimes he'd forget to tell us to go home, and we would be afraid to ask him. And sometimes it might be daylight before we could go home."

As an arranger: "I moonlighted as an arranger at $2.50 per song. A contemporary bandleader and a good friend of mine, Jimmy Gallagher, for whom I arranged songs regularly . . . says 'Owen was actually a $1.50 arranger, but he charged $2.50.'"

Recording artist: "Jim Bulleit, who had organized Bullet Records, asked me to record a single called *Zeb's Mountain Boogie* with my orchestra. It was country and, frankly, I figured our group was too sophisticated to cut a country song. Country music then was strictly hillbilly and I wanted little part of it . . . Jim insisted, so I agreed with the stipulation that I be allowed to use the name of Brad Brady and His Orchestra. He approved and released ten thousand copies that sold quick-like.

"When Jim told me he intended to press another batch, I said, 'If it's okay with you, use the name Owen Bradley and His Orchestra on the label.' I, Owen Bradley, an old hambone, wanted the recognition. *Zeb's Mountain Boogie* sold about seventy-five thousand copies and [in those days] seventy-five thousand was considered a hit."

In 1940, seeking some stability in his life, Bradley got a full-time musician's job at radio station WSM. Shortly thereafter he had to go into the service, and in the U.S. Maritime Service he played piano with the Ted Weems Orchestra. It was late in 1945 that he returned to Nashville, "and that's when all the good luck started."

Bradley's "luck" consisted of a lot of hard work. He returned to his musical chores at WSM radio, working with such young artists as Dinah Shore and Snooky Lanson. He continued arranging and reestablished a band to play at local engagements (the Bradley band continued through 1964). And he produced his first record.

"The late Francis Craig," he said, "a very popular local orchestra leader, had scored a big hit with *Near You* for Bullet Records. Craig needed a follow-up. He and Jim Bulleit came up with *Beg Your Pardon*, and Jim asked me to handle the recording session."

In 1947, he began to work as a part-time producer with Decca Records' Paul Cohen. "I owe a lot to Paul for whatever success I may have achieved . . . He gave me the opportunity to use some of my own ideas and educated me in the art of producing."

Cohen would come to Nashville from New York, Bradley recalled, "stay two weeks, and record various acts. As things progressed, he would call me up and say, 'I can't come down. Would you call up Ernest Tubb and take Ernest into the studio?' With a great artist like Ernest Tubb, you just go into the studio and be real quiet and learn how to work a stopwatch."

A lot of the Nashville recordings in the late forties were done in the ballroom studio in the old Tulane Hotel, run by moonlighting WSM engineers. There, Bradley worked his first gold record session. The artist was Red Foley.

"Unless I'm mistaken," said Bradley, "*Chattanoogie Shoe Shine Boy* was the first song of any consequence with which I came near being a writer. I did more arranging on that song than writing." The key to Bradley's arrangement was the rhythm of what sounded like a snapping shoe shine rag. Credit for that, Owen insisted, must go to drummer Farris Coursey. "He beat his legs off until they turned purple. He worked so hard that he had to change legs; it's a good thing he had two legs."

More and more Cohen was turning production tasks over to Bradley and, in the final analysis, Bradley would be responsible for the recording successes of Patsy Cline, Loretta Lynn, Brenda Lee, Conway Twitty, and a host of others. But the recording business doesn't lend itself to mathematical certainties, and Bradley delights in telling stories about the goofs.

There was the case of Buddy Holly. "That was sort of a disaster, I guess," he told music writer Chet Flippo. "Paul and I felt we should record him country. I remember the sessions—Paul said, 'Look, just call our regular guys and do it country.'

"We'd go in to record him, but Buddy had a feeling to go a different direction; he heard a different drummer. I don't know whether Decca dropped him or not [Decca did, Flippo pointed out], but he turned up . . . on Coral. This time he was doing it the way he heard it, and this is the way it should have been done in the beginning. It was good to see that happen—he proved he was right. But, see, we had no real experience doing what I call rock."

There was the case, too, of young Loretta Lynn. Dorothy A. Horstman wrote in *Stars of Country Music*: "The Wilburns (Teddy and Doyle) tried hard to get her a recording contract, going from Capitol to Columbia and, finally, to Decca . . . Loretta recorded a song called *Fool Number One* as a demo, and when Decca A&R man Owen Bradley heard it, he wanted the song, but not the artist. The Wilburns made a deal to give him the song for Brenda Lee to record in exchange for a recording contract for Loretta."

In 1958, Cohen left Decca to become the head of Coral Records, and Bradley got his job. On his own, then, Owen produced his first million seller with Brenda Lee's *Sweet Nothin's*.

In the early fifties, Owen and his brother, Harold, a superb session guitarist, began to talk about the future of television and music. And they decided to build a film studio; to be first in a business that seemed destined for big things.

"The first studio we built was . . . at the Teamsters' place out at Second and Lindsley. A film studio. We were only there six or eight months because the guy raised the rent." They moved to Hillsboro Village, not far from what is now Music Row. For whatever reason, and some of it had to do with lack of experience in film, the venture was not successful. They had a lot of recording equipment left over; it seemed a natural thing to build a recording studio.

They had several locations, but they eventually wound up on Sixteenth Avenue South, just a few blocks from Division Street, in a Quonset hut. "We had problems with the sound rolling around in there, so I got a bunch of old velour curtains. We finally got it down to where it worked just beautifully. It wasn't scientifically worked out; it was just a little at a time."

The Bradley Quonset hut studio was a success. By 1961, when *Billboard* magazine named Owen Country and Western Man of the Year, the Bradley studio was averaging about seven hundred sessions a year.

Columbia Records acquired the Quonset hut studio, and it remains an active studio today. Bradley is proud of what was built there: "I don't think Columbia has touched it acoustically since they bought it. It has no real acoustics because it's dead—that was the beginning of the dead studios."

The success of the studio also was the beginning of Music Row, where Bradley had considerable real estate holdings. Publishers began headquartering on Sixteenth Avenue South, and songwriters and musicians and other record companies. More studios were added. The Row became the center of Nashville's music business. In 1967, the Country Music Hall of Fame, built at the head of Sixteenth Avenue South, was opened; BMI built a new headquarters there. But it all started with the Bradleys and their Quonset hut studio. Today, the street is renamed; it's called Music Square East.

The Quonset hut was followed, in the mid-sixties, by a rural studio near Mt. Juliet, Tennessee, called Bradley's Barn. "My son, Jerry, wanted to learn a little about the business," Owen explained, "so I built a little demo studio up close to my boat on the lake. The next thing you know, we were getting people out there to record. . . ."

Jerry Bradley learned well at the Barn. He later went on to run RCA-Nashville.

In October of 1980, a fire, apparently caused by faulty wiring around a fluorescent light fixture, totally destroyed the barn studio. Estimated loss: a half million dollars. Perhaps the most cherished item lost in the blaze was a ledger that contained the name of every artist and every song recorded there.

In the same month, Bradley went to Chicago to receive a special Human Relations Award from the American Jewish Committee. He was cited for "leadership in the effort to overcome prejudice and bigotry and for devotion to the cause of understanding among all people based on the universal recognition of the rights of the individual and the value of human dignity."

That, without question, is Owen Bradley.

So, too, is the man who loves to talk about pleasant memories: "I remember what a thrill it was playing on all the late Hank Williams recording sessions—at his request. I don't know why. At best I was only a fair piano player."

Owen Bradley, born Westmoreland, Tennessee, October 21, 1915.
Married, Mary Katherine Franklin, 1935. (Two children: Patsy, Jerry.)

I was fortunate to live through that period when we wiped out the line between western and pop. It became so big so fast that they had to differentiate between this new music and true western music, so then began calling it 'country and western' and, pretty soon, just 'country' music. None of us ever dreamed that our songs would go pop.

24

Pee Wee King

Elected to the Country Music Hall of Fame: 1974

When Pee Wee King walked from the front row of the audience in the Grand Ole Opry House, on an October evening of 1974, to mount the stairs to the stage and acknowledge his election to the Country Music Hall of Fame, he shed a few tears.

And he said: "God, it's been fun."

Fun was the hallmark of King's career. Good times, bad times, indifferent times—he enjoyed himself. His natural enthusiasm for performing, his smiling, round face, his disarming frankness, pointed to only one thing. He was having fun.

There were no hang-ups with him. He readily accepted the nickname of Pee Wee, an appellation that might have offended other men of small stature (he's five feet seven). There were never any pretenses about his being born a country singer; no story invented to put him in a cotton field or behind a plow. He was from a Polish family in Wisconsin, and he'd tell anyone who was curious that his real name was Julius Frank Anthony Kuczynski.

Yet, with his long-time partner, Redd Stewart, he created a song that might be the most important single copyright in the history of country music—*Tennessee Waltz*.

The story of Pee Wee King starts in Abrams, Wisconsin, a small community about thirty miles north of Green Bay. Actually, he had been born in Milwaukee, "but when I was young," he said, "my parents moved to a farm in Abrams . . . Dad had come from that area and so had my mother. And their parents originally had come from Poland . . . My dad played violin and concertina. He thought it would be an asset to him, as I grew up, to play sometime in his band—it was called the Midnight Four Plus One."

Young Frank Kuczynski learned to play the concertina, and he took violin lessons ("not fiddle—violin"). Somehow, an accordion found its way into the Kuczynski household, along with some unclaimed accordion lessons, and Frank was hooked. Thus, there was never really any doubt that he would be an entertainer. He grew up that way.

He was performing in Milwaukee under the name of Frankie King in 1934 (he was an admirer of the big band leader, Wayne King) when J.L. Frank, a promoter of country and western shows, heard of him. Frank hired him to play in a band with a new singer named Gene Autry during a Midwest tour. Later that year, Frank brought him to Louisville to join Autry on radio station WHAS. The group was called the Log Cabin Boys.

There were three members in the band whose first names were Frank. "Since you're the shortest one here, we're going to call you Pee Wee," Joe Frank told him. The name stuck.

Appearing on the Louisville station was a duo known as the Sunshine Girls. They were Lydia and Marie Frank, the stepdaughters of Joe Frank. Lydia remembers: "Pee Wee called me for a date. We all worked together, but he was always teasing my sister. So when he called, I said, 'You must want Marie.' But he said he was calling me."

During that same period, King met a "bashful little kid who played the fiddle. His name was Redd Stewart and he had a little group over on WGRC called the Kentucky Wildcats. We needed a fiddle player so Mr. Frank called him and he came to work for us."

By that time, Autry had left the Log Cabin Boys to pursue a new career in motion pictures. And King started a group he named the Golden West Cowboys. In 1936, the year he married Lydia Frank, Pee Wee was working in Knoxville on station WNOX, the starting point for a lot of country stars, including Roy Acuff, Archie Campbell, and Chet Atkins.

In 1937, Joe Frank placed King and his Golden West Cowboys on the Grand Ole Opry, an association that was to last ten years. Pee Wee's days on the Opry were not without a bit of controversy. "When we were first on the

Opry," Redd Stewart recollected, "horns, drums, and electrical instruments weren't allowed. You can give Pee Wee credit for being one of the first to break down those barriers." Magazine writer Lana Ellis added this point: "A barrier was broken the day President Franklin Roosevelt died. When the Opry musicians tried to find a way to express their grief, King suggested a solo of *Taps* played on the trumpet. The forbidden instrument was heard that night and the public reaction was favorable. The trumpet stayed."

Pee Wee himself remembered another change. "I believe that we were the first country entertainers in Nashville to join the musicians union local . . . Many of the Opry members started becoming union members, although it was two or three years before the Opry became completely unionized . . . So I guess I had something to do with getting the Opry unionized."

During his period on the Opry, King also began to appear in movies. "When Autry left us in Louisville, he promised he'd give us a call when he got to be a star in Hollywood," Pee Wee laughed. "Well, he did. The big one for me was Gene's *Gold Mine in the Sky* in 1938. When Gene went into the service, I did two westerns with Johnny Mack Brown and two with the Durango Kid."

In the days that Pee Wee and his band played the Grand Ole Opry they received no pay for the WSM show. Money had to come from personal appearances they could promote during the *Opry* broadcasts. On one of those appearances, at the Kiel Auditorium in St. Louis, a disc jockey approached King backstage. "Pee Wee," he said, "there's a boy here who should go to work with you. He's wasting his time in St. Louis. He's got a fine voice and a heck of a personality. His name is Eddy Arnold."

King met him, liked him, and offered Arnold a job. Eddy accepted. "He didn't even ask how much we were going to pay him," Pee Wee said. "So he drove into Nashville in his little ol' Plymouth and stayed with Joe Frank and me. Eventually, he brought his mother to Nashville. He was a wonderful asset."

Some years later, King told an interviewer that the country music industry owed much to Arnold: "He was our first bridge to the pop field as an artist in his own right. He took a bit of criticism for this, but I always admired him. He took his own songs, like *Anytime* and *I'm Sending You A Big Bouquet of Roses*, and introduced them to nightclub and supper club audiences. That's when country artists began having country records that were pop hits and country writers stopped having to depend exclusively on pop artists to make their songs big sellers."

King knew about that kind of thing. He might have been thinking of his own classic, *Tennessee Waltz*. His own recording of it, and an almost simultaneous recording by Cowboy Copas (once a member of the Golden West Cow-boys, incidentally), never sold a million copies. It wasn't until pop singer Patti Page got the song that it became a major hit—on both country and pop charts—and sold millions.

King tells how the *Tennessee Waltz* was created: "It was a Friday night in 1946 and we were coming back to Nashville from Texarkana. The luggage truck was the easiest place to concentrate . . . Bill Monroe's *Kentucky Waltz* was playing on the radio and Redd said, 'You know, it's odd, we make a living in Tennessee, but nobody's ever written a Tennessee waltz song! And so we took the old melody that we were using as our theme—the *No Name Waltz*—and Redd started writing lyrics on the back of a match box cover. Redd used to smoke cigars. This was one of the reasons he never rode in the limou-sine—the boys in the limo didn't want the smoke. We used to keep the dome light on in the luggage truck, and I'd make notes—what we'd have to do, what wardrobe to take, where we're going to stay. Anyway, on the back of this match box cover—a big nickle box of matches—Redd had written the lyrics. And we kept putting it together, putting it together."

When they got back to Nashville and turned the song into Acuff-Rose, Fred Rose did one bit of editing. Stewart's original phrase was "Oh, the Ten-nessee Waltz, Oh, the Tennessee Waltz, / Only you know how much I have lost." That was changed to "I remember the night and the Tennessee Waltz, / Now I know just how much I have lost."

In 1965, *Tennessee Waltz* became the official song of the State of Tennes-see. "Governor Frank Clement once told me," Pee Wee said, "that no matter what country he went to, the minute they knew he was coming, the orchestra learned the *Tennessee Waltz*. And, of course, it was so great when Governor Clement got to do the keynote speech at the Democratic convention in 1956 and they brought him onto the platform with it. I have never heard a bad rendition of it—there's no way anyone could butcher it . . . The other big thrill I get out of it is when the University of Tennessee football team is playing on net-work television and they have halftime. Then you see that big marching band playing the *Tennessee Waltz March*.

"Redd and I were in Boston once, waiting for the elevator, when the door opened; just like on cue, the Muzak sound system began playing the *Ten-nessee Waltz*. And Redd turns to me and says, 'King, this is going too far now, man!'"

(The *Tennessee Waltz* has accounted for nearly five hundred recordings and sales of perhaps seventy million copies.)

King has some four hundred songs to his credit and, surprisingly, his fa-vorite is a jazzy, non-country thing called *Bonaparte's Retreat*. "It was the first thing Redd Stewart and I did that was really successful, so I think there's a little nostalgia or sentiment attached to it."

Pee Wee had a gold record in 1951 with his pop *Slow Poke* written with Chilton Price, a Louisville broadcasting record librarian.

In 1947, King decided to leave the Grand Ole Opry. He wanted to get into television, and he had an offer from WAVE in Louisville. Within a short time he was doing four television shows each week—in Louisville, Chicago, Cincinnati, and Cleveland. And for thirty-nine weeks, he had a network show on ABC television. That was in 1956.

King's career was changing, however. His manager and father-in-law, J.L. Frank, died in 1952; the road was getting tougher; the inroads of rock 'n roll were changing musical tastes. In 1962 he gave up the four weekly TV shows; in 1969 he broke up the Golden West Cowboys. His attention was turned to packaging shows for fairs—an enterprise in which Pee Wee King and Redd Stewart are still featured on the stage.

So the fun that Pee Wee mentioned in his Hall of Fame acceptance speech still continues. And so does the pride when he hears, again and again, the haunting refrain of the *Tennessee Waltz*. For Julius Frank Anthony Kuczynski, a.k.a. Pee Wee King, it's a sweet life.

Julius Frank Anthony Kuczynski, born Milwaukee, Wisconsin, February 18, 1914.
Married, Lydia Frank, 1936. (Four children: Marietta, Frank Jr.; twins, Gene and Larry.)

Look at me, I'm not funny. But I've built up the fact that I love to perform, and the people know I love it. That sort of thing is contagious, and it's more valuable than being able to sing or being funny or anything else.

25

Minnie Pearl

Elected to the Country Music Hall of Fame: 1975

It is Saturday night at the Grand Ole Opry House in Nashville. Roy Acuff, an impish grin on his face, rears back and shouts: "Cousin Minnie Pearl!" He stretches out the words, making them elastic, so that they cover the tripping, dancing entrance of a woman in a gingham dress, white stockings, shoes held together with safety pins, her hair piled on top of her head under a ridiculous flowered, straw hat on which a price tag dangles from the brim.

"How-dee!" she shouts into the microphone.

The audience roars back: "How-dee!"

"I'm just so proud to be here!" Minnie Pearl responds. And everyone in the audience knows she really is.

As Acuff stands at another microphone, lovingly playing straight man for her, Minnie launches into a familiar routine—as familiar as the hit songs that come from the Opry stage each weekend. If the fans come to hear Acuff sing, once again, *Wabash Cannonball*, they also come to hear Minnie Pearl tell the stories, once again, of her family and friends at Grinder's Switch, Tennessee.

"I had a birthday just the other day," she begins, "and they had a cake with a birthday candle for every year of my life. And some idiot lit them candles. Seven of the guests was overtook by the heat." (Laughter)

"It's the biggest fire they've had at Grinder's Switch since Ceph Joneses' barn caught fire. Ordinarily, the barn would have burned out before noon. But the fire department kept it burning all day long." (Laughter)

"We got a fire engine at Grinder's Switch got my name on it. It's named for me."

Acuff, giggling: "Is that right?"

"Yeah, it's named for me—the fire engine. 'Cause it's always ready and seldom called for." (Laughter, building to applause) "That ain't no laughin' matter. That's sad." A change of pace: "Roy, I wanted to bring my brother."

Acuff: "Your brother?"

"Well, I wanted to bring him," Minnie continues, "but every time I take him somewhere, folks they just run from him. The last time I brought him up here some fella pointed a finger at Brother and said: 'What's the matter with that ole boy? He got spots all over his face. Has he got the small pox?' And I said: 'No, Brother ain't got the small pox. We just been trying to learn him to eat with a fork.' " (Loud laughter) "Brother and a friend of his named Handsome Peabody . . . that's his name."

Acuff, laughing: "That's a new one on me."

"Well, you stick around. There'll be a whole lot of new things about me you don't know."

Acuff: "I imagine."

"Well, sir," Minnie goes on, "Handsome Peabody is Brother's best friend, and they decided they'd haul hay from Kentucky down here. And they got 'em a truck and they was buyin' the hay for ten dollars a bale, and sellin' it for ten dollars a bale."

Acuff, incredulously: "Why . . . that wasn't no good."

"Finally, Handsome said: 'Why, we ain't makin' no money. Wonder what's the trouble?' And Brother said: 'Maybe we need a bigger truck!'"

The laughter rolls across the big Opry House audience and Acuff claps his hands delightedly. Minnie launches into a fast chorus of *Careless Love* ("I only know two keys," she tells the audience. "One of 'em's 'C' and the other one ain't.") and skips off the stage to heavy applause.

Acuff always brings her back for an afterpiece; they've done dozens over the years. This time Acuff says to her: "You possibly won't like me for this, I know, but I don't think anyone will have hard feelings. Did you ever notice how small Dolly Parton's feet are?"

"How small her *feet* are?"

"Yes . . . her feet."

"No. I wonder what causes that?"

"I really don't know," Acuff answers shyly, "but I think nothin' won't grow in the shade too well."

Minnie feigns shock at the slightly risque punch line—which she had given to Roy in the wings prior to the show—and skips off again. As she takes her final bow, she gives a comic gesture that brings a roar from the crowd and must make the radio audience of the *Grand Ole Opry* wonder what is happening.

Over the years, *that* Minnie Pearl has become a very real person, even to the woman named Sarah Ophelia Colley Cannon who created her. She speaks of Minnie in the third person: "She thinks she's cute. I don't think I'm cute, but she thinks she's cute, and I love getting into her skin and feeling cute. At times she comes off pretty funny, I think, and that's when I don't get in front of her and just let her handle it. If I do that she just opens up like a flower. But just let me say 'We've got so and so here, let's not use that gag,' and then I can't find her. She just takes off and she's just a little wisp or something backstage. She's gone, and there I stand with my bare face hanging out and her hat on. She never gets tired, though. I've wondered.sometimes what she thinks about having to get into that costume and work over and over."

Sarah Colley (*not* Minnie Pearl) was born in Centerville, Tennessee, the fifth daughter in the family of a prominent lumberman. Centerville is some fifty miles southwest of Nashville, and very close to a 'community' of two houses, an old barn, and a train switch—Grinder's Switch. Tom Colley made a tomboy of his youngest daughter, teaching her to whistle and how to recognize trees and birds. Her mother, known affectionately in Centerville as Aunt Fannie Tate Colley, was a cultured lady who organized book circles, played the organ at church, and had strong views on how proper young ladies should behave. She didn't want her daughters to walk around the town square, for example, because they would have to pass the smelly town stable.

As a child, Sarah showed interest in the stage; her mother gave her "expression" lessons. And on occasional trips to Nashville, while her mother went shopping, Sarah would sit in the Palace Theater watching vaudeville shows.

"I didn't realize at the time that this was going to be my life's work," she told interviewer Laura Eipper, "but I had this funny feeling about watching this one gal work. Her name was Elviry Weaver and she was a lot like Marjorie Main or Marie Dressler—a comic heavy. It was pure slapstick comedy and I ate it up. I'd sit through three or four shows. I'd sit there and see the lights. I didn't see that it was tawdry and I didn't see that half the canvas was off the backdrop and that it was in tatters. I didn't see that these were tired vaudevillians that had to get themselves back up together for the four o'clock show. I thought it was delightful . . . that she could make people laugh."

When Sarah graduated from high school, she was enrolled in Ward-Belmont College in Nashville, an elite finishing school for young ladies. When she graduated in 1932, after majoring in speech and drama, she went back to Centerville to teach. It didn't really work. After two years she took a job with the Wayne P. Sewell Producing Company in Atlanta, traveling the South and producing amateur musical comedies in remote rural areas.

"It gave me a chance," Minnie recalls, "to really make a study of country girls. I became Minnie Pearl in 1936 at Brenlea Mountain in Baileyton, Alabama, at a show. I was staying in a mountain cabin and met a fine old mountain woman there who told so many tales and funny stories. After ten days with her, I began to quote her, and people would laugh. She was like Granny on *Beverly Hillbillies*, a sprightly, brittle, hardy woman with a bun of hair on the top of her head. She told me once: 'I've had sixteen young 'uns. Never failed to make a crop.'"

Sarah kept working on the character and the hill dialect, and by 1940 (she was twenty-eight) she felt secure enough in Minnie Pearl to audition for a spot on the *Grand Ole Opry*. WSM manager Harry Stone and program manager Jack Stapp heard her—and hired her. Stapp said later: "We thought she was just great."

She knew, however, that the Minnie Pearl character needed work, and important help on that came from Roy Acuff. In December of 1940, Acuff asked her to join his road show—at fifty dollars a week. ("Well, that was just . . . my word, that was an enormous amount of money! I was making ten at the Opry.") She had never been on the road with a country music band and, as a matter of fact, really was not too familiar with country music. And there was something missing in her act.

"There was one night," Minnie remembers, "that we stopped at an all-night truck stop and there was a juke box, and I had a few beers, and I got up on the floor and started doing this dumb old dance that I do on the stage now. They all started laughing and Roy said: 'Minnie, why don't you do that on stage?' I stopped immediately and said, 'Oh, I couldn't do that. That's silly!' He said: 'That's what I've been tryin' to tell you, Minnie. Be silly. That's what they pay to see. Turn loose, Minnie.' Roy Acuff taught me that important lesson. Make a fool. Self-deprecation. He took a stiff, real frightened, plastic comic—a drama student who thought she had comedic talent—and made her into a crazy, carefree hillbilly comic."

Minnie also credits comedian Rod Brasfield for adding to her character and for teaching her the nuances of timing. Brasfield, from Smithville, Mississippi, joined a traveling tent show at sixteen, and later worked with the famous Bisbee Comedians troupe. He joined the Grand Ole Opry in 1944 and, in essence, Brasfield and Pearl became a team, the comedy stars of the radio network portion of the Opry, the *Prince Albert Show*, with Red Foley as a straight man foil. They also worked together on what was called *Purina's Grand Ole Opry*, a live-to-kinescope television series in the fifties.

Brasfield was a visual comic, with an elastic face, and a penchant for slapstick. But Minnie remembers him as an unselfish partner, a comedian who was perfectly willing to give his fellow worker the key punch lines. Here's a small sample of one of their routines:

(Brasfield enters, dressed in an ill-fitting, long, striped bathing suit, swim fins on his feet, carrying an inflated inner tube.)

Rod: "I'm a-goin' swimmin' with the purrtiest woman I ever seen."

(Minnie enters behind him, wearing a Gay Nineties swim suit that covers her from the neck to the ankles.)

Minnie: "How-dee, Rodney!"

Rod: (turning to her in surprise) "Well, I declare, if it ain't Jane Russell!" (double take) "An' it ain't! . . . Hey, Minnie, are you goin' swimmin' in that there swim suit?"

Minnie: (coyly) "Yes, do you think it's too daring?"

Rod: "Well, I don't know. Did anybody dare you to wear it?"

Minnie: "You're a big 'un to talk. Look at that what you got on."

Rod: (proudly) "Ain't it a fit?"

Minnie: "A fit? It looks more like a convulsion to me."

Rod: "This here's my divin' suit."

Minnie: "Well, you oughta know about the dive."

Rod: "How's that?"

Minnie: "You've been in plenty of 'em."

Rod: "Oh, Minnie, hush!"

Minnie: "Listen, Rodney, tell me how you feel about these girls that go out in these swim suits like I've been lookin' at down yonder at the lake. Do you like bathin' beauties?"

Rod: "I don't know, Minnie, I never bathed one."

Minnie: "Rodney, there are some girls down there that had on swim suits . . . well, I ain't never saw nothin' like it. One of 'em had on what Uncle Nabob called a hobo bathin' suit."

Rod: "Hobo? What in the cat hair is in a hobo suit?"

Minnie: "No visible means of support."

Corny? Yes. Entertaining? Also, yes. Simple, innocent routines of that sort have been the backbone of rural humor, primarily because country shows are designed as family entertainment.

When Sarah Colley was developing the Minnie Pearl character, her father advised her to "keep it kind." And that's been the hallmark of Minnie Pearl's humor. She tells funny stories about her family and friends in Grinder's Switch —Brother, Sister, Uncle Nabob, Ceph Jones, Lem Perkins, Mammy, Hoke Weatherby, her shy boy friend, Hezzie—and the audience laughs. But the humor is never bitter: "Brother's not a failure—he just started at the bottom and likes it there."

"The folks come to see me," she says, "because we share a mutual affection. We like to enjoy human frailties."

The cornerstone of the Minnie Pearl character is that she can never get a man, but she keeps trying. In real life, Minnie Pearl was married in 1947, at the age of thirty-five, to a commercial pilot, Henry Cannon. He flew Minnie to many of her personal appearance dates. "I'm the luckiest gal in show business," she joked. "I married my transportation."

Joking aside, the marriage has been a very successful one, and Minnie Pearl has become one of the most durable stars in country music. She has played venues from tent shows to Las Vegas to Carnegie Hall. And she's proud (not vain) about what she has done.

"There's a poem I keep on my desk:

> *A bell's not a bell 'til you ring it,*
> *And a song's not a song 'til you sing it.*
> *Love in your heart wasn't put there to stay.*
> *Love isn't love 'til you give it away.*

"Laughter is the same way," Minnie Pearl says. "The first thing you think of when you hear a joke is to want to tell it, to share it. . . ."

Sara Ophelia Colley, born Centerville, Tennessee, October 25, 1912.
Married, Henry R. Cannon, 1947.

*Paul Cohen did more than anyone else to start the record-
ing business in Nashville. Paul was the guy who brought the
record business to our town. He . . . contributed more, a
lot more, than he ever took out of the industry.*
                                        —Owen Bradley

26
Paul Cohen

Elected to the Country Music Hall of Fame: 1976

Country music's recording history, starting in the twenties, was written in
colorful chapters by the exploits of Ralph Peer, Frank Walker, Eli
Oberstein, Uncle Art Satherley, and others. They were the men who
went out into the hills, to the small crossroad towns, into hotel rooms and gar-
ages in cities across the nation, and recorded artists on portable equipment.

They were pioneers. But so, too, were the men who saw the growing needs
of the fledgling recording industry, who understood that stability was necessary if the business was going to prosper, who reasoned that the public would
continue to buy records only if the technical quality improved.

Paul Cohen, a Chicagoan, was one of those.

When Cohen got into the business in 1927, at the age of nineteen, he
worked for the Columbia Gramaphone Record Company. At the time, there
were only two recording centers—New York City and its environs and Hollywood—where the recording industry was progressing in parallel lines with the
motion picture industry.

As the thirties began and the Depression widened, the record business was one for entrepreneurs. Two of them surfaced in Chicago in the persons of Jack and Dave Kapp. They ran a store in Chicago; the worsening economic climate closed it in 1932. Jack took a job with the then-dominant American Record Company. Dave became a talent manager of sorts. In 1934, as entrepreneurs will do, Jack found himself running the new Decca Recording Company, an offshoot of English Decca. His brother, Dave, was enlisted to head the country music division.

One of the first young men they hired was Paul Cohen. That was in August of 1934; he was a salesman for Decca Records. In 1935, he moved to Cincinnati as the Midwest branch manager.

Dave Kapp, in the meantime, went on the road seeking out talent. He made two trips through the South each year. Formal records of those journeys were not kept. "If we had known we were making history," Kapp once said, "then we would have taken more photos and kept better documentation. . . ."

It is known, however, that he signed Jimmie Davis in 1934; he recorded Milton Brown and the Brownies, Bradley Kincaid, and the Carter Family. And in April of 1940, he conducted an historic recording session with Ernest Tubb in the Rice Hotel in Houston. Tubb was to become one of Decca's most enduring country music stars.

Through the thirties, the Kapps built Decca into one of the strongest record companies in the nation. They had a large, well-rounded catalog, headed by Bing Crosby. In the country field, in addition to Tubb and Kincaid and Brown and Davis, they had Cliff Bruner, Johnnie Lee Wills, Rex Griffin, and Bill Carlisle.

In the early forties, Dave Kapp turned the country division over to Paul Cohen. Almost immediately, Cohen started to look at Nashville—because of its vast talent pool drawn by the Grand Ole Opry—as a possible recording center. Just as important, perhaps, was the availability of good recording engineers. He didn't move to Nashville, but he made frequent trips to the city, and he lined up a strong aide in Nashville in the person of Owen Bradley, then WSM's musical director.

The turning point came in the spring of 1945, when Cohen decided to record one of Decca's brightest young stars, Red Foley, in Nashville. He selected WSM's downtown Studio B for the session. What is known of that session is that it happened either in March or April of 1945. Even the titles of the songs recorded are in doubt. Foley recalled, somewhat tentatively, that three of the four songs he recorded were *Tennessee Saturday Night, Blues in the Heart,* and *Tennessee Border*.

Country music historian Robert Shelton, in his entertaining book, *The*

Country Music Story, wrote: "Whenever the first date of the first commercial session in Nashville is established, some sort of public celebration will be in order."

(As an aside, the old National Life and Accident Insurance Company building, in which Studio B was housed, fell under the wrecker's ball in 1981).

Later in 1945, Cohen also took Ernest Tubb to Studio B for a session. The date was September 11, and Tubb cut two sides: *It Just Don't Matter Now* and *When Love Turns to Hate*. Thus, Cohen firmly established the pattern of using Nashville as a recording base. Others were to follow his example rather quickly.

Tubb is proud of the role he played in it: "Two sound engineers at WSM, Carl Jenkins and Aaron Shelton, wanted to set up an independent recording studio, and they came to Red Foley and me to ask if we could persuade Decca to do some recording there . . . Jenkins and Shelton eventually established Castle Studio in the Tulane Hotel, which was the first recording studio as such in Nashville. I recorded *Blue Christmas* there. WSM objected to these outside activities by Jenkins and Shelton, so they sold the studio and stayed with WSM."

The Tulane Hotel studio was used frequently by Cohen and by Bradley. RCA's Steve Sholes, one of the first to see the wisdom of Cohen's pioneering, recorded in Nashville for the first time in 1946 at yet another private studio run by the Brown Brothers. That one had been built at Fourth and Union Streets, on a site that had once been the law offices of Andrew Jackson.

Cohen began calling Nashville "my second home," and he built a very strong roster of country stars for Decca. Included were Kitty Wells, Webb Pierce, Bill Monroe, Patsy Cline, Red Sovine, Bob Wills, Loretta Lynn, Jimmy Wakely, Brenda Lee, Tex Williams, Spade Cooley, Rex Allen, Tubb, Foley, Davis, and a one-time country singer named Bill Haley.

In 1958, Cohen left the Decca country A&R job and went to work for Coral Records; Bradley succeeded him. In 1960, Cohen finally moved to Nashville to begin his own independent label, Todd Records. Later he joined his old boss, Dave Kapp, at Kapp Records, and his last job was as Nashville operations manager for ABC-Paramount Records.

He became ill in 1970, and entered a hospital in Bryan, Texas. Diagnosis: Cancer. He died there on April 1. In an ironic twist, on that same day Hubert Long, one of Nashville's leading talent agents and a colleague of Cohen in the establishment of the Country Music Association, posted a letter to a gift shop in Bryan, directing that a gift be sent to Cohen every day he remained in the hospital and designating the names of prominent people in Cohen's Music City that were to be put on the cards. The gifts were never to be delivered.

The true influence of Paul Cohen in the country music industry is reflected in the number of people with whom he worked who have been elected to the Country Music Hall of Fame: Ernest Tubb, Red Foley, Bob Wills, Bill Monroe, the Carter Family, Jimmie Davis, Patsy Cline, Kitty Wells, and his protégé, Owen Bradley.

Paul Cohen, born Chicago, Illinois, November 10, 1908; died Bryan, Texas, April 1, 1971.
Married; one son: Paul, Jr.

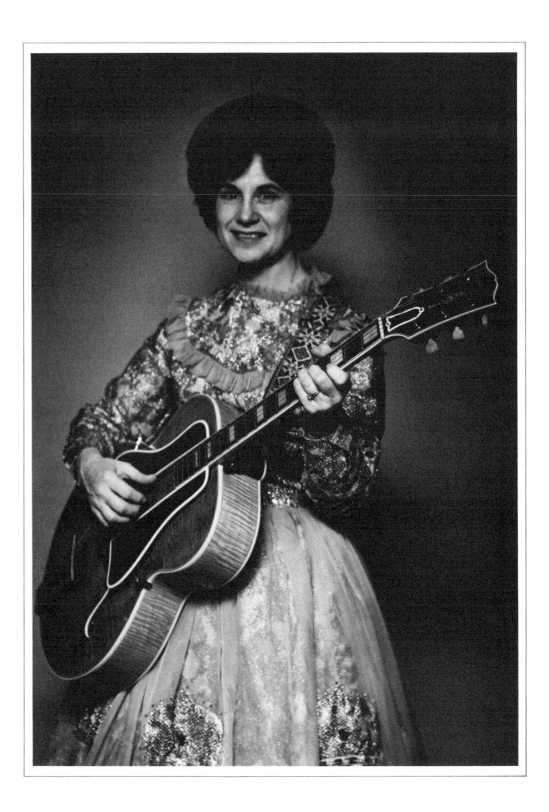

Of course I was proud of 'Honky Tonk Angels'—but I still couldn't get used to the idea that I, personally, Kitty Wells, had a hit record out . . .

27

Kitty Wells

Elected to the Country Music Hall of Fame: 1976

Kitty Wells is a paradox. Almost a stereotype of the wife-mother, she broke the mold of that image with one spectacular recording—*It Wasn't God Who Made Honky-Tonk Angels*—and became the first female superstar in country music.

It wasn't a defiant act. It just happened. But, as country music historian Bill C. Malone contends, "Kitty emerged to dominate the country field for years and to alter its course forever . . . she sang a memorable (and, to some, shocking) set of lyrics which placed the blame for nearly every broken heart squarely on the male. . . ." Another noted country music authority, Douglas B. Green, put it this way: ". . . she was the first important woman singer to tackle in song the issues that so disturbed postwar America: infidelity, divorce, and drinking . . . her willingness to deal frankly with these new and emotion-charged problems, combined with her touching singing style, earned her the title of Queen of Country Music . . . [Kitty] paved the way for the acceptance of women singers in general, something that was long overdue in country music."

189

There was virtually nothing in her background that would have suggested that she would someday revolutionize the country music industry.

She was born in 1919, the daughter of a railroad worker, in Nashville. Her name was Muriel Ellen Deason, and she was one of six children. One writer has called her childhood circumstances "average"; another used the word "unexceptional." What may have distinquished the Deason family from others in the south Nashville neighborhood was that there was always music around. She sang in church as a youngster and began playing the guitar at the age of fourteen.

As a teen-ager, Muriel and her sisters, Mabel and Willie Mae, along with a cousin, formed a musical group called the Deason Sisters. They played numerous community functions, mostly for no pay, and also sang regularly on the *Old Country Store* program on radio station WSIX.

She began dating a young cabinet maker/guitarist named Johnny Wright, who had moved to Nashville from Mt. Juliet, Tennessee. They married in 1937 (Muriel was only eighteen) and their first professional experience together was as Johnny Wright and the Harmony Girls on WSIX. The third member of the trio was Johnny's sister, Louise.

It wasn't music that supported them, however, during those Depression days. Wright worked at the Davis Cabinet Company for fifteen dollars a week, and Muriel was employed at a clothing factory, the Washington Manufacturing Company, ironing shirts for nine dollars a week.

In 1939, Johnny teamed with his brother-in-law Jack Anglin, who had married Louise Wright, as the Dixie Early Birds on WSIX. By 1940, the decision was made to go into music full time; they formed the Tennessee Hillbillies, later renamed the Tennessee Mountain Boys. They first went to radio station WBIG, in Greensboro, North Carolina, but it didn't work out. Nearly broke, they wrangled a thirty-dollar advance from WCHS in Charleston, West Virginia, and went there to be regulars on what was called *The Old Farm Hour*. Muriel was with the group, singing sometimes, but certainly not featured. The Wrights' first child, Ruby, had been born, and Muriel was pregnant again when they traveled to West Virginia.

The entire troupe lived in two rooms in Charleston; Muriel and Johnny, with the baby, Ruby, plus Jack and Louise in one room; the other three members of the Tennessee Mountain Boys in the second. And while they were in West Virginia, the Wrights' second child, Bobby, was born.

In June of 1942, they moved on to WNOX in Knoxville, Tennessee. But wartime gasoline rationing made it almost impossible to keep any kind of personal appearance schedule, and they had to move back to Nashville. Johnny Wright got a job at the DuPont plant; Jack Anglin was inducted into the service.

A year later, the Wrights were back at WNOX to try again on the *Mid-Day Merry Go Round* show, a program that spawned Roy Acuff, Pee Wee King, Bill Carlisle, and Archie Campbell. Their new group included Johnny, Smilin' Eddie Hill, a young fiddle player named Chet Atkins, and Muriel in a more prominent role. It was there that Muriel was renamed. Johnny reasoned that Muriel Deason Wright was too difficult for the fans to remember. He called her Kitty Wells, a name taken from an old mountain folk song, *Sweet Kitty Wells*.

It wasn't an easy life. With Knoxville as their base—and later Raleigh, North Carolina—they toured widely, traveling in a car, dragging a trailer loaded with their instruments and luggage. But when the war ended, they got their first big break. Anglin returned, teamed up again with Wright and Eddie Hill, and they were hired as regulars on the *Louisiana Hayride* radio program in Shreveport, which ranked second to the *Grand Ole Opry* and the *National Barn Dance*. It was 1948, and the act was "Johnny and Jack, featuring Kitty Wells." They starred on *Louisiana Hayride* for four years before an offer came to join the Grand Ole Opry in Nashville.

Up until that time, Kitty was not widely recognized as a solo performer, and certainly not as a solo recording artist. "In 1949, about the time Johnny started recording for RCA," she recalled, "I sang some gospel songs for them. But that was before a girl (any girl) had really got started in the recording field. And the fact is, they didn't really get the records out—at least in more than a trickle. I guess it was reasonable from their viewpoint. They were afraid the records wouldn't sell, and they'd be stuck with them."

(There had been a few girl singers who had received some measure of public acceptance: Patsy Montana, who had a million-selling pop record, *I Wanna Be a Cowboy's Sweetheart*, in the thirties; Molly O'Day, Rose Maddox, Martha Carson. But none had reached major star status.)

Decca Records executive Paul Cohen, a pioneer in the Nashville recording industry, saw something special in Kitty and signed her to a contract. She was not wildly enthusiastic. "I really thought it would be the same thing all over again," she said. "I'd just do a record session and that would be it. The record probably would be released, but that would be the last you'd hear of it."

Circumstances conspired to make it otherwise. Hank Thompson had a big hit on the country charts with *Wild Side of Life*, a song that suggested that men were led down the primrose path by ladies of easy virtue called "honky-tonk angels." Songwriter J.D.Miller, who had a fine commercial touch, wrote an "answer" song—a *woman's* answer, putting the blame on men. He brought *It Wasn't God Who Made Honky-Tonk Angels* to Kitty. She liked it, Johnny Wright liked it, and so did Decca producer Owen Bradley, who had been assigned to the session only because Paul Cohen was out of town on other business.

"It was really a familiar melody," Kitty remembered, "and it had been used for a great variety of lyrics. The Carter Family used it (*I'm Thinking Tonight of My Blue Eyes*), and Roy Acuff (*The Great Speckled Bird*). Actually, I didn't think much about Hank Thompson's song—or that it needed an answer. I guess it just turned out to be the right song at the right time."

Overnight, it was a hit. It quickly became the first solo record by a female singer to reach number one on the country music charts. Kitty Wells was a star.

But not just because of one record. Later in 1952 she went to number one again with *I Heard the Juke Box Playing* and *A Wedding Ring Ago*. And the parade to the top of the charts continued—1953: *I Don't Claim to Be an Angel, I Gave My Wedding Dress Away, I'm Paying for That Back Street Affair*; 1954: *One by One* (a duet with Red Foley), *Release Me*; 1955: *As Long as I Live* (with Foley again), *Making Believe, Whose Shoulder Will You Cry On?*; 1956: *How Far Is Heaven?* (a duet with her daughter, Carol Sue), *Searching, You and Me* (with Foley once more), 1957: *Repenting*; 1958: *I Can't Stop Loving You, She's No Angel*; 1959: *Amigo's Guitar, Mommy for a Day*; 1960: *Left to Right*; 1961: *Heartbreak U.S.A.*; 1962: *We Missed You*; 1964: *Password, This White Circle on My Finger*; 1965: *I'll Repossess My Heart, You Don't Hear*.

In addition there were dozens of others that reached the Top Ten on the charts, including several duets with Webb Pierce and Roy Drusky. Kitty Wells had not only broken the trail for other female country singers; she had built a four-lane highway.

She was voted the number one female country artist for eleven consecutive years by *Billboard* magazine, for ten consecutive years by *Cashbox*, the top female artist of the decade by *Record World*, and she was also the first female country singer to win an award from *Downbeat* magazine, which usually confined itself to jazz and pop music. In 1954, Tennessee Governor Frank Clement created a Tennessee Womanhood Award for her, and twenty years later the Nashville Business and Professional Women named her Woman of the Year.

In the midst of all of that success, there was also tragedy. Jack Anglin, who had remained with Johnny Wright and Kitty, was killed in a one-car accident in Nashville in March of 1963. Ironically, he was on his way to a memorial service for singer Patsy Cline, who had been killed several days earlier in a private plane crash that also took the lives of Hawkshaw Hawkins, Cowboy Copas, and Copas' son-in-law, Randy Hughes.

Kitty's greatest honor came in 1976 when she was inducted into the Country Music Hall of Fame. Roy Acuff told a reporter at that time: "Kitty has always been thought of as a wonderful lady in show business as well as wife and mother. She is highly respected by everyone who knows her, because of her everyday conduct, on the stage and off. As the old saying goes, there will be a lot of water over the dam before country music will be blessed with a finer lady and more loyal person."

Her performing style was—and is—surprising to many people who are not familiar with the details of country music. "Kitty Wells sang in a restrained, physically immobile manner," Bill Malone has written, "and with simple dignity. Although her clear, nasal voice was immediately recognizable, her performance was marked by no vocal or physical tricks. But when she sang in country dance halls, people clustered reverently around the stage to both see and hear the 'queen of country music,' whose success opened the door for other women stars, like Loretta Lynn, to appear and thrive."

Loretta recognized that, of course. "When I first started singing," she said, "I tried to sound too much like Kitty. I have gotten away from it, but . . . Kitty Wells is still my favorite girl singer."

Kitty continues to play nearly two hundred personal appearance dates a year, with a touring troupe billed as the "Kitty Wells—Johnny Wright Family Show." They cover more than 100,000 miles annually in a customized Silver Eagle bus known as the Kittyhawk.

In 1979, in action designed to coincide with her sixtieth birthday, Kitty and Johnny announced the formation of their own record label, Ruboca—a name formed from the first two letters of the names of their children: Ruby, Bobby, and Carol Sue. All of the children have been performers, Bobby most prominently. Kitty's first single release on Ruboca, *Thank You for the Roses*, was written by Jack Anglin's brother, Jim.

Thank You for the Roses, her first new recording in three years, quickly made it to the *Billboard* "Hot Country Singles" chart.

That was not surprising. Kitty Wells has never had a single release that didn't chart.

Muriel Ellen Deason, born Nashville, Tennessee, August 30, 1919. Married, Johnny Wright, 1937. (Three children: Ruby, Bobby, Carol Sue.)

Happiness is a friend who has usually been around, but heartbreak and sorrow are old acquaintances of mine. I've tasted success, and gorged on failure. I've walked on red carpets and waded mud. Every person I know, as far as I'm concerned, is my friend. If I have an enemy he's kept it a secret from me.

28

Merle Travis

Elected to the Country Music Hall of Fame: 1977

Chet Atkins, universally regarded as one of country music's finest guitar players, named his daughter Merle.

Doc Watson, perhaps the best folk guitarist in the world, named his son Merle.

Both men named their progeny out of respect to the talent and friendship of a guitar picker out of Muhlenberg County, Kentucky—Merle Travis. The Country Music Association, when it inducted Travis to the Hall of Fame, called him "a man of seemingly limitless talents"—guitarist, songwriter, actor, cartoonist, writer.

It may be that he is most proud of his talent as a writer. And, because of his modesty and his innate honesty, perhaps the best way to chronicle the career of Merle Travis is to use only the words he has written, or spoken, about himself.

"I was born November 29th, 1917, in Rosewood, Kentucky . . . If you'd look for it on the map you wouldn't find it. It's not there. You'd find Greenville, though. It's the county seat. It's in southwestern Kentucky, almost exactly be-tween Nashville, Tennessee and Evansville, Indiana. . . .

"Just before the turn of the century, William Robert Travis married a black-eyed, black-haired girl whose name was Laura Etta Latham. A year and a half later my oldest brother, Taylor, was born. Two years from then my only sister, Vada, was born. Thirteen years passed and my brother John Melvin appeared on the scene, and I cropped up a couple of years after that . . . .

"The Rob Travis family never lived in a house with electricity, plumbing (inside or out), we never had a radio, and we never had rugs on the floor. Dad never owned a car in his life, we had no horses or mules, our lights were coal-oil lamps and our drinking water from a spring. Mom cooked on a coal stove, and the house was heated with a coal fireplace. . . .

"There was no money, and new clothes, bought on credit at Beech Creek Coal Company store, came seldom. When they did, it was new overalls for us menfolks and a few yards of cloth. Mom made our shirts and her own dresses from the cloth . . . Our clothes were patched over patches (this is a fact, not a poor attempt at a joke). But we stayed clean, and always had enough to eat, except a few times during coal mine strikes. . . .

"The first house I could remember living in was owned by a good ole Negro couple that we called Uncle Rufus and Aunt Rowena Littlepage. They had been slaves before the War Between the States and were quite old when we moved to the old Littlepage place at the top of Browder Hill. Uncle Rufus was a kind and colorful old gentleman. His white hair and black skin, his mild manner and wisdom were right out of a story by Joel Chandler Harris, or a song by Stephen C. Foster.

"It was in this old pre-Civil War house that I discovered music.

"Dad traded his brother, Uncle John Travis, out of an old five-string ban-jo. I was completely fascinated by the instrument, and hounded Dad by the hour to play it . . . Dad played what today's folklore enthusiasts call the 'rapping style' of banjo playing . . . This rollicking style . . . is very much alive today, thanks to folks like Grandpa Jones and . . . Bashful Brother Os-wald. . . .

"I learned to pick the banjo that way when I was about eight. I'm sure the word talent shouldn't enter here. I was merely imitating Dad. I fancied myself exactly like him when I'd rare back with the old five-stringer and yelp in my squeaky little voice the song I'd heard him sing. . . .

"My first guitar was 'Taylor' made. My brother Taylor made it out of what wood that he could find, and it played pretty good. I figured out a few chords and learned a few basics off the phonograph to . . . Vernon Dalhart, Carson Robison, and Jimmie Rodgers records.

"When I got big enough to run around by myself, I'd walk down to Drakesboro, which was three miles, to the Pentecostal meetings. And there were two guys, Mose Rager and Ike Everly, that had a way of playing a guitar with a thumb pick and their first finger. I thought that it was the prettiest music I had heard in my life. So I went home and found a piece of celluloid that was a comb originally, and I scraped it down thin enough to put in hot water and shape into a thumb pick. And I tried to play like they did. That's how I learned to pick. . . .

"Ike married a lovely Muhlenberg County girl, and they had two sons. When the boys were still very young the Ike Everly family moved to Iowa, and all of them performed on the radio. I had a letter from Ike while they were in Shenandoah. He said his two boys wanted to be entertainers, but he wasn't sure just how well they would do. In 1956 we had a little get-together in Drakesboro at Mose Rager's house. Ike and his family were there. Ike's boys sang a few songs. He said they were planning to make some records. I thought they sang very well. So did millions of other folks a short time later when their records were played around the world. They used their real names, Don and Phil, the Everly Brothers. . . .

"When I was sixteen I did what many boys were doing in the thirties . . . I joined a Civilian Conservation Corps camp that President Roosevelt came out with to help us out of the Depression. I was paid thirty dollars a month, but I had to send twenty-five back home, so I ended up making five dollars a month.

"I saved enough money to buy myself a Gretsch guitar, which was the first decent guitar I had. I caught a freight down to Evansville, Indiana, where my brother lived and went to a music store [to buy the guitar]. . . .

"A boy named Junior Rose and I hoboed all over the country with our instruments. He played the mandolin and I played the guitar. . . . We thumbed rides on the highways, rode freight trains, and even bummed rides on river boats. My guitar was always with me. We'd play on street corners at night and ask for donations from people who would gather around to see what was going on.

"'We're trying to make our way to Texas,' I'd lie, 'I have a sick sister there. If any of you folks would like to help us, just pitch any loose change you have in your pockets here in front of us.'

"Then in Evansville, in 1935, my brother got me on radio station WGBF to play a tune at a marathon dance. I played *Tiger Rag* just as much like Mose Rager as I could. . . .

"This broadcast led to a job with a band who played on the same station. This was something to write home about. I was on the radio! The boys in charge of the band were Elgie and Freddie James. There were five of us all together. The name of the group was the Knox County Knockabouts. They were talented musicians and singers. I imagine we sounded fairly well. There was no pay for playing on the radio, but we were allowed to announce our engagements. . . .

"After a time the band broke up. I hitchhiked back . . . home. A few weeks passed and I got itchy feet again. A few days later I was on top of an L&N boxcar leaving the Drakesboro depot heading back to Evansville—with my guitar beside me.

"Another band took me on. They were doing the same thing the Knock-abouts did. There was one exception. A combination car salesman and radio announcer by the name of Aud Rhodes was personal manager for the group. We were the Tennessee Tomcats. Aud was something of a super salesman and smooth talker. . . .

"He'd say on the air, 'If any of you would like to have this band out to your schoolhouse or fair to entertain, drop us a post card.' Then, we'd go out and play schoolhouses, dances, and little fairs. And, when we'd get back, Rhodes would say, 'Well, we didn't do very good, boys,' then pay us thirty-five cents apiece. . . . But now that I look back, Rhodes did pretty good for those times booking us.

"Now, Clayton McMichen, who was the hottest thing in the country at that time, was playing a school in Greenville, and I walked six miles to see him. After the show I went backstage and got a chance to play for him. He said he might get in touch with me some day to play with his band.

"We had a big flood in Evansville in 1937, when a telegram came from McMichen. So I got my overalls and my guitar and conned a guy into taking me across the river in a rescue boat. I got on a train and went to Columbus, Ohio, to meet McMichen. . . .

"I had no idea where to go when I got there, but I wasn't long in finding out. The whole town was plastered with placards advertising the GREAT NATIONAL FIDDLER'S CONTEST, between CLAYTON McMICHEN AND NATCHEE THE INDIAN! With special added attraction, the famous Delmore Brothers. . . .

"That was a great day for me. It was my first meeting with Alton and Rabon Delmore. We later became the closest of friends until the end of their lives. That was the day I met Cowboy Copas. He played the guitar for Natchee the Indian and never sang at all.

"'Hello, son,' Clayton said to me. 'I'm proud to have you with us.' He looked me over, and put his hand on my shoulder. 'By grannies, I think I'll just call you Ridgerunner.' . . .

"Later, I joined the Drifting Pioneers at WLW in Cincinnati. And with

Grandpa Jones and the Delmore Brothers, we worked as the Brown's Ferry Four . . . Syd Nathan (he started King Records) down on Central Avenue in Cincinnati ran a used record store, and me and Grandpa Jones would go down there and buy records. One day Syd said, 'Why don't you boys make your own records?' We said, 'Ain't nobody asked us.' Syd said, 'Well, I'm asking you. I'm gonna start a record company.'

"Jones said we couldn't do it because we were under contract to WLW, but Nathan said we could 'slip out of town to do it.' We did and recorded as the Sheppard Brothers. Can you imagine trying to camouflage Grandpa Jones' voice? . . .

"I was in Cincinnati until the war came along, and I went to the Marine Corps. I don't talk too much about it; I wasn't no Sergeant York. . . .

"When I got back to Cincinnati, there wasn't anyone I knew. . . . Smiley Burnette was playing the Albee Theater there, and I went backstage to talk to him. We went out to eat, and he sat down and looked at the snow on the street and said, 'I had rather live in California and eat lettuce than live here and eat caviar.' I said, 'Really?' Well, he left, and the next day I got to thinking about it and borrowed ten dollars apiece from about everybody at the radio station. Then I rode a sit-up train all the way to California. I lived there about twenty-three years. . . .

"In California I was on the radio, worked a lot of pictures and made records for Capitol. . . . Cliffie Stone was my A&R man at Capitol, and he wanted me to record an album of folk songs. I said, 'I thought Bradley Kincaid and Burl Ives have already sung all the folk songs.' Stone said, 'Write some.' I said, 'You don't *write* folk songs.' He said, 'Well, write some that *sound* like folk songs.'

"So that's what I did. The reason that I wrote that bunch of junk is basically that I had to."

(Note: That "bunch of junk" included *Sixteen Tons, Dark as a Dungeon*, and *Nine Pound Hammer*.)

"About *Sixteen Tons* . . . people come up to me and say, very seriously, 'Every word of that song is true.' And I say, 'Really?' Why, the whole thing's a fun song. You know, the guy picks up the shovel the day he's born, and he ain't gonna let no high-tone woman make him walk the line. Why, in the first place, it takes *two* men to load sixteen tons of coal. . . .

'And *Dark as a Dungeon*—I had a date with a girl down in Redondo Beach . . . I thought, dad gum, I got to get along and write some songs for that album. And it was dark, and I thought, 'The streetlight's on—what the heck, it's light enough to write by.' It was a dark and cold night; I figured there must be something there. I pulled over and got out a piece of paper and pencil and wrote, 'It's dark as a dungeon way done in the mine.' Then I thought of all the Irish songs that go, 'Come all you fair and tender ladies,' and I got, 'Come all you young people so young and so fine, and seek not your fortune way down in the mine.'

"And some people say, 'Hey, sing *Dark as a Dungeon*. Boy, you must have really been inspired to write that!' And I think about sitting under a streetlight after a date with a pretty girl—that's inspiration. . . .

"Inspired songs ain't worth a dime. I heard that from Johnny Mercer. Some songwriters are inspired by their sick mother or their girlfriend that's left them. But a songsmith like Harlan Howard or Cindy Walker, Dallas Frazier—you say, 'I need a song Tuesday.' 'Well, what sort of song?' 'A sad love song about a girl who came back when she's been gone.' He says, 'I'll have it for you tomorrow.' And they write it. They don't have to be inspired; they're songsmiths."

(Travis' low-key self-evaluation tends to obscure his real accomplishments. As a songwriter he had hits with *Divorce Me C.O.D.; So Round, So Firm, So Fully Packed; I Am a Pilgrim; Smoke! Smoke! Smoke! (That Cigarette)*, with Tex Williams; *No Vacancy*, with Cliffie Stone; as well as the aforementioned "folk" songs, *Sixteen Tons, Dark as a Dungeon*, and *Nine Pound Hammer*.

As an actor, he appeared in some forty westerns, with the likes of Tex Ritter, Eddie Dean, Charles Starrett, Smiley Burnette, Rod Cameron, Jimmy Wakely, and others. There was also his acclaimed cameo role as a guitar-playing soldier singing *Re-enlistment Blues* in the 1953 top film, *From Here to Eternity*.

As a guitarist, his album with Chet Atkins, *The Atkins-Travis Traveling Show*, won the Grammy for the best country instrumental performance in 1974. He also has a gold album for his picking on the Nitty Gritty Dirt Band's classic album, *Will the Circle Be Unbroken?*

Merle was a pioneer in the electric guitar field, and was believed to be the first artist to play a solid body guitar in public, a Bigsby electric he designed himself. (One of his other design innovations was having all the tuning "machines" on the same side of the headstock, now a trademark of Fender guitars.)

As 1982 began, Travis was still "very active in the business. . . . I don't play the beer bars every night, but I play concerts and colleges and clubs. I'm very lucky to be able to pick and choose where and when I play. . . .

"And I live now in Oklahoma—in the Cherokee Nation over by Tahlequah; down at the end of a road without a house in sight. . . .

"Music has been very good to me . . . I never took a lesson; never gave a lesson . . . I don't ever remember actually sitting down and practicing playing the guitar. You can tell that by listening to me! But, then, I don't remember sitting down to drink a lot of water. The guitar was there, and when I felt like it I'd grab it and pick around on it. Just as I'd pass the water bucket and, if I was thirsty, I'd take a drink. . . .

"You hear music everywhere on the guitar. There's hardly anywhere you put your fingers there's not a chord."

A final word from Chet Atkins: "I'd probably be looking at the rear end of a mule if it weren't for Merle Travis."

Merle Robert Travis, born Rosewood, Kentucky, November 29, 1917. Married, Betty Morgan. (Three daughters: Pat, Cindy, Merlene.)

. . . If you look back, I never did have any one record that really took off; some of them, like 'Old Rattler' and 'Mountain Dew,' would continue to sell steadily over the years, but I never had any really smash hit.

29

Grandpa Jones

Elected to the Country Music Hall of Fame: 1978

Hey, Grandpa," someone in the audience shouts, "what's for supper?"

The old man on the stage answers immediately: "Cornbread, turnip greens, candied yams, butter beans, blackberry cobbler, and all things rare, and the more you eat, the more to spare."

Louis Marshall Jones is among the last of the character performers in country music. His "Grandpa" guise has served him well since he was only twenty-two years old, for a period of more than forty-six years.

Yet, in spite of the comedic aspects of his costume and the national recognition as a funnyman he has gained on the long-running *Hee Haw* television show, Jones doesn't consider himself a comedian. ". . . am I a comedian? Well, no. It's just that I was a singer working by myself—no band or anything. And with my voice, maybe my singing got boring quicker. At any rate, I couldn't just sing one song right after the other, so I started putting little jokes in between. Now I've been using the same jokes for years, and the times I've tried to change them it doesn't go over as well."

Grandpa, with his distinctive drop thumb banjo style, considers himself a country music performer, with the emphasis on the word *country*.

"Really, if *Hee Haw* hadn't come along," he told an interviewer after his election to the Country Music Hall of Fame, "I'd probably be a-plowin' right now. 'Cause since they put so much pop and rock in country music, a lot of old pickers like me has fell by the wayside. It's not that we haven't got listeners. It's because the radio stations are afraid to play our stuff. The only thing you can get now is the top 50, the top 20, the top 10, the top everything. There's so many people out there that ask us, 'Where can we hear country music?' We can't tell 'em. Not even in Nashville."

Jones came by his country music heritage naturally. Born in 1913 in Niagra, Kentucky, a small town near the Indiana border, he was the youngest of ten children. His father, a sharecropper, has been a fiddle player; his mother played the concertina. But it really wasn't music that dominated their home; it was work.

"Back then you raised tobacco," Jones recalled. "Thought you'd starve to death if you didn't raise tobacco, where we were from. You had to do everything by hand then—plant it, burn the plant beds, plow it with a walkin' plow, hoe it. I hated it. But I think it does you good to be poor when you start out. You enjoy a lot of other things better."

The Jones family moved around a lot while young Marshall (he was rarely called Louis) was growing up. "We moved about every two years. We moved so much that every time the wagon backed up to the door the chickens laid down and crossed their legs."

On one of the farms on which they lived, Grandpa remembers, "a saw mill was set up to take out some of the lumber that was plentiful there at the time. The workers lived in tents and one came to the house askin' to leave his git-tar so the moisture wouldn't hurt it.

"I got to sneakin' in and foolin' with that git-tar when I was about ten, and that was my first real introduction to a musical instrument."

When the worker left, so did the guitar, and the youngest Jones could only dream about having one of his own. His recollection is that a brother came home with a guitar for Marshall. "I like to went wild, seein' that git-tar, 'cause I'd been wantin' one for so long. He got it at some old junkyard called Cheap John's. Paid seventy-five cents for it."

With that guitar, and with his friend Miff McKinley, also an amateur musician, Jones began playing local dances and parties.

In 1928, the family moved again, this time to Akron, Ohio, where the elder Jones hoped to get a job in the rubber plant. Marshall was enrolled in

Akron's West High School, where he was a painfully shy lad. But the city life was to provide him with his first break. The year was 1930.

"There was a week-long amateur contest held in the Keith Albee Theater," Grandpa said. "It was sponsored by Wendell Hall, the old red-headed musicmaker who had that famous record, *It Ain't Gonna Rain No More*. There were four hundred an' fifty contestants an' he'd go through an' weed 'em out every night. At the end of the week I won first place. The two songs I sang were *Dear Old Sunny South by the Sea* and *Goin' Back to Texas*.

"I won fifty dollars in ten-dollar gold pieces, so of course I went right out an' bought a better git-tar!"

The very next day he was given a radio show on WJW in Akron. It was an early morning stint, and he was billed as "The Young Singer of Old Songs." It wasn't long before he teamed up with harmonica player Joe Troyan, and they made their way to Cleveland. In 1934, a Cleveland newspaper columnist wrote: "Word from WHK . . . reveals big things about Zeke and Harve, better known as Marshall Jones and Joe Troyan . . . Jones has more than 500 songs of the hillbilly type in his library. Troyan hails from Cambridge, Ohio, and can do more tricks with his harmonica than a big-time magician. He carries 100 different harmonicas with him and can play two at a time."

That act drew the attention of Warren Caplinger and Andy Patterson, who were recording artists in the twenties and were then talent scouts for the popular *Lum and Abner* radio show. Jones and Troyan became members of the house band for *Lum and Abner*. When the show moved from Cleveland to Chicago, the young musicians elected to move to WBZ in Boston where they joined the troupe of Bradley Kincaid, a superb Kentucky folksinger and an early star of the *National Barn Dance*. Marshall Jones' career was to change completely.

"We'd play the little theaters in New England (with Kincaid)," Jones reminisced, "performin' between pictures. Up on the East Coast as far as Maine an' then drive back an' play an early mornin' radio show. I never got enough sleep an' Kincaid would say, 'Come on an' get up here to the microphone; you're just like an old grandpa.'

"Of course, I talked this way back then an' people got to writin' in an' askin': 'How old is that old man? He sounds like he's eighty.' So we got the idea of makin' an old man out of me."

To enhance the new "Grandpa" image, Kincaid gave him an old pair of mountain boots to wear; he told Jones they were already fifty years old. Lines were drawn on his face to suggest wrinkles, and a well known blackface comedian of that era, one Bert Swor, helped Jones to rig up his first mustache.

From that time on—it was 1935 and Marshall Jones was only twenty-two—he was billed as "Grandpa Jones."

The boots, resoled at least three times since then, are still used. And the mustache of 1982 is real. Obviously, the boots are dear to him. There's one story that, some years ago, while Grandpa was playing a park in Maryland, a drunken woman broke into his dressing room and made off with the boots. Jones was furious. When he found the woman, she had passed out on a hilltop above the park—with his boots on. "I tried to pull them off," he said, "and I guess I drug her halfway down the hill."

Musicologist Charles Wolfe, writing in the *Journal of Country Music*, reported: "In 1937, when he was twenty-four, Grandpa published his first song, a sequel song called *An Answer to the Maple on the Hill*, with the M.M. Cole Company, then one of the country's leading sheet music publishers. He also struck out on his own, getting a job at WWVA's *Wheeling Jamboree*. He spent the next five years at various West Virginia stations, working by himself and with a vocal trio. Up until this time, Grandpa's style was quite different from that to which today's fan is accustomed. Accompanying himself on guitar instead of banjo, he specialized in sentimental songs and material learned from his mentors, Bradley Kincaid and Jimmie Rodgers. Moving from WWVA to WCHS (Charleston) to WMMN (Fairmont), Grandpa continued to perfect his style, working with artists like Hugh Cross, Buddy Starcher, and Cowboy Loye (Loye D. Pack).

"The earliest known recordings of Grandpa date from this period, a couple of 1940 transcriptions from the WMMN's *Sagebrush Round-Up*, and they are quite revealing. On one, he sings *Rainbow's End*, a mellow cowboy song, with a trio called the Grandsons; on another, he joins a quartet to do a . . . version of *Turn Your Radio On*; on a third, he leads the cast in the program's theme song, *Raise a Ruckus Tonight*, and on a fourth he does a sentimental number called *They Needed an Angel*. Though he had recently been taught by Cousin Emmy to flail the banjo, no banjo is heard on these early recordings."

In 1942, Jones moved on to WLW, Cincinnati, to join the Boone County Jamboree. There he met Alton and Rabon Delmore, Merle Travis, and Ramona Riggins, later to become his second wife. He also met a record store owner, Syd Nathan, who had an idea about starting his own record label.

Grandpa recalled: "One day Nathan took Merle Travis and I up to Dayton. He said there was a studio up there he could use as he didn't have one yet an' there was none in Cincinnati. I remember we recorded upstairs over the Wurlitzer Piano Company. We cut a few sides an' comin' back Syd said, 'What'll we call the company?' We decided on King Records. 'King of them all,'

Syd said. Merle an' I sang a duet an' called ourselves the Sheppard Brothers, but the master was damaged an' never came out. The first King record to be released was me singin' *Raining Here This Morning* an' *I'll Be Around If You Need Me*."

The war intruded on Grandpa's career; in the Army he tried to get assigned to Special Services, but wound up, instead, as an M.P. in Germany. But he did organize a band called the Munich Mountaineers and broadcast daily over the Armed Forces Radio Network.

By 1946 he was back in Cincinnati. There he continued to record on King and, in 1947, two of his best numbers were released: *Mountain Dew* and *Old Rattler*. By that time the banjo was prominently featured. He also became a member of the Brown's Ferry Four, a gospel quartet begun by Alton Delmore (he still does similar material with the *Hee Haw* gospel quartet).

The Grand Ole Opry beckoned from Nashville, and that was his next stop, going on tour with the Pee Wee King tent show. And in 1949, Connie B. Gay, the Washington, D.C., country music promoter, lured Grandpa and Ramona to the nation's capitol.

Bill Littleton, Nashville editor of *Performance* magazine, told a Grandpa Jones story of that era: "Connie took Grandpa out to the airport one afternoon, and Grandpa was supposed to fly up to Connecticut . . . to do a gig that paid about $250. Well, about six o'clock, the promoter called Connie and said, 'Where's Grandpa? We met the plane, and he wasn't on it.' And Connie said, 'Of course he was on it. I took him to the airport.'

"What had happened was that Grandpa had gone into the men's room with a comic book, lost track of time, and missed the plane. But Connie had no idea what had happened and called the airport and had him paged. Sure enough, in a few minutes, Grandpa came to the phone. Connie, all exasperated, you know, said, 'Grandpa, what in the hell are you doing?!' And Grandpa, real calm and collected, said, 'I'm settin' here readin' a two hundred an' fifty dollar comic book.'"

Jones moved on again—to the *Old Dominion Barn Dance* in Richmond, Virginia; back to the *Grand Ole Opry*; a brief return to Washington to take over a television show vacated by Jimmy Dean, and, then, in 1959, back to the *Opry* to stay.

His recording career had similar peaks and valleys. In January of 1952, he moved from King Records to RCA Victor in Nashville, and had some modest success with *Mountain Laurel, Old Blue, Standing in the Depot,* and *Stop That Ticklin' Me.*

RCA A&R man Steve Sholes thought there was a chance that Grandpa would appeal to a broader audience, and he urged him to do topical material. That led to such records as *T.V. Blues, That New Vitamine,* a duet with Minnie Pearl of *Papa Loves Mambo,* and *I'm No Communist.* They were, to be kind, unimpressive sellers.

"Steve didn't understand the kind of stuff I ought to do," Grandpa said, "and he'd bring these things that I just couldn't do at all. I just lost interest. He brought in one time a thing called *Hey, Liberace.* It was ridiculous, an' I told him so. I said, 'I can't do that stuff.' I don't think he liked it too well. I got the axe pretty soon after that."

Jones moved to Decca, then Monument. He had one brief hit with the old Jimmie Rodgers tune, *T for Texas,* and recorded a Christmas narrative, *The Christmas Guest,* which sells well on a seasonal basis. "Fred Foster tried everything under the sun at Monument to get us some hit singles, but it just didn't happen."

It was Foster, an enthusiast for old-timey country music, who put Grandpa in touch with CMH (Country Music Heritage) Records in California. Jones found a home, because CMH deals with the realities of the limited, but enthusiastic, audience for the country music of the earlier era.

In a sense, Grandpa Jones was rescued by *Hee Haw,* a phenomenon of television that began in 1968. Suddenly, it seemed, Louis Marshall (Grandpa) Jones was a national star; a whole new generation "discovered" him.

"I don't think I amounted to too much until then," Jones told writer Alanna Nash. "I don't think I amount to much now, but what I'm talkin' about is I don't think many people knew about me until *Hee Haw.* Before that, my fee was very low. Now I can go out an' ask a decent price, accordin' to the other entertainers. Oh, *Hee Haw* has done more for me than anything. You're known everywhere on that tube."

He found out, in October of 1978, that he "amounted to something." That's when he was elected to the Country Music Hall of Fame.

Minnie Pearl said of him: "He may play that role of Grandpa, but Louis Marshall Jones is a highly intelligent man. He reads a lot; he's well-educated, and he's just plain smart. He's intellectual. He pretends like he's not, but he is."

And *Hee Haw* colleague John Henry Faulk commented: "Jones is blessed by not having that mad, driving, competitive ambition that marks a great many stars . . . I think that's one of his principal assets, and probably the reason he lives so well and so comfortably. He insists on being a human being first and an artist second."

Louis Marshall Jones, born Niagra, Kentucky, October 20, 1913.
(One daughter, Marsha, by a previous marriage.)
Married, Ramona Riggins, 1946. (Three children: Eloise, Mark, Alisa.)

Hubert Long was class, and just by being in the music business he made it better.

—Bill Anderson

30

Hubert Long

Elected to the Country Music Hall of Fame: 1979

He had plans for Nashville.

Hubert Long sat in his lavishly decorated apartment in the SESAC building he had built in 1969 and talked of Music City also becoming a motion picture center. Nashville, he believed, had a lot to offer to film producers. "Certainly, the talent is here," he said.

Three years later he was dead, but the dream didn't die with him. Today, the State of Tennessee is actively promoting the area as a movie production base. And the talent pool is even greater.

Long knew about talent. Talent booking and management was his life—his whole life.

"He never married," one of his "Stable of Stars," Bill Anderson, said, "and it always seemed to me like those of us that he represented were like his kids. And we could always reach him. There was no time I couldn't find him in five minutes, anywhere in the world."

He wasn't the first talent agent in Nashville, but he may have been the first who saw country music and its stars as an *international* commodity. And without question, there was a time when Hubert Long International, Inc., was the biggest and most successful country music talent agency anywhere.

There was little in his early life to suggest what he might become. He was born in Poteet, Texas, in 1923, the son of a farmer and part-time oil field worker. Poteet was noted as being the strawberry capital of the world. When Hubert was of high school age, the family moved to Freer, Texas, where he played both the trumpet and the drums in the high school band.

As with most American males of that age group, his graduation from high school was accompanied by his induction into the Armed Forces. World War II found him in the U.S. Navy, and he spent three years in the South Pacific.

Returning to Texas from the service, he got a job in the record department of a dime store in Corpus Christi. The business appealed to him, and he expanded the store's record department; in a matter of weeks he had boosted the weekly sales five times over. New opportunities arose, and he left Corpus Christi for a job as a regional sales representative with Decca Records in San Antonio. When Hubert's immediate boss at Decca left that company to join RCA Victor, he took Long with him.

He was attending the Houston Fat Stock Show on RCA business when he met Thomas A. Parker (later Colonel Tom Parker), the manager of RCA's leading country music star, Eddy Arnold. Parker was impressed by the enthusiasm of Long and hired him, almost immediately, as a publicity-advance man for "The Eddy Arnold Show."

Hubert was now in country music with both feet, and the job with Arnold took him to Nashville for the first time. When Colonel Tom turned his attention to a young singer named Elvis Presley, and Arnold went his own way, Long moved to Shreveport, Louisiana, to become the manager of the *Louisiana Hayride* show. He had "gone to school" on Parker's management techniques, and in Shreveport he found and signed two promising singers—Faron Young and Webb Pierce. They were the first artists represented by what would become, in 1953, the Hubert Long Talent Agency in Nashville. Hank Snow, Ferlin Husky, Johnny and Jack, Kitty Wells, Roy Drusky, and Skeeter Davis soon swelled the ranks of the agency.

Long became a force in the growing Music City scene; his commercial sense took him into real estate (he was at one time the leading property owner on Music Row), record production, personal management, and music publishing. In 1959, he opened Moss Rose Publications, named after the street on which he then lived. That was followed by the establishment of Woodshed Music, Stallion Music, Husky Music, Buckhorn Music, Pawnee Rose Publications, and Ramblin' Rose publications—plus Music City Advertising.

Other stars were added to the Long roster: Bill Anderson, David Houston, George Jones, Tammy Wynette, LeRoy Van Dyke, Charlie Walker, Jan Howard, Mel Tillis, Ray Price, Del Reeves, Jim Ed Brown, Mother Maybelle Carter, and many other performers. Long represented the newer breed of manager; he had a reputation for "feeling" the market potentials of an artist, both in the United States and abroad. By 1969, as the expansion continued, the business became Hubert Long International.

His enthusiasm, little diminished since the dime store days, made him one of the organizers of the Country Music Association. He was the first man ever to serve as both president and chairman of the board of the CMA.

He became one of the most active leaders in the annual Music City Pro-Celebrity Golf Tournament. He was a lifetime member of the Tennessee Association of Country Gentlemen, the group of community leaders who provided the financial backing for the charity golf tournament.

In 1972, he became ill and underwent surgery for removal of a brain tumor. Several months later he died in Nashville's Baptist Hospital. He was not yet fifty years old.

Fellow talent agent Bob Neal commented: ". . . the music business here has lost one of its finest and most energetic leaders."

The Hubert Long Agency was acquired by Dick Blake, a close friend, and Dick Blake International remains as one of the top talent agencies in country music. Others from the Long agency went on to form their own substantial talent agencies, including the late Shorty Lavender, Bill Goodwin, and Louis Dunn. Thus, the Hubert Long influence was perpetuated.

Mrs. Jo Walker-Meador, the long-time executive director of the Country Music Association, said of Long: "He was the CMA's first treasurer, and my offices were next door to his for the first couple of years. During those first years, I used a lot of his equipment but mostly his brainpower to get things started . . . Country music has lost one of the best friends it ever had."

Hubert Long, born Poteet, Texas, December 3, 1923; died Nashville, Tennessee, September 7, 1972.

*When you walk out on stage you forget anything else. You
go into a completely different world. Costumes are a part of
it, because, as you know, 'flash' is a part of your act. . . .*

31

Hank Snow

Elected to the Country Music Hall of Fame: 1979

Hank Snow has been a dues-payer in life—first class.
There seems to be a syndrome of "hurt" in country music, and
Snow is almost a perfect laboratory example of it. Someday scholarly re-
searchers may name it the *Snow syndrome*—a phrase that will be used to explain the apparent corrolation between having experienced the most difficult
realities of living and the ability to sing country songs.

Snow himself, in his quiet, standoffish manner, might reject all of that
kind of thing as mere blathering, but, deep inside his loner's soul, he would
recognize the truth of it.

Hank was born in 1914 in Liverpool, a small town in the Canadian province
of Nova Scotia. At eight, there was the trauma of his parents' divorce and the
complete break-up of the family. Two of his sisters went to an orphans'
home; a third sister—the eldest—was sent to work in a shoe factory. Young
Hank was placed in the home of grandparents, where he wasn't really wanted
and where he became a victim of physical abuse.

His mother was the only stable element in his unhappy life, and he ran away from his grandparents to return to her; at the time she was employed as a housekeeper in Liverpool. His mother was his model. "My mother was completely organized all the time," he told an interviewer. "Years ago, I guess even before I was born, my mother was a piano player. She used to play for the silent pictures, you see. She was very talented."

The mother was also a Vernon Dalhart enthusiast, and his records were part of Hank's early days. So, too, was a mail order guitar, complete with a 52-lesson "how-to-play-the-guitar" instruction book. "That was for her," he said, "but it came in handy for me, too."

Hanks's return to his mother was not idyllic, however. She remarried and they moved to Lunenberg, a fishing village seventy-five miles from Liverpool. What might have been a new beginning turned into a nightmare. His step-father beat him—frequently, sadistically. It got so bad that the day came when his stepfather physically threw him out of the house. He was twelve years old.

"My escape from all the turmoil and poverty of that particular time," he recalled, "was going to sea. That was my escape at that time. Which took care of about four years of it."

Thus, at sixteen, tougher and more self-reliant (the year was 1930), he was back in his mother's home briefly. His recollection has it that he was practicing his guitar one day when his mother came home with a Victor record by Jimmie Rodgers: *Moonlight and Skies.* The impact of that record, of hearing the distinctive Rodgers blue yodeling style, convinced the teen-ager that his final escape would be as an entertainer.

But it was tough. He worked in fish plants, as a delivery boy, a lobster-man, a Fuller Brush salesman, a stevedore—anything to exist. And he persisted in his ambition to be a singer in the Jimmie Rodgers mold. That persistence got him a nonpaying radio show on CHNS in Halifax, which eventually led to a sponsor and a Canadian network show.

In 1936, again because he persisted, Hugh Joseph signed him to a recording contract with RCA's Canadian division. The first record he cut under that contract included two of his own songs: *Lonesome Blues Yodel* and *Prisoned Cowboy.* The label said he was "Hank, the Yodeling Ranger."

"The one was a Jimmie Rodgers type thing," he said. "It was a blues; actually you'd think it was one of Jimmie's songs it was written so close . . . My first session I did in an old church in Montreal that wasn't being used any more—see, RCA Victor at the time was remodeling their studios or something. I always thought that brought me some luck."

"Some luck," but not a great deal of it. The record wasn't really a hit; his first royalty check was for $2.96. His real luck was still a long way down the road: fourteen years away.

Also, in 1936, he married. His wife, Minnie, was a six-dollar-a-week choco-late dipper at the time. And the reality of his position as an entertainer, even though he had a network show and a recording contract, is illustrated by the fact that their son, named Jimmie Rodgers Snow (later to be an evangelist preacher), was born in a charity ward of a Salvation Army hospital.

Hank played his first professional, in person engagement at the Gaiety Theater in Halifax "for three dollars a day, three performances, which was a dollar each. My wife made me a little neckerchief in yellow and red, a little ban-dana. Took a pair of black dungarees and she sewed a white strip of cotton up each side. And that's what I did my first performance in the theater with."

Snow admits that, initially, his "road work wasn't that great." His recollec-tions of those days form a classic picture of the development of an enter-tainer.

"My wife used to act as my advance man. She'd go ahead and put up the posters and arrange for the little halls that we'd play in and then join up with us and sell tickets at the door. We'd go in beforehand and line up probably ten or twelve shows in an area. You'd get those little old schoolhouses and halls for three and four dollars a night, charge fifteen cents admission—that was big money then. One of our top crowds would have been, oh, five hundred; we figured we were really setting the woods on fire then.

"I think I played every honky-tonk and beer joint . . . well, probably I'm stretching it a little bit when I say every one, but I've played with no dress-ing room, dirt floors, no stage, standing on the dance hall floor, you name it. And any time I played the clubs back then, you had to drink with these people. I was never a habitual drunkard, and I thankfully didn't turn out to be an alcoholic, but . . . to be sociable with them you'd go to their table and have a drink with them. I quit alcohol completely . . . the 31st of March, 1970. And I wouldn't want to go that route no more."

Snow, who said his greatest honor in life was becoming a United States citizen, did not play the U.S. until 1944, when a fan named Jack Howard ar-ranged two weeks of personal appearances in the Philadelphia area. That led to other appearances in the States, and in 1946 he had a radio program on WWVA, Wheeling, West Virginia.

He also acquired a horse named Shawnee somewhere along the way, and that trick animal became a part of his act. He learned to ride it through sheer determination. And there were dreams that he might make it as a movie cow-boy. He went off to Hollywood for a period in his career that he remembers only with disgust. It broke him. Since he had a few friends in Texas, he headed for Dallas; when he got there in the fall of 1948, his wife and son with him, he had eleven dollars and no job.

In Texas, he met Ernest Tubb, with whom he had corresponded for almost a decade. They were drawn together, of course, by their mutual admiration for Jimmie Rodgers. Tubb helped him, and so did a Texas fan, Bea Terry, who badgered a local disc jockey into giving play to Hank's latest Canadian release, *Brand on My Heart*.

The RCA contract in Canada did not extend to the United States; to further his recording career in this country he had to persist again. And he did. His first U.S. recording session was arranged in Chicago. One of the songs he cut (and one which he never really liked) was *Marriage Vow*, and it was a modestly good seller after its release in December of 1949—good enough to keep RCA interested in him.

On January 7, 1950, Snow made his debut on the Grand Ole Opry, largely due to the inside maneuverings of Ernest Tubb. "I don't mind telling you," Hank remembered, "that I bombed. The people just sat there while I sang. And sat. No applause, no nothing, almost. Just sat." Opry officials weren't terribly enthusiastic either. "Harry Stone was going to let me go," Snow said. "Yeah, they were getting ready to leave me go, because actually then you had to have a hit record even to get on the Opry, so I was very fortunate."

It was a hit record that saved Hank Snow at the Opry and stabilized his entire career. His recording of *I'm Movin' On*, a song in the Rodgers railroad genre, was such a sensational hit that it stayed in the number one position on *Billboard*'s country charts for an unprecedented forty-nine consecutive weeks in 1950 and 1951. To put things in perspective, that was a period when Hank Williams, Red Foley, Ernest Tubb, Tennessee Ernie Ford, and Eddy Arnold were the big names on the country charts.

Other hits followed: *Golden Rocket, Rhumba Boogie, Now and Then There's a Fool Such as I, I Went to Your Wedding, I Don't Hurt Anymore, Let Me Go Lover, Yellow Roses, Miller's Cave, I've Been Everywhere*.

He became an international star. He had a highly successful European tour in 1961, and toured Japan in 1964 ("In the history of my career I have never played before a greater audience"). In 1966, he and his band spent eighteen days in Vietnam.

In 1974, Snow's contract with RCA was renegotiated to extend through 1987. The significance of that is that he will be under contract with one record label for fifty years—longer than any artist in any musical field.

Hank's style on stage is unique. He has persisted (persistence is what has motivated his entire career) in wearing the most garish, rhinestone-studded costumes on the stage. "Flash," he calls it, and he is a great admirer of pianist Liberace, because of the use of that same "flash." He was an admirer, too, of the young Elvis Presley, and it was he who arranged for Presley's only appearance on the Grand Ole Opry.

Bill C. Malone, the noted country music historian, wrote of him: "Two qualities that have always distinguished Hank Snow are his versatility and his thorough professionalism. No country singer has been more adept at singing both the slow, romantic ballad and the fast, upbeat tune, and his performances have been distinguished by his clean, crisp flat-picking guitar style. With faultless enunciation (listen to his version of *I've Been Everywhere*) and a mellow, resonant baritone voice distinguished by a Canadian accent which begs to be imitated, Snow developed such a much-admired and oft-imitated style whose influence has been detected in singers as varied as Johnny Cash and blue-grass vocalist Charlie Waller."

Offstage, Snow is reserved; some say even cold. He admits to that, telling interviewer Peter Guralnick: "I am a loner, that is so right. They have got tired of sending me invitations in this city, because they know better. I'm not conceited, I'm not stuck up. I'm just reserved and actually a loner. I've been on my own since I was twelve . . . I always said it was the greatest education; you couldn't get an education like that in no college, there's no way. It prepared me and taught me to be thrifty, it taught me to be business-minded, and it taught me to . . . be completely organized. . . . So I think it was a great education, and I became well disciplined through all of this."

His tragic early days also taught him to be compassionate. He created the Hank Snow Foundation for the Prevention of Child Abuse, and a great deal of his time is spent in that effort. It is the hallmark of the latter years of his career.

A summation of Hank Snow?

"I always worked very hard at my business. Some of 'em don't."

Clarence Eugene Snow, born Liverpool, Nova Scotia, Canada, May 9, 1914.

Married, Minnie Blanche, 1935. (One son: Jimmie Rodgers Snow.)

I've been very successful, but I don't ever try to analyze the reasons for it. I just feel that folks will enjoy my brand of country music and that this is not 'here today and gone tomorrow' success.

32

Johnny Cash

Elected to the Country Music Hall of Fame: 1980

Dyess, Arkansas, is dying. Yet, paradoxically, it will live forever.

The tiny community was born of necessity during the Great Depression, brought into being by the federal government to resettle poor families who needed the promised twenty acres of delta land, the mule, and the small frame house just to survive. The reason for its existence has long been dead. Indeed, the memory of why Dyess became a reality in the first place has almost flickered out—except in the mind, and the songs, of Johnny Cash.

Cash was a child of the Depression in the South, which was something vastly different from the Depression in northern industrial cities. From the age of three to eighteen, John R. Cash lived in Dyess, picked cotton there, laughed there and cried there, and learned to sing there. From Dyess, he went on to become one of the most durable stars in country music, the recipient of fame and wealth. *Five Feet High and Risin'* and *Pickin' Time* are classic anthems to Cash's growing up days. They project a believability that has characterized all of Johnny's music.

Few country music performers have had such a powerful believability; it is responsible for a lot of the myths that have grown up about Cash. His songs of prison—*Folsom Prison Blues, Starkville City Jail, I Got Stripes, San Quentin, Give My Love to Rose*—are so realistic that people can see him behind bars (Contrary to the generally accepted legend, Cash's time in jail was limited to one night after an arrest for being drunk in public). His railroad songs—*Hey, Porter, Rock Island Line, Orange Blossom Special, City of New Orleans*—are certainly performed by a railroad man (which he was not). His cowboy songs—*Don't Take Your Guns to Town, The Ballad of Boot Hill, Hardin Wouldn't Run*—suggest personal experiences as a gunslinger in the Old West. His gospel songs—*Land of Israel, He Turned the Water into Wine, Belshazah, Come to the Wailing Wall*—leave no doubts in the minds of listeners as to his faith in God. Even his comedy hits—*A Boy Named Sue* and *One Piece at a Time*—are perceived to be autobiographical.

Johnny Cash, the actual man *and* the image, is real to the audiences, and so are the songs he sings.

After graduation from high school, Cash joined the Air Force in 1950, serving most of his hitch in Germany. There he bought his first guitar, learned to play it, and did a lot of playing and singing in the barracks—mostly country songs and gospel tunes. On July 4, 1954, he was honorably discharged. "I had a crooked nose from a fight with a paratrooper in a honky-tonk," Cash wrote in his autobiography, *Man in Black*, "a scar on my cheek left by a drunken German doctor who couldn't find a cyst he was trying to remove, and a left ear with the hearing temporarily impaired because a German girl stuck a pencil in it. Otherwise, I was in good shape to come back to my people and to a San Antonio girl named Vivian Liberto, whom I married a month later."

John set up housekeeping in Memphis, at first trying to make a living as a door-to-door appliance salesman. By his own admission he was a dismal failure. He tried to get a disc jockey job, then spent a few months in a radio announcer's school. A turn in the road came when his brother Roy introduced him to two auto mechanic friends—electric guitarist Luther Perkins and bass player Marshall Grant.

"We three became friends," Cash recalled, "and 'made music' together practically every night at Roy's house or at mine. Friends and neighbors started coming in and listening, and we'd sing and play until the early hours of the morning, night after night, just for the love of it."

Memphis was the place to be in those days for anyone with musical ambitions. Sam Phillips, owner of Sun Records, was beginning to stir things up, especially with a young singer named Elvis Presley. Through persistence, Cash wrangled an audition with Phillips and eventually cut a record with two original Cash songs: *Hey, Porter* on the "A" side and *Cry, Cry, Cry* on the "B" side. It was released in mid-May of 1955, and the Johnny Cash career was launched. Cash and the Tennessee Two began to play personal appearances around Memphis and into Arkansas, Louisiana and Texas, billed with Elvis Presley and Carl Perkins, a rockabilly star with Sun Records.

In 1956, Cash's *I Walk the Line* was released by Sun and sold more than two million copies. The Grand Ole Opry beckoned in July of '56, and other hits followed: *Guess Things Happen That Way, Ballad of the Teenage Queen, Ways of a Woman in Love, Home of the Blues*.

Those were exciting days at Sun Records. Cash remembered one day when Carl Perkins and Elvis Presley were in the studio with him, and Phillips entered to introduce a new piece of talent, Jerry Lee Lewis. Somehow, the four of them began to sing gospel songs, and Sun producer, Jack Clement, turned on the tape recorder. "I have never heard the tape from that impromptu session that day," Cash wrote later, "but I have been told that a tape exists, locked away in a bank vault in Memphis, of a rough, unrehearsed quartet of would-be singers who, with no commercial reasons in mind, gathered around the piano back in the summer of '55 and put their hearts into eight or ten good songs."

Cash's career prospered, but the pressures of it began to brew trouble. He freely admits that he began to build a dependence on amphetamines—Dexedrine, Benzedrine, Dexamyl. And as that dependence grew, so did his erratic behavior. He began to miss concert dates; on some appearances (as with one important one in Carnegie Hall) he could not sing at all, because of laryngitis brought on by a combination of the drying agent in the amphetamines, cigarettes, and alcohol.

One memory is particularly vivid for Cash: "One Saturday night, in Nashville for an appearance on the Grand Ole Opry, I arrived at the Ryman Auditorium having taken pills regularly for weeks. My voice was gone . . . I was down to about 165 pounds. . . . The band kicked off a song, and I tried to take the microphone off the stand. In my nervous frenzy, I couldn't get it off. Such a minor complication, in my mental state, was enough to make me explode in a fit of anger. I took the mike stand, threw it down, then dragged it along the edge of the stage, popping fifty or sixty footlights. The broken glass shattered all over the stage and into the audience. The song ended abruptly, and I walked offstage and came face to face with the Grand Ole Opry manager. He kindly and quietly informed me, 'We can't use you on the Opry any more, John.'"

Cash's marriage collapsed during this period. But with all of the tribulations, his recording career prospered; he had signed with Columbia Records in August of 1958. He had major hits with the singles, *Don't Take Your Guns to Town* and *I Still Miss Someone*. And albums such as *The Fabulous Johnny Cash*,

Hymns by Johnny Cash, Songs of Our Soil, and *Ride This Train* were big sellers.

John was also an important concert act; the addition of the young Statler Brothers and the traditionalist Carter Family to his show made it the most sought after in country music.

In 1968, his personal life turned around. He defeated his drug problem, with the constant help of Dr. Nat Winston, June Carter, and June's parents, Maybelle and Ezra Carter. (Cash would dedicate his book, *Man in Black*, to "Ezra J. Carter, who taught me to love the Word.") On March 1, 1968, Johnny Cash and June Carter were married in Franklin, Kentucky.

In 1969, Cash became even a bigger star when he began his weekly television series on the ABC network. In October of that year, he dominated the Country Music Association's awards show as no individual has done before or since. The report in the trade paper, *Variety*, summed it up best:

". . . The NBC-TV hour could have been aptly named the Johnny Cash Show. Of the ten presentations, Cash walked away with five. This was in addition to performing *A Boy Named Sue* and *Daddy Sang Bass*, latter with the Carter Family, Statler Bros., Carl Perkins and The Tennessee Three, all regulars on Cash's vidseries. By the time Cash received his third award (Male Vocalist), he opened his acceptance speech with 'Just in case I don't see you again tonight . . .' Two awards later, he had given up on acceptance speeches and trudged up to receive the accolade as though punching in for work on a time clock. If there were an award for best performance during the award show, Cash would have won that also."

To complete the record, the CMA awards John won that triumphant night were: Male Vocalist of the Year, Single of the Year (*A Boy Named Sue*), Album of the Year (*Johnny Cash at San Quentin*), Vocal Duo of the Year (Cash and June Carter), and Entertainer of the Year.

Grammy awards, given by the National Academy of Recording Arts and Sciences, were also important to Cash in the latter part of the sixties: For the singles of *Folsom Prison Blues* and *A Boy Named Sue*, for two duets with June, *Jackson* and *If I Were a Carpenter*, and for the liner notes he wrote for his own Folsom Prison album and for Bob Dylan's *Nashville Skyline* album.

And then there was Johnny Cash the actor. In the seventies he brought the same versatility to the screen that has marked his music: a hard-bitten gunfighter (in a movie with Kirk Douglas), a convincing murderer (in a *Columbo* episode with Peter Falk), a con-man preacher who repents (in a *Little House on the Prairie* episode with Michael Landon), an exploited American Indian (in the Public Broadcasting drama, *Trail of Tears*), and as a narrator of his own motion picture, *Gospel Road*.

Perhaps his most significant role was as the lead in a CBS made-for-TV movie titled *The Pride of Jesse Hallam*. His was the role of an illiterate Kentucky coal miner who, when forced to go to the city to earn a living, cannot cope in modern society. His sensitive portrayal of a proud man who learns to read and write won him plaudits from the critics.

In 1980, when Cash celebrated his twenty-fifth anniversary in show business, *Country Music* magazine devoted an entire issue to Cash. (At the same time he starred in a two-hour CBS television special pegged to his silver anniversary.) In the special issue, the reality of Johnny Cash came through in the tributes written about him. Some examples:

Record executive Fred Foster—"One of the most vivid threads in the tapestry of Cash is the Christian one. Shortly after his return from the Holy Land where he had filmed *Gospel Road*, Johnny told me the following story; one, I might add, that has left an indelible mark on my spirit. He said that one day, after many days of hard work, he was walking (wearily, I'm sure) along the shore of the Sea of Galilee. He sat down on a rock overlooking the shore, and the magnitude of Christ and what He had done for mankind filled his very being. He suddenly had the feeling that our Lord had sat upon this very rock. He took a pinch of the dust from beside the rock and placed it on his tongue, as visions of the Last Supper burned in his brain. He told me that was the sweetest Communion he had ever taken. I have never taken one since that I don't think of Johnny's words."

Larry Gatlin (in a letter addressed to Cash)—"Even if you were not Johnny Cash, the All-Time #1 Super Star of Country Music, you would still be J.R. Cash, the All-Time #1 Human Being, and for that, more than anything, I love ya!"

Record producer Billy Sherrill—"I first met Johnny Cash in the early sixties, when I was working for Sam Phillips in Nashville. My duties were receptionist, secretary, janitor, and mixer for the studio. One night after midnight, after twelve hours of demo sessions (no hits), I was preparing to leave. I met John at the elevator, and he told me he had just finished an album at another studio and he wanted me to stay and play it for him. I was very tired and in no mood to listen to anything, so I politely declined to play it. He said O.K., so I locked up and we both left. After I was out of sight, John returned to the studio, politely kicked the door in, and listened to his album."

"Cowboy" Jack Clement, producer, songwriter, singer—"Johnny Cash is a music man, and that is the highest compliment I give. It has been said of Johnny Cash that he cannot tune a guitar and that he sings awful. And at times this is true. But there are times when Johnny Cash's guitar is pure pluperfect; and there are times when Johnny Cash sings like Johnny Cash better than anybody in the whole zip-adee-doo-dah world . . . John is a fair rhythm man upon occasion. Upon other occasions, he is brilliant, the only beat around. The only show in town."

United States Senator Howard H. Baker, Jr.—"Johnny Cash is a true national treasure. The clear, simple melodies of his music have touched the lives of countless people throughout the world. It is music in the finest country tradition, but John has given universal voice to the trials and triumphs, the hopes and disappointments, the love and lost love common to all men and women."

John R. Cash, born Kingsland, Arkansas, February 26, 1932.
Married, Vivian Liberto, 1954. (Four daughters: Rosanne, Kathy, Cindy, Tara.) Divorced.
Married, June Carter, 1968. (One son: John Carter.)

Country music today is not just a 'backwoods phenomenon,' which many people believed it to be during the early years of this century. Today, country music is solidly entrenched in the mainstream of music throughout the world, and IS, in fact, 'popular' music!

33

Connie B. Gay

Elected to the Country Music Hall of Fame: 1980

In 1937, a twenty-three-year-old native of Lizard Lick, North Carolina, unsure of the direction in which his life was going, spent some time as a street-corner pitchman.

His product was a pocketknife sharpener, purchased for five cents apiece from a carnival supplier in Chicago, and "sold for a quarter in hick towns and for fifty cents in sucker towns like Washington."

That taught the young man something—that the so-called sophistication of the big city was a myth. But he wasn't quite sure how to use the newfound knowledge.

Time passed.

In the mid-forties the same young man was a producer and news announcer on the U.S. Department of Agriculture's *National Farm and Home Hour* radio show. Occasionally, he would play a country music record on the program. And when he did, there was always a noticeable increase in the mail.

That taught him something, too. In his mind there was, somehow, a corrolation between the ability to sell the five-cent knife sharpeners for fifty cents on a city street corner, and the growing realization that country music had a wider appeal than most people thought.

"Slowly it dawned on me," Connie B. Gay said, "that there were lots of people like me from places like I came from living here in Washington. I thought, now I'd like to take that music out of church basements where a few people square danced to it, and put it into the cash register."

And that's exactly what he did.

He brought country music to the city.

He took country music uptown.

And in the process—accompanied by a promotional campaign unparalleled in the business—he put it into the cash register. *His* cash register; one that played a fifty-million-dollar tune.

A colleague said: "Connie was two years, maybe more, ahead of everyone else. He figured there was money in country music back when everybody—I mean everybody, all the smart boys—knew there wasn't anything in that hillbilly crap. He got in ahead of them, and he stayed ahead of them until he quit."

In 1973, after he had retired, an interviewer asked him: "Connie, to what do you owe your success?"

"To a mule and Adolf Hitler," Gay replied. "When I was a boy in Lizard Lick, North Carolina, I spent enough time behind a mule that I knew I didn't want to be behind that smell all my life. And Adolph Hitler—well, when the war started, Southern boys went north to train, Northern boys went south, and everybody got a taste of everybody else's music. By the time the war was over, everybody was listening to hillbilly music."

Lizard Lick, where Connie Gay was born as one of ten children (the seventh son of a seventh son—a lucky omen, some believe), is some eighteen miles east of Raleigh. The circumstances of the Gay family was poor—very poor. A living had to be scratched out of only seventeen acres. The way out of the poverty of Lizard Lick, it seemed clear, was to get an education.

When he graduated from Wakelon High School in Zebulon, Connie journeyed the short distance to Raleigh to enroll in North Carolina State University. The treasurer asked him if he had any money and, with some pride, Connie told the official that he had $2.52.

"With that much money," the university treasurer said lightly, "you ought to be able to make it."

Connie made it. He ran the college switchboard at night, he worked for a dry cleaner during the day, and he managed a college swing band called Jimmy Gerow and his N.C. State Collegians.

In 1935, at the height of the Depression, he graduated from North Carolina State with a B.S. degree in Agriculture. There followed a series of jobs with the U.S. Department of Agriculture: as a soil scientist, organizer of farm cooperatives, a stint in Puerto Rico and another in the Virgin Islands, aimed at increasing crop production for the war effort; Congressional liaison officer, speech writer (he wrote some of the agricultural elements of President Roosevelt's famous "fireside chats"), and producer, writer, and on-the-air commentator for the *National Farm and Home Hour* network broadcasts.

By 1946, Gay was determined to test his theories about the city appeal of country music. "Do you believe in extrasensory perception?" he once asked a newspaper interviewer. "I do. I have had dreams, hunches, little voices that tell me to get into this, get out of that. Somehow I always knew what to do."

But country music in urban areas? It seemed to most to be the wrong move at the wrong time. There was a postwar economic slump underway; the really smart people were getting out of radio and into that new TV thing. Gay, however, now thirty-two and with a thousand dollars he had saved, began a half-hour noontime show on radio station WARL in Arlington, Virginia, serving the metropolitan Washington area.

The date (it's an important one in country music's history) was Thursday, November 7, 1946. The show was called *Town and Country Time*.

"Frank Blair (later a star on the NBC *Today* show) was running the program end of the station," Connie remembers, "and he thought I was crazy. Everybody knew you couldn't sell a country disc jockey show; not in a city, not in the nation's capitol.

"But I told him I didn't want any salary—and I never took a penny from the payroll in nine years—I would just take a percentage from the sponsors. A *big* percentage, but then there weren't any sponsors in sight. . . ."

He broadcast from the basement of his home on North Lincoln Street. "It took off like Blaylock's bull," Connie said. The program was soon expanded to three hours (WARL would become the first urban station to go full-time country). "I couldn't beat the sponsors off with a stick. It was Katie-bar-the-door from then on. The show would sell anything. But I always kept half the commercial time for selling Connie B. Gay."

And that was selling something special.

Item: Connie B. Gay excursion trains to the Grand Ole Opry in Nashville from Washington, Baltimore, Philadelphia, New York, and Boston.

Item: Monthly Connie B. Gay country music moonlight cruises on the Potomac River. One of the performers on one of the cruises was named Elvis Presley. Connie got him for two hundred fifty dollars.

Item: Connie B. Gay country music concerts at Griffith Stadium.

Item: Chartered country music square dance trains from Washington and Baltimore to Paw Paw, West Virginia.

Item: The Connie B. Gay Hillbilly Air Show at Bailey's Crossroads, Virginia; stunt men in the air, country music on the ground. Fifty-five thousand paid customers.

And then there was Constitution Hall.

Owned by the high-toned Daughters of the American Revolution, Constitution Hall had housed an annual national folk festival prior to Pearl Harbor, and the DAR ladies were under the impression that that was the type of show Connie Gay had in mind when he approached them to rent the hall. He did nothing to dissuade them of that impression.

On October 31, 1947, Gay sold out Constitution Hall, by invitation only, to Cabinet members, Senators, Congressmen, the "best society" of Washington, for a six-dollar top.

"Oh, the other promoters laughed when I started to work on that," Connie remembered. "They were going for maybe a dollar top and fifty cents for the kids. Well, two dollars was always my bottom price for a concert. I knew what the people I had were worth, and I wouldn't sell them for less. If you wanted to hear Eddy Arnold, Minnie Pearl, Rod Brasfield, T. Texas Tyler, Judge George D. Hay, Cowboy Copas, and Kitty Wells, you had to make it worth their trouble—and mine. I grossed twenty-two thousand dollars that night."

His success with the one-nighter at Constitution Hall convinced Connie that he ought to push on. In the summer of 1948, he rented the hall again, this time for a weekly series of concerts. One Washington reporter wrote: "Soon the directors of the DAR were getting disturbing reports. There was something positively low-brow and historically unauthentic about a mountain song titled *When It's Toothpicking Time in Falseteeth Valley*. That was one of the troupe's favorites.

"Connie was filling the hall, which is a phenomenon in the summer. The directors began to fear that their temple of music would become known as 'Connie's Barn.' They doubled the rent. But that didn't discourage Connie. They finally asked him to leave. But not before he had crowded the hall for twenty-seven consecutive weeks—a record for any Washington concert series."

It would seem that Gay's successes would have brought other promoters on the run, eager to cash in on what he had uncovered. But that was not the case.

"There was still this cornpone image, this redneckism, they didn't like," Gay said. "They went with rock and roll, but they stayed out of country until country and rock began to come together. A lot of other promoters put me down. Like Liberace said, I cried all the way to the bank."

Upon the early success of his *Town and Country Time* on WARL, Connie went to the U.S. Patent Office and registered the phrase "Town and Country" as a trademark. Then he began to merchandise it through the Town and Country Network, a syndicated radio series that eventually went to some eighteen hundred stations. There was also a Town and Country syndicated TV film show, and a live television show on WMAL-TV in Baltimore, initially with Jimmy Dean as the host.

But Dean, Gay was convinced, was destined for bigger things. He put together a deal for a network *Jimmy Dean Show* on CBS; Connie owned it outright for a time and then sold it to the network. He also developed and owned *The George Hamilton IV Show* on ABC-TV, and a country show titled *Gaytime* on NBC-TV.

Simultaneously, he was buying radio stations. At one time or another he owned WQMR, Silver Springs, Maryland; WTCR, Ashland, Kentucky; WVQM, Huntington, West Virginia; WTCS, Fairmont, West Virginia; KLRA, Little Rock, Arkansas; WYFE, New Orleans, Louisiana; WFTC, Kingston, North Carolina; KITE, San Antonio, Texas; and WGAY, Washington, D.C.

He had bought WGAY (those were already the call letters when he acquired it) for $464,000. As an afterthought, the seller let him have the sister FM station for one dollar more. On that FM station, then, Gay pioneered another sound that became known as the "beautiful music" format.

Success, of course, breeds pressure. And Connie Gay was not immune from it. He told *Washington Star* feature writer Gwen Dobson: "You know, I'm Baptist, and we didn't do a lot of drinking around home and when I came up here [to Washington] I was what you'd call a social drinker. And then . . . I couldn't get enough . . . both hands . . . morning, noon and night . . . I was really on the sauce . . . I could consume up to a gallon a day.

"I remember so well, I was in New York, so I went over to the Lenox Hill unit of Alcoholics Anonymous and told them about 'this friend of mine' . . . you know that's what they all say . . . and AA saved me."

He was to face another trauma, however.

"My wife had gone out early to shop and I was upstairs shaving when I noticed this puff under my jaw . . . about the size of an egg . . ." Doctors diagnosed it as cancer of the lymphatic system; the cure rate was poor.

"Within days I was in the hospital and I'll never forget it. As any radio man would—I looked at the clock. The hands were straight up at noon when I went under and when I woke up they were straight down at 6:30 P.M." The doctors told him that if he went five years without a recurrence it would be regarded as a cure. That was in March of 1966.

The battle with alcoholism, which wrecked his first marriage, and his brush with cancer gave him pause. He began to ease up on his hectic schedule and, by 1972, he had disposed of his radio stations, the promoting had stopped, he was no longer working on the Town and Country Network. He had retired.

But the memories were still there. He recalled how, in December of 1957, he and a small group of country music friends were sitting around a hotel room bemoaning the demise of an organization of country music disc jockeys. "I said we should start a new organization and broaden it to include the rest of the people in country music. The idea was to take this music, which was sort of provincial, and make it into a worldwide music, to take it out of the closet and bring it uptown."

From that meeting the Country Music Association was formed, with Connie B. Gay as its founding president.

There are memories, too, of the stars he helped along the way.

Roy Clark: "Roy's an absolute entertainment genius—he's the alpha and omega in this business. A marvelous man. But I had to fire him one time because he couldn't hear his alarm clock and kept coming to work late. I guess now that he's a star, he's got enough people to get him up for work."

Patsy Cline: "She came down to my National Championship Country Music Contest in Warrenton, Virginia, in 1951, while she was working in a drugstore in Winchester, and won that contest. She had stardust all over her; she never failed to just absolutely tear the audience apart. She was the greatest singer I have ever known."

Charley Pride: "I gave Charley his first square meal in Nashville . . . his clothes, boots, and an LBJ string tie. I have followed his career with great interest. He's a tremendous performer."

But memories, as dear as they are, do not tempt him to return to the country music fray.

"Those days are gone." A smile.

"I'm like an old farmer in North Carolina who said he quit farming, and he wouldn't tell a mule to get up if it sat in his lap. That's about the way I am."

Connie Barriot Gay, born Lizard Lick, North Carolina, August 22, 1914.
Married, Hazel Anne Pleasant, 1936. (Two children: Jan, Judy Ann.) Divorced.
Married, Katherine Regina Comas, 1961. (Two daughters: Cecilia, Caroline.)

I could write a song and go home and live with it and re-edit it and re-edit it until the words became a . . . what did Hemingway call it? . . . a sword, not a word, a cutting sword . . .

—Bob Nolan

34

Original Sons of the Pioneers

Elected to the Country Music Hall of Fame: 1980

There is no more enduring sound in country music (and, in this case, the phrase "country and western music" is perfectly applicable) than the tight and beautiful harmonies of the Sons of the Pioneers.

The sound began in 1933; it is alive, and vital, and still new, in the eighties.

When the electors of the Country Music Hall of Fame decided to honor the original Sons of the Pioneers in 1980, the task was to determine just who were the *original* members of the group. It was easy enough to identify Len Slye (a.k.a. Roy Rogers), Tim Spencer, and Bob Nolan as comprising an initial act known as the Pioneer Trio. That, truly, was the beginning of it all.

Yet, in the early days, the Sons of the Pioneers was a rapidly evolving entity, and the Hall of Fame electors dealt with the dilemma by deciding that six men could be called "originals." Slye, Spencer, and Nolan, of course, plus brothers Hugh and Karl Farr and Lloyd Perryman. No one, not even the most thorough researcher in the country music field, could argue with the selections. Those six set the pattern; they were responsible for creating a sound like no other in American popular music.

237

Even in the eighties, after having lasted through nearly a half century of personnel changes, the unmistakable Sons of the Pioneers sound persists. There have been other "Sons"—Pat Brady, Ken Carson, Shug Fisher, Ken Curtis, Tommy Doss, Dale Warren, Deuce Spriggens, Roy Lanham, Rusty Richard, Billy Armstrong, Bob Mensor, Luther Nallie, Billy Liebert, Rome Johnson, plus an occasional alternate—but there has been only one sound.

It could be convincingly argued that at least two of the Sons of the Pioneers deserve individual recognition in the Country Music Hall of Fame. One, quite naturally, would be Roy Rogers, "King of the Cowboys." The other would be Bob Nolan, a songwriter of prodigious talent, the poet laureate of the West. But that argument is for another day.

One by one, then, here's how the "originals" came together.

Bob Nolan was born in 1908 on an isolated farm in the wilds of the Canadian maritime province of New Brunswick. To get supplies they had to make a 180-mile raft trip down the St. John River to the Bay of Fundy. "We probably had one month out of the year that we went to school," Nolan told interviewer Bill Bowen, "and it was five and a half miles away. I trotted the whole distance—half of the time with a Canadian lynx stalking me all the way."

At the age of twelve he was sent to Boston, Massachusetts, to live with his aunts and to go to school. Earlier, his father, Harry, although a Canadian citizen, had enlisted in the U.S. Army and had been gassed in Belleau Woods. Mustered out, he went to the desert country near Tucson, Arizona, to regain his health. Young Bob joined him in 1922; he was fourteen.

He went to high school in Tucson, where he attracted the attention of University of Arizona athletic authorites by pole vaulting fourteen feet, a world class mark in those days. Before he entered college, however, he was injured in a motorcycle accident, and he had to turn his athletic interests to weight-lifting and swimming. At the university, Nolan majored in music and English literature. He wrote a poetry column, ironically titled *Tumbleweed Trails*, for the university student newspaper. But wanderlust grabbed him and he left school.

He became a drifter, exploring the desert country, studying the plains, and living in the mountains. It was a love affair with the beauties of nature. That experience would inspire many of his best songs, including *Cool Water, Way Out There*, and *The Song of the Bandit*.

His father had moved to California and, in 1929, Bob joined him. There he tried to start a musical career, first taking a job with a traveling chautauqua troupe and singing his own songs, many of them converted from his poems. Chautauqua work wasn't steady, however, and paid little, and he took a life-guard job on the beach in Venice, California. It is part of the Bob Nolan lore that, in a lifeguard swimming competition, he beat out a Honolulu swimmer named Clarence Crabbe ("Buster" Crabbe, a gold medal winner in the 1932 Olympics and later one of the famous movie Tarzans).

In 1931, with the Depression engulfing the nation, Nolan lost his lifeguard job. His attention was drawn to a newspaper advertisement telling of vocalist auditions for a western group called the Rocky Mountaineers. In his audition, Bob sang his first composition, *Way Out There*, and when he began his distinctive yodel a member of the Mountaineers said: "I've heard enough—he's hired."

The man who spoke was Leonard Slye, later to be known around the world as Roy Rogers. Slye was born in 1911 in Cincinnati, and grew up on a small farm near Portsmouth in southern Ohio. His musical education began early, because his father played the mandolin and guitar. After the economic crash of 1929, the elder Slye couldn't make it on the farm; in 1931, he and his son, Len, went to Tulare, California, to work as migratory fruit pickers. They quickly learned that "golden California" was overrun with poverty-stricken fruit pickers and farm workers from all corners of the nation.

Len turned to music to make a living, beginning with an act called the Slye Brothers, which were Len and a cousin. He also worked briefly with Uncle Tom Murray's Hollywood Hillbillies before becoming active with the Rocky Mountaineers.

It was a struggle. The Mountaineers played on radio station KGER in Long Beach and at various local social events, but there was little money coming in. More than once Slye and Nolan made forays into rural San Fernando Valley for fruits and vegetables, just to have something for the band members to eat.

By the fall of 1932, Nolan was discouraged by the lack of progress being made with the Mountaineers and left to take a job as a caddy at the Bel Air Country Club. Tim Spencer was signed on as Nolan's replacement.

Spencer was born in 1908 in the mining community of Webb City, Missouri, the son of a fiddle-playing mining engineer. At the age of three, Tim made his debut by singing *Joy Bells* at the Webb City Methodist Church. Later he joined his brothers (Roy, Ray, Forbes, Leo, Glenn, Kenneth, and Dean) as a double quartet, singing at church functions.

Tim was only five when the family moved to Springer, New Mexico, near the foothills of the Sangre de Cristo Mountains. They were homesteaders. But it really didn't work out as had been anticipated, and young Tim grew up in the small Oklahoma town of Pitcher.

He was determined to pursue a career in music; his father wasn't sure it made sense. There was a time, when he was only thirteen, that Tim ran away from home in a dispute with his father over a banjo the youngster had purchased on credit. The elder Spencer found him working in a hotel restaurant in Dallas and brought him back to Oklahoma.

Nevertheless, Tim's interest in music didn't die. He made periodic trips to Kansas City and Tulsa to see some of the radio artists of the time. His heroes were William S. Hart and Tom Mix and Hoot Gibson. He was certain the movies were beckoning him. By 1931, his father relented and Tim was placed on a train to California, probably because an older brother, Glenn, was already living in Los Angeles.

Tim got a job with Safeway Stores, working in one of their warehouses. But that was only to make enough money to subsist. Every spare moment was spent visiting radio stations where western groups were playing—he soon knew the names of the members of every western group in the area—and there were a lot of them.

Again, there was a newspaper advertisement. The Rocky Mountaineers were looking for a baritone who could yodel. Tim knew that it must be Bob Nolan who was being replaced, and he hurried to see Len Slye and audition for him. He had never yodeled before, but he did for the audition and Slye hired him.

Still, the lightning refused to strike. The Rocky Mountaineers didn't make it. Neither did the International Cowboys, for whom Slye and Spencer worked. And the O-Bar-O Cowboys, yet another unsuccessful western band, didn't help the Slye-Spencer career either.

It's not clear just who motivated the move, but in September of 1933 Len Slye and Tim Spencer made their way to the Bel Air Country Club to once more enlist the talents of Bob Nolan. Nolan recalled that Tim was such a good salesman that he talked them into each putting fifty dollars in the pot to start a new group. They began what they called the Pioneer Trio.

Len was working at the time with Jack LeFevre and His Texas Outlaws on radio station KFWB, and the three young men moved into a boarding house near the station. Cost: $7.50 a week, and that included two meals a day.

In every spare moment, the Pioneer Trio worked on its distinctive sound, rehearsing interminably. Len sang the lead and played guitar, Tim sang tenor and also played the guitar, and Bob sang baritone and played bass fiddle. Within a month they thought they were ready and arranged for an audition at KFWB. Nolan's *Way Out There* was the final song of the audition. They were hired, for thirty-five dollars a week, to be part of the Texas Outlaws show.

All three were writing songs, Nolan and Spencer leading the way, and Nolan was loosely responsible for the arrangements. Good things were beginning to happen for them. For one thing, a *Los Angeles Examiner* columnist heard their arrangement of Billy Hill's pop western hit, *The Last Roundup,* and picked it as a "best bet."

KFWB, conscious of their growing popularity, gave them their own shows (plural)—three hours a day. They had an 8 to 9 A.M. show as the Pioneer Trio, another 5 to 6 P.M. as the Gold Star Rangers, and then appeared with the Jack Joy Orchestra for another hour in the late evening.

They began to look for an additional member for the group, someone who could provide some instrumental breaks in their routine. A fiddle player, perhaps. And, in early 1934, they hired a Texas fiddler named Hugh Farr.

Farr was born in 1903 in the small central Texas town of Llano. His parents, Tom and Hattie Farr, were enthusiastic amateur musicians, performing frequently at neighborhood parties; Tom on the fiddle, his wife on the guitar.

Later Hugh would say that when he was born, after the Farrs had had five daughters, his father shouted: "Well, I'll be darned! There's my fiddler!"

By the age of seven it was clear that Hugh had an unusual natural talent for music. He quickly learned to play the guitar and worked with his father at Saturday night dances.

The fiddle would come a couple of years later. The story is told that Hugh asked his father if he could stay home from school one day, promising that he would spend the time learning to play the fiddle. His father agreed. When Tom Farr returned home that night he found that the youngster had not only mastered the fiddle, but he had memorized almost every song his father could play.

The fiddle became Hugh's instrument, and in a few years he was playing engagements in numerous Texas communities, accompanied by a younger brother, Karl, who had become a fine guitarist.

In 1925, the Farr family moved to Encino, California. Hugh was twenty-three. He got a job working on the building of the North Hollywood High School, and when that project was completed, he began playing with a group at a bar called Mammy's Shack in Sherman Oaks. He played there for three years, until the place burned down.

He worked next with Len Nash and His Country Boys, then as a KFOX staff musician, with Sheriff Loyal Underwood and the Hollywood Range Riders, and with Jack LeFevre and the Texas Outlaws. That's how he met the members of the Pioneer Trio.

When he joined them in 1934 he played fiddle, of course, but he also added his bass voice to the vocal ensemble.

During that period, the name of the group was changed to the Sons of the

Pioneers. One story has it that the change came from a slip of the tongue when KFWB announcer Harry Hall introduced them. Whatever the truth of that, the name *was* changed.

In the same year they made their first commercial recordings for the new Decca company, initially cutting *Way Out There*, *Moonlight on the Prairie*, *Ridin' Home*, and *Tumbling Tumbleweeds*, all written by Nolan.

In 1935, the highly popular *Tumbling Tumbleweeds* was selected as the title song for Gene Autry's first starring movie for Republic Pictures. And Warner Brothers Pictures (owner of radio station KFWB) used the Sons of the Pioneer's voices on numerous animated cartoons. That was the year, too, that Hugh Farr's guitar-playing younger brother, Karl, was added to the organization. It was now a quintet.

They began to appear in movie short subjects and then made their first full-scale westerns with Charles Starrett at Columbia: *The Gallant Defender* and *The Mysterious Avenger*.

In 1936, things were even better. They appeared in Paramount's *Rhythm on the Range*, which starred Bing Crosby; they were special guest stars at the Centennial Exposition in Dallas, they became regulars on the KNX Hollywood Barn Dance, they did two films with Dick Foran at Warner Brothers, another with Autry at Republic, and signed with Columbia Pictures to star in the Charles Starrett western series.

September of 1936 saw the first break in the ranks. Tim Spencer, apparently because of an internal disagreement, left the Sons of the Pioneers (he would return in 1939), and he was replaced by nineteen-year-old Lloyd Perryman, a guitarist and a fine singer.

Perryman was born in 1917 in the farming community of Ruth, Arkansas, and grew up in Zion, Arkansas, where his father operated a small general store. His was not a musical family in the same sense of the Farr Family, but he did get a guitar at the age of nine, which he learned to play but never developed the knack of tuning properly.

In the winter of 1928, the Perryman family moved to Wasco, California, not far from Bakersfield. In high school there, Lloyd began to be seriously interested in music, appearing in several musical shows at school and singing on an amateur program on radio station KERN in Bakersfield.

He also became enamored of a country group he heard on the radio from Los Angeles, the Beverly Hillbillies. His determination to emulate them put him aboard a southbound freight train in 1932; he was fifteen years old.

In Los Angeles, he auditioned for Bonnie Newahee and His International Cowboys, then appearing on KGER. In that band at the time were Len Slye and Tim Spencer, just prior to their decision to convince Bob Nolan to start a new group. Perryman didn't get the job with Newahee, but he was recommended to Bert Crowe and the Sierra Mountaineers, who hired him.

The following year he joined a new group being organized, Cyclone and His Four S Cowboys. It failed. Then his big break came—there was an opening on the Beverly Hillbillies, at that time the premier country group in Los Angeles. It turned out to be only a temporary opening. There followed stints with the Texas Outlaws at KFWB, with Jimmie LeFevre and His Saddle Pals, and with at least five other bands in the L.A. area.

Stability came when Bob Nolan contacted him and asked him to fill in for Tim Spencer. In the final tally, Lloyd Perryman would be with the Sons of the Pioneers longer than any of the others—forty-one years, if you include the time out for military service during World War II.

Those six, then, are the Original Sons of the Pioneers honored in the Country Music Hall of Fame: Slye, Spencer, Nolan, the Farr brothers, and Perryman.

In 1937, there was another important defection from the group when Leonard Slye left to accept a contract to be a cowboy actor at Republic Pictures. Roy Rogers was born. His replacement in the "Sons" was Pat Brady.

And so it has gone. Recording stars, radio stars, movie stars, television stars, with a vastness of material unmatched by any other group. The complete story is told in *Hear My Song: The Story of the Celebrated Sons of the Pioneers,* an outstanding book by Ken Griffis, published in 1974, and revised in 1977, by the John Edwards Memorial Foundation at the Folklore and Mythology Center of the University of California at Los Angeles.

Yet, the story of the Sons of the Pioneers is open-ended. Their superb sound has continued down through nearly a half century.

Leonard Slye (Roy Rogers), born Cincinnati, Ohio, November 5, 1911.

Robert Clarence Nobles (Bob Nolan), born New Brunswick, Canada, April 1, 1908; died June 15, 1980.

Vernon Harold (Tim) Spencer, born Webb City, Missouri, July 13, 1908; died April 26, 1974.

Thomas Hubert (Hugh) Farr, born Llano, Texas, December 6, 1903; died March 17, 1980.

Karl Marx Farr, born Rochelle, Texas, April 29, 1909; died September 20, 1961.

Lloyd Wilson Perryman, born Ruth, Arkansas, January 29, 1917; died May 31, 1977.

Oh, if I had the wings of an angel,
Over these prison walls I would fly . . . .

35

Vernon Dalhart

Elected to the Country Music Hall of Fame: 1981

On September 14, 1948, the night checkout clerk at Bridgeport, Connecticut's Barnum Hotel died in the Bridgeport Hospital of a coronary occlusion. He was sixty-five. Thirty-three years later he was inducted into the Country Music Hall of Fame—some say many years too late.

The modest words on the Hall of Fame plaque of Vernon Dalhart proclaim: "Marion Try Slaughter [his real name] . . . was the first popular singer to demonstrate the wide appeal and economic potential of country music."

If ever there was an understatement of a performer's value to an industry, that sentence is it. Vernon Dalhart recorded music's first million-seller record in the mid-twenties: *The Prisoner's Song,* backed with the *Wreck of the Old 97.* Even more stunning is the fact that from 1915 to 1938, he was responsible for nearly five thousand releases and reissues, fully two-thirds of them genuine country material, that sold as many as seventy-five million copies!

Professor Walter Darrell Haden, Dalhart's biographer, put it in perspective: "At the time when Chicago studio broadcast experiments were about to become the WLS National Barn Dance and well before the show could develop a country recording star with any sort of national following, Dalhart had millions of country records sold around the world. Before the Grand Ole Opry was even a gleam in the eye of George D. Hay, Vernon Dalhart recordings were international harbingers of a half-century of commercial country music to follow."

Certainly, what muddied the waters and kept the industry from seeing clearly what was Dalhart's prodigious contribution to country music, was his propensity for using pseudonyms on many of his records. The exact number may never be determined, but it is known that there were at least one hundred ten pseudonyms used on almost as many different record labels. Some examples:

as Al Craver, *Sentenced to Life Behind These Gray Walls*, on Columbia.

as Mack Allen, *At Father Power's Grave*, on Harmony.

as Tom Watson, *I Wish I Was Single Again*, on Velvetone.

as Tobe Little, *Picture That Is Turned Towards the Wall*, on Okeh.

as Hugh Latimer, *Pick Me Up and Lay Me Down in Dear Old Dixieland*, on Perfect.

as Sid Turner, *Go 'Long Mule*, on Pathe.

as Warren Mitchell, *Alabamy Blacksheep*, on Regal.

as Harry Britt, *Hide Me Always in the Hills of Virginia*, on Domino.

as Dick Morse, *It Ain't Gonna Rain No More*, on Oriole.

as Walter Clark, *You Can't Blame Me for That*, on Melotone (Australian).

as Walter Hyde, *You're in Kentucky, Sure as You're Born*, on Apex (Canadian).

even as a woman, Fern Holmes, *There's a New Star in Heaven Tonight—Rudolph Valentino*, on Silvertone.

and as Mr. X, *Just a Girl That Men Forget*, on Radiex.

Then, too, there were pseudonyms like Jeff Calhoun, George Morbid, Val Veteran, Gwyrick O'Hara, Carlos B. McAfee, Josephus Smith, Joe Kincaid, Vernon Dell, Frank Dalbert, James Ahern, Lou Hays, and on and on. Putting together the Vernon Dalhart recording history has been a discographer's nightmare.

Marion Slaughter was born in 1883 in Marion County in northeast Texas, about three miles from Jefferson, the county seat. It is said that his father, Robert, and his uncle, Will Slaughter, grew "domestic cattle . . . cotton, peas, and corn" on a 500-acre ranch. While he was still a young boy, the family moved into Jefferson itself, where his father was a sometime hotel keeper and Baptist preacher. Jefferson was a tough town in those days, and his father was killed in a saloon during a knife fight with a brother-in-law, one Bob Castleberry.

Details on Marion's early life are sketchy, but it is known that he spent at least one summer as a cowpuncher in northwest Texas. It's also known that he took piano lessons in Jefferson, sang at various community affairs, and developed some proficiency as a whistler and as a player of the mouth harp. When he was about sixteen, his mother moved to Dallas; during that period he studied at the Dallas Conservatory of Music. Before he was twenty he married a Canadian girl who had come to Dallas, Sadie Lee Moore-Livingston, and they had two children.

In 1910, he challenged New York City, taking a stage name—Vernon Dalhart—from the two Texas towns between which he had worked as a cowboy. He worked in a music store, selling and delivering pianos, and he sang as a paid soloist in New York churches and funeral homes. By 1912, he had landed a minor role in the Puccini opera, *Girl of the Golden West*; in 1913, he sang in the Century Opera Company's production of Gilbert and Sullivan's *H.M.S. Pinafore*, both in New York and on the road. Dalhart also sang the lead role of Lieutenant Pinkerton in Puccini's *Madame Butterfly*.

Thus, the tenor from Texas was well grounded in opera and operettas when the recording industry was started. In 1915, with jobs scarce, Dalhart answered a newspaper advertisement: "Wanted: Singers for Recording Sessions." He went to East Orange, New Jersey, for an audition and was hired, allegedly by Thomas Alva Edison himself. But it wasn't until 1917 that the Edison company released Dalhart's first recording on a Blue Amberol Cylinder: *Can't Yo' Heah Me Callin', Caroline?* By that time, he also had a release on Columbia Records titled *Just a Word of Sympathy*. There was little thought of artist exclusivity in those days, and apparently Dalhart recorded anywhere he could.

On July 13, 1924, country music history was made. Dalhart, his recording fortunes in a decline, persuaded Victor Records to let him record a country song, *Wreck of the Old 97*. On the "B" side of the thick 78 rpm disc he put a hastily prepared version of *The Prisoner's Song*. When released in November it was an immediate hit, a record that sold like no other record before it. Major controversy surrounded the record, as well, most assuredly because it was such a sensational success.

For one thing, *Wreck of the Old 97* was not a new song; indeed, the tale of the 1903 wreck of the Southern Railroad mail train, in which the engineer and twelve others were killed, had been recorded by Virginian Henry Whitter in 1923 on the Okeh label. And Dalhart, in his version, not only copied Whitter's lyrics but duplicated his nasal style as well. More than fifty persons were to claim its authorship, and in the thirties two suits over the song's copyright reached the U.S. Supreme Court.

But *The Prisoner's Song* caused the biggest flap, because it was the "B" side of the Victor release that was the unqualified, and surprising, hit. There are any number of versions of who was responsible for the song.

Dalhart's version is that during a break in the July 13 recording session, he and his cousin, Guy Massey, adjourned to a hotel room nearby and simply wrote the song; Massey the lyrics and Dalhart the tune. That was the version he gave later to a newspaper columnist. Earlier, he claimed that Massey had written the entire song, and he did copyright it in Massey's name alone in the fall of 1924.

A different version of the story was given by Nathaniel Shilkret, Victor's musical director, to music historian Jim Walsh. Shilkret said Dalhart had pleaded for the session. "Come on and give me the date," the singer was supposed to have said. "I need the money!" When a song for the "B" side came into contention, Dalhart submitted a song he said was written by his cousin; "some penciled notes," Shilkret remembered, without music.

"The manuscript, as he submitted it, was a mess," Shilkret told Walsh. "It was only long enough to fill about half a record. I told him it couldn't be used as it stood, but that I thought it might be fixed up to do. He agreed for me to take it home with me. I wrote some verses and ground out a simple, mournful tune to fit the words.

"When I submitted the finished result to Dalhart he was well pleased. But neither then nor when the record became the biggest seller ever made up to that time did he offer to give me as much as a cigar. . . .

"The original manuscript may have been written or copied from some source by Dalhart's cousin, Guy Massey, but it was unusable and not worth recording as it stood. Dalhart himself had nothing to do with writing it. There would have been no 'Prisoner's Song' record if it had not been for my altering, editing, and adding to the manuscript."

Carson J. Robison, a singer-songwriter-musician who was on the session with Dalhart, told Bill Walsh that Dalhart had represented the song as public domain. "We recorded it," Robison wrote in a letter, "and shortly afterwards Dal copyrighted the song in his name and stuck Victor for royalties. As far as I can learn, he collected from Shapiro-Bernstein (music publishers) approximately $85,000 which represented 95 percent of all royalties. Guy Massey got five percent and died . . . a few years later practically penniless. In later years when Dal was doing everything he could to get back on records, he was a guest star on 'We, the People,' and I cringed when I heard him tell how he went home one night and composed *The Prisoner's Song*. The man never composed a note of anything in his life. . . ."

There were other voices in the controversy, but today it is clear that the song had folk origins. Riley Puckett recorded the traditional ballad under the title of *All Bound Down in Prison*. It's also known in folk circles as *I Have A Ship on the Ocean, Meet Me in the Moonlight, Prisoner Walls,* and several other titles. And going back even farther, the American folk song apparently stems from an old English song, *Here's Adieu to All Judges and Juries*.

Controversy aside, the fledgling recording industry was astounded by the selling power of *The Prisoner's Song*. Other artists moved to cover the hit, and Dalhart himself cut the song in sessions for perhaps thirty other labels. It sold throughout the world. Dalhart told an interviewer that his recordings of *The Prisoner's Song* sold more than twenty-five million copies, and it's believed today that he did not exaggerate. He also earned royalties on more than one million copies of sheet music sold of the song.

Vernon Dalhart became a rich man. He had a big English Tudor home in fashionable Mamaroneck, New York, with a solarium, servants, and an underground garage for expensive cars. His son was given a Stutz Bearcat for a high school graduation present. He was in demand everywhere—at recording studios and on personal appearance tours.

Biographer Walter Haden wrote: "A kind of a one-man recording industry in his busiest years from 1924 to 1928, the singer and his services were in such demand that he not infrequently cut three different sessions a day to keep up with the market for his recordings."

His recording of *The Death of Floyd Collins* was another million seller, and he also had major hits with *The Letter Edged in Black, Golden Slippers, My Blue Ridge Mountain Home, Lucky Lindy, The Convict and the Rose, The Little Rosewood Casket, The Dream of the Miner's Child, The Crepe on the Old Cabin Door, The Wreck of Shenandoah, The John T. Scopes Trial, The Sinking of the Titanic, I'd Like To Be in Texas When They Roundup in the Spring, Little Black Mustache, Billy the Kid*. Title after title—some of them released on twenty-five different labels. And more.

The stock market crash in 1929 cost Dalhart dearly; his personal fortune began to disappear, and the subsequent general Depression cut heavily into record sales. Vernon Dalhart had seen his best years. From 1933 until May 1, 1938, he didn't record at all. In '38, then, he cut six sides for Victor's Bluebird label. One of them was the first published song, *Johnnie Darling*, written by a young Texan named Red River Dave McEnery. Another was titled *Lavender Cowboy*, which was blacklisted as "blue," meaning dirty. Dalhart was never to record again.

The last years were bitter ones for him. He got a job as a night watchman at the Bullard Company in Bridgeport, Connecticut; "war work," he called it, ". . . a nice easy job." And at that time, in 1942, he was still trying to interest

Columbia Records in letting him record again. In 1946, he was employed by the Harry Hawley Voice Studio in Bridgeport. His advertisement for his "voice placing" and "professional coaching" listed his credits in opera *(Il Trovatore, Cavalleria, Pagliacci, Aida)*, and oratorios *(Holy City, Messiah, Persian Garden)*, and light operas *(H.M.S. Pinafore, The Mikado, Naughty Marietta, The Merry Widow)*. But not a word about *The Prisoner's Song* or *Wreck of the Old* 97, or any of the other recorded hits he had. There were few students.

His next job was at the Barnum Hotel. And there was no glory at the end.

So what was the significance of Vernon Dalhart, nee Marion Try Slaughter? He broke the trail and plowed the ground that first brought commercial success to country music. The startling sales of *The Prisoner's Song* and *Wreck of the Old* 97 in 1924, and the other country music hits that followed in the next several years, encouraged the young recording industry to seek additional talent in the country field.

Record company talent scouts roamed far afield in the wake of Dalhart's success. And before 1930 they had recorded:

Jimmie Rodgers.

And the Carter Family.

And Ernest "Pop" Stoneman.

And Carl T. Sprague.

And Uncle Dave Macon.

And Sam and Kirk McGee.

And Gene Autry.

And Roy Acuff.

And Bradley Kincaid. And hundreds more.

Vernon Dalhart had opened the door, and the country music industry marched through it.

Marion Try Slaughter, born Jefferson, Texas, April 6, 1883; died Bridgeport, Connecticut, September 14, 1948.

Married, Sadie Lee Moore-Livingston, 1901. (Two children: Janice, Marion Try III.

I was always a bug about radio . . .

36

Grant Turner

Elected to the Country Music Hall of Fame: 1981

It's a fact that one of the best known personalities on the Grand Ole Opry never sings a note and never fingers a chord. Yet, the fans seek him out to shake his hand, to ask for his autograph, and to hear firsthand the friendly voice that has come into their homes for nearly fifty years.

That would be Grant Turner, the dean of Opry announcers.

It's a fact, too, that he very nearly didn't come to the Opry at all. In 1944, when he was contemplating the offer from WSM radio in Nashville, he was also mulling over a radio opportunity in Cincinnati. "I often wonder what would have happened," he said, "had I gone there instead of coming here."

Turner's road to the premier country music show in the nation began in Abilene, Texas, where he was born in 1912. What he remembers most distinctly about his youth is that he was fascinated by radio. "My grandmother had a radio and I wanted one of my own. So I built a crystal set . . . When I was sixteen, they were going to move a station from Breckenridge, Texas, to Abilene, so I went and helped them move. We put up the transmitter, and we used a windmill as a tower.

253

"The studio we put in the lobby of the Grace Hotel. It's still there."

On that early Abilene station Grant, as a teen-ager, got his first lesson about country music stardom when Jimmie Rodgers, the Singing Brakeman, came to town. Turner recalls: "Jimmie was in the neighborhood to take part in a jewelry auction. He got $750 for that. Of course, he was a big recording artist back then. He didn't really care about show dates. He went around autographing his records.

"The Studebaker dealer found out that he was in town and paid him $250 for an hour show on the station. That was a lot of money in those days.

"He was a chain smoker. I remember the yellow stains on his fingers. He didn't have a strap on his guitar. He stood up to perform and he just put one foot up on a chair and put his guitar across the leg."

For a time, young Grant thought he would be a newspaperman. He went to Hardin-Simmons College and studied journalism. And when he graduated he held newspaper jobs in Texas, eventually moving to the *Dallas Morning News*. But radio had not lost its appeal. There followed announcing jobs in Sherman and Longview, Texas, and in 1942 he moved to WBIR, in Knoxville, Tennessee.

He was called Tex in Knoxville, where he worked with such country music stars as Carl Butler, Johnny and Jack, Kitty Wells, and Bill Carlisle. He was to work with them all again in Nashville.

His first day on the job at WSM was June 6, 1944—D-Day, the Allied invasion of France. "It was all you could hear. Radio really covered things back then. We stayed on for two or three days with that kind of coverage.

"The old WSM," he reminisced, "was like a small Radio City. There would be writers, song pluggers, stars, and musicians around all the time. Performers were always dropping by. You felt you were in the center of a lot of activity. Now, of course, most of that activity is centered around the Opry House."

Turner had not been brought to Nashville to work on the Grand Ole Opry; he was a staff announcer. But he got a call from George D. Hay, the Solemn Old Judge, who was the majordomo of the Opry. "Well, the Judge had me go down to the Opry. There was a bench on the side of the stage. He said, 'I want you to watch and tell me what you think.' I had heard the Prince Albert segment of the Opry over the network back in Texas, but it never occurred to me that I would ever be on the Opry."

Hay must have been impressed with Grant's perceptions of the Opry, because he put him on the staff; he became Judge Hay's protégé.

After nearly fifty years of association with the *Grand Ole Opry* broadcast, there are some incidents that remain crystal clear. Turner, in chatting with Nashville newspaperman Max York, let his memories carry him back:

"There was the time that Bob Wills was on the Opry playing *San Antonio Rose*. I guess this woman got carried away, because she fell right out of the balcony and landed on the stage. . . .

"I never had much experience with firearms, but one night Rod Brasfield was looking for someone to shoot a blank pistol. He asked me to do it, and I said I would. Rod had this gag where he would talk to Red Foley about this new feed he had for laying hens. It was called Lay Or Bust.

"Well, as he turned to leave, I was supposed to fire this pistol, and he was supposed to say something about the rooster getting in the feed. That pistol went off and it scared me half to death. You can't image how much noise it made. . . .

"I'll never forget the night I came out of the Opry House and saw Grandpa Jones and Ramona talking with Stringbean and his wife. They were having so much fun. I never saw a happier couple. I was going to stop and say something to them, but they were busy talking. I think they were planning to go fishing.

"That was just a short time before Stringbean and his wife were murdered—that very night. . . .

"I remember when Patsy Cline was in an automobile accident. She was out of action for months and months. Then, they brought her down to the Opry and wheeled her out on the stage. She didn't sing, she just greeted the crowd. She still had scars on her forehead. You can't imagine the feeling in the place. Everybody in the audience and all of us on the stage were so proud to see her. . . ."

Turner's job at the Grand Ole Opry made him a serious student of country music, and like his mentor, Judge Hay, did before him, he expressed concern about the loss of real country music identity. "I have a feeling we are losing so many of the old-time musicians, the old-time comics, that we've already turned the corner. I know that tastes are changing; a lot of the younger fans don't understand the country idiom, the expressions from the soil, that are contained in some of the best of the old songs."

Turner sighed. "The truth is that if something isn't done to turn it around, well, it's all going to sound like pop music. The term *country music* won't mean anything anymore."

The Opry's chief announcer believes, however, that country music will prevail. He is aware of the constant assaults that have been made on the genre. "I can remember times," he told an interviewer, "when there were empty seats at the Opry. You remember back when Elvis Presley came along? He and the other people in that rock 'n roll era took away some of the [Opry] audience. I remember one Saturday night. It was a Christmas Eve. I guess it was pretty cold that night. But there was hardly anybody there in the Ryman Auditorium. Some of the best shows are during the holidays when all the stars are home in Nashville. But that night nobody came to see them.

"Yes, I was worried about the Opry at that point . . . but now, we're getting new people all the time . . . And I think the Opry will go on as long as it keeps replenishing the supply of pure country music."

In Turner's recollections Hank Williams stands out like a beacon. "Hank had so much going," he said, "that people could hardly keep up with him. He wrote some of his best songs at three o'clock in the morning, even with a party going on around him.

"I always thought the songs came from a tormented soul. There were many bad scenes when alcohol and drugs got hold of him; sometimes they turned him against his audience. But those people understood him. And that's one thing about the country music audience: They understand the music and the performers. And they're loyal."

Grant Turner, born Abilene, Texas, May 17, 1912.
(One daughter, Nancy, by a previous marriage.)
Married, Lorene Hughes, 1956.